Grant Fowlds is a South African conservationist with a unique commitment to everything endangered. Grant's vision is to try to fill the shoes of the late elephant whisperer Lawrence Anthony and his recent undercover filming of a tusk and horn auction in Vietnam demonstrates that he is on the right track.

Graham Spence is a journalist and editor. Originally from South Africa, he lives in England. Together he and his brother-in-law, conservationist Lawrence Anthony, wrote *The Elephant Whisperer*, the story of the incredible relationship forged between one man and a herd of wild African elephants. Other books with Lawrence Anthony include *Babylon's Ark: The Incredible Wartime Rescue of the Baghdad Zoo* and *The Last Rhinos: The Powerful Story of One Man's Battle to Save a Species*.

Also by Grant Fowlds and Graham Spence
Saving the Last Rhinos

By Graham Spence (with Lawrence Anthony)
The Elephant Whisperer

Rewilding Africa

Restoring the Wilderness on a War-ravaged Continent

By Grant Fowlds
and Graham Spence

ROBINSON

ROBINSON

First published in Great Britain in 2022 by Robinson
This paperback edition published in 2024 by Robinson

1 3 5 7 9 10 8 6 4 2

A CIP catalogue record for this book
is available from the British Library.

ISBN: 978-1-47214-575-8

Typeset in Caslon Pro by SX Composing DTP, Rayleigh, Essex
Printed and bound in Great Britain by Clays Ltd, Elcograf S.p.A.

Papers used by Robinson are from well-managed forests
and other responsible sources.

MIX
Paper | Supporting
responsible forestry
FSC® C104740

Robinson
An imprint of
Little, Brown Book Group
Carmelite House
50 Victoria Embankment
London EC4Y 0DZ

An Hachette UK Company
www.hachette.co.uk

www.littlebrown.co.uk

To the conservation legends and my friends Beyers Coetzee, Chris Holcroft and Peter Rutsch who tragically passed away during the writing of this book – this story is the legacy you left us.

Acknowledgements

I am deeply indebted to some talented individuals whose genius this book has been shaped by:

Graham Spence, author and ghost writer, who is able to convey my real stories into print.

The services of Gary Wright, friend and agent, have propelled me from a field conservationist to a storyteller through two books, including *Rewilding Africa*.

My brother, Dr William Fowlds, whose inspiration in the rhino field has to take credit for so many of my experiences. The success of Amakhala Game Reserve and its members has been enormous in changing the shape of a landscape from farming to wildlife and tourism.

My adventures and philanthropy have been nurtured by Kingsley Holgate and Sheelagh Antrobus – from rhino art to early childhood development.

The dedication of this book is to my fallen comrades and I wish to express my gratitude to Una Coetzee, widow of Beyers; Desire Dudley, partner of Peter Rutsch and the family, together with Jac and Ashli Holcroft, whose father was such an inspiration in such a brief journey in conservation.

ACKNOWLEDGEMENTS

Every story is unique and the kind and generous friendship Peter Eastwood of Tanglewood, New Zealand, has provided me, through rhino art, gorilla conservation and thicket restoration, is commendable.

My unsung Zululand heroes in this book are Richard Mabanga, Sibonelo Zulu, Mdiceni Gumede, Thulani Thusi, Abe Nzuza and Nunu Jobe. They, and several others, have taught me the power of culture and given me the confidence to be one of them in the field of work and across the racial divide.

To Dr Jacques Flamand, friend and mentor, who I admire for his work in the black rhino range expansion, finding more habitat for this iconic species.

To my cousin, Warne Rippon; his wife, Wendy; daughter, Hannah; and the tremendous Buffalo Kloof team, for a great conservation legacy in the making.

It has been a privilege to work with John Kahekwa in the Democratic Republic of Congo and the Pole Pole Foundation, together with his loyal family in Kahuzi Biega National Park. His accolades of being a Tusk for Africa winner and, in 2021, an Earthshot Prize finalist, are richly deserved.

Over the last few years the Mawana owners, the Van der Walt family (all four siblings), have played a significant role in a vision yet to be determined at Loziba Wilderness. Many people have played a role in this project.

Recent serendipitous work and friendship synergies with sculptor Andries Botha have been life changing, as have projects with Joe Pietersen and his brother Willem from Nkombe Rhino.

To my Swedish mentor and *Power Goals* author, Christina Skytt, whose constant inspiration to write a bestseller has been unwavering since my first book, *Saving the Last Rhinos*.

The Covid pandemic led to some trying financial times and Chris Small and Carlien Roodt became my closest business compatriots in the formation of Project Rhino Alliance.

I have greatly enjoyed connecting with Americans who care about conservation, like Ellie Leaning, Nevvar Hickmet and Lisa Goldsmith, and the UK golden girls, volunteers Jennie Munro, Rebecca Hunt and Sarah Cobden-Ramsay.

The blessings of octogenarian parents' support in Bill and Rose Fowlds, together with a dedicated management team of Steve and Kerry Maartens at Leeuwenbosch, my ancestral home, are truly appreciated.

My story will not end with this book. The sequel is being penned with some interesting conservationists who have been very much part of my success: the eccentric John Varty, legendary filmmaker and visionary; Pongola Game Reserve, Thula Thula family and team Ven Africa – whose land and conflicts form part of the daily work in conservation; my loyal friend Declan Hofmeyr, who shares some common goals on corridors and wild connections; and long-time friend Dereck Milburn, with whom I have shared so much in almost a decade, as well as interesting connections to rhino in Uganda.

In conservation, a close and dedicated family is imperative due to long periods away from home. My wife, Angela, daughters Jess, Georgi and Alice, together with new additions in son-in-laws Richard Harris and Kyle Steyn, and the gift of our first grandchild, Madison, make the trip home so meaningful.

Africa needs conservation heroes. Some of them are in this book.

Grant Fowlds
South Africa, November 2021

Contents

CHAPTER ONE

Cruel Planet

Una Coetzee's voice was scratchy with worry. 'I have a bad feeling about this, Grant.'

Her husband Beyers had been tracking elephants that had broken out of the Mawana game reserve, and trumpeting had been heard in the vicinity. Elephant trumpet blasts echo for many miles across the African bush, usually indicating that the animals are either agitated or excited.

Or if they are about to attack.

Now Beyers was missing somewhere in the rugged and remote valley dissecting the Thaka River. No one had heard from him for several hours, and Una wanted to speak to him before flying back to Johannesburg from Durban.

'I'm just about to board the plane,' she said. 'Should I take a later flight?'

I thought about that briefly. Beyers was one of the most capable people I knew. He was the equivalent of an alpha Special Forces operative in the bush with serious weaponry and tracking skills. He had twice been a world field archery champion. If anyone could get himself out of trouble, Beyers could.

'Go home, Una. Your kids are waiting for you.'

I told her I had seen Beyers the night before at Mawana, her family's game reserve nestling in one of the wildest areas of the KwaZulu-Natal province in eastern South Africa. He had been in fine form, entertaining not only myself but sculptor Andries Botha. Andries, a legend in arts and environment circles, was in the wilderness area to sculpt a memorial honouring the life of the iconic conservationist Ian Player and his African mentor, Magqubu Ntombela.

Beyers and I, along with the Van der Walt family who owned Mawana, were in the throes of rewilding the former cattle ranch and other surrounding farms to create a world-class game reserve called Loziba Wilderness. There were thirty-two elephants roaming free on the land, beautiful animals that would be vital for our future plans. However, fences surrounding the reserve were in disrepair and there was a constant threat that the herd would break out, wreaking havoc in nearby village croplands – or, even worse, causing loss of life. The Van der Walt family had already been served a non-compliance order stipulating that, if the elephants escaped, the provincial conservation authority Ezemvelo KZN Wildlife would destroy them.

The 'sword of Damocles' was no mere over-dramatic idiom for these animals. They were literally living on borrowed time. As a result, we had a computerised tracking collar fitted on to the matriarch and the senior bull so we knew exactly where the herd was at all times. This was vital if we wanted to keep the elephants alive.

On this particular breakout, we saw to our dismay that the animals were about to invade a neighbouring farm. Beyers had to act fast. With his brother-in-law Johannes van der Walt, he immediately decided to drive from Pretoria to chase the elephants out of the danger zone.

Una begged him not to go. She had a premonition of impending disaster and pleaded that he should let people already on the reserve handle it.

Unfortunately, on the day of the breakout, the farm manager had quit so Beyers had little option but to track the elephants himself. Also, not many people could handle these risky situations as efficiently as him. He had successfully coaxed the elephants back to Mawana several times – in fact, he had done just that the week before. Most times he did so by firing shots into the air to turn the animals, or else used what we called the 'Mawana band'. This was basically a motley group of beaters banging old tin drums and making such a racket most self-respecting creatures would head for the hills.

Both the Mawana band and rifle shots were moderately successful, but Beyers believed we needed something more dramatic, something that would permanently frighten the elephants off adjacent properties. For this, he was going to use heavy-duty thunder flashes that he had recently bought from a firearms dealer.

The computer tracking the matriarch's electronic collar indicated that the elephants were moving on to land owned by Dlemeveni Sithole. We knew him well. The son of a manual labourer, he was now a successful businessman and the sole large-scale black farmer in the area. Despite his remarkable rags-to-riches story, Mr Sithole was a humble yet inspiring man, and thankfully also a conservationist. However, his patience had been tested before by marauding elephants and we didn't want that to happen again.

As I told Una, Beyers had invited myself, Andries and fellow sculptor Jess Bothma to spend the previous night at Mawana, where we had sat around the log fire under the stars until late.

Andries is also the founder of the Human Elephant Foundation and his immense artistic flair is heavily influenced by environmentalism. He and Beyers found instant rapport as Beyers eloquently outlined our Loziba dream of rewilding former farmland into a ruggedly pristine wilderness. It was almost impossible not to get caught up in Beyers's enthusiasm. His absolute zest for life was infectious. He also lived on the edge, paragliding and flying microlights for fun, and his passion for the bush was unparalleled.

The next day we visited Mr Sithole, telling him we were aware that the Mawana elephants were nearby and we would chase them off. Gracious as ever, Mr Sithole thanked us. We then drove to another neighbouring farm, managed by Brandt van Jaarsveld, to fetch his son Hendrik, who would be assisting Beyers in tracking the herd. Twenty-one-year-old Hendrik was out here on holiday as he now lived in the United States, but was keen to get back into the African bush. Beyers also brought along three farmworkers to repair any fences the elephants had broken.

It was Tuesday 18 February, 2020. Andries, Jess and I had to be back in Durban that day, so we said our goodbyes as Beyers and his companions trekked down into the Thaka Valley. I watched the untamed thornveld and acacias swallow them up. It is a panoramic vista I never tire of; big-sky wilderness stretching to infinity with the ancient dust of Africa swirling in the gusts.

We got into my battered old Toyota Yaris, which I believe has rattled over more rutted bush tracks than any other small car in history ever has or will. Caught up in the primal purity of the moment, Andries started telling me what an impression Beyers had made on him. They had the same vision, the same love of elephants, felt the same magnetic pull of wild places. He said he would try to raise the cash needed for the game-proof fence that would secure the future of the Mawana elephants once and for all. I told him it was a lot of money – about half-a-million US dollars for a single power strand, and many millions more for a full electric barrier. It was money we simply didn't have, which was why Beyers had to resort to Wild West 'rodeos' whenever the animals broke out.

We heard a rifle shot. Then another . . . a few more. About five in total.

I dialled Beyers on my cellphone. 'I heard some shots. Have you seen them?'

'*Ja*, but the ellies are not moving fast enough. I'm now going to bring in the big boys.'

In other words, the thunder flashes.

In hindsight, I should have said that as a conservationist I wasn't convinced that was the best plan. Loud noise is a proven method of moving animals, but sometimes it can overly unsettle them, particularly highly intelligent animals such as elephants.

Instead, I said, 'Beyers, maybe you don't have to do that. The herd is now out of the danger zone. They're heading home.'

Beyers paused before replying. He knew what I meant but, on the other hand, timing was crucial. If he didn't get the elephants back to the Mawana reserve and safety within the next twelve hours, the entire herd could be destroyed. For Beyers, that was unthinkable.

'I just want to get them through the valley,' he said. 'Then I can relax. I don't want them to come back here again.'

It was the last time we spoke.

A few minutes later, the first thunder flash went off. A billowing cloud of acrid smoke exploded into the air and even some rocks moved. It was almost like dynamite. This big bang was big, all right.

Perhaps that was the problem. Perhaps, in the team's understandable eagerness to get the threatened elephants to safety, they were pushing them too hard. We'll never know.

What we do know is that Beyers, Hendrik and one of the farmworkers, Thobani Masondo, continued following the herd. Beyers took a video on his cellphone, and it's clear that, while the elephants were still going in the right direction, they were moving slowly. Looking back, that could have been the first warning sign. The animals should have been running at full speed with all the noise and smoke from the thunder flashes. But they weren't.

Later that afternoon I dropped Andries and Jess off at their car parked outside my house. That's when Una phoned to say she couldn't get hold of Beyers.

I told her not to worry. I told her how cheerful Beyers had been the night before, and how capable he was in the bush. He knew exactly what he was doing. The fact he was not answering his cellphone was probably due to a flat battery or lack of any signal that deep in the sticks.

'Beyers loves this sort of thing,' I said. 'This is his life.'

But as the afternoon wore on, something started to niggle. We have a Mawana elephant group chat on WhatsApp, and no one – not just his wife – had heard from Beyers. Una was now extremely concerned as she boarded the plane. She repeated to me her dire premonition.

At about 4 p.m. Brandt van Jaarsveld phoned me. His son had just contacted him. Hendrik was in a terrible state. For the past hour, he and Thobani Masondo had been running for their lives.

'There's big trouble,' said Brandt. 'Hendrik says the elephants attacked them. They went mad – screaming and trumpeting. We don't know where Beyers is.'

I went cold with dread. Had Una's intuition been correct? 'You mean he's dead?'

'I don't know,' Brandt said. 'Hendrik says he may be injured. We're going back to look now.'

Una was on the plane so there was no way to get hold of her. But what would I tell her if we did? I was still hoping against all odds that Beyers had somehow escaped, just as Thobani and Hendrik had.

To keep Una out of the loop until we had clarification, I called everyone else on the WhatsApp group individually and told them to maintain phone silence.

Two hours later, Brandt phoned to say he and Hendrik had arrived at the scene of the attack. With them were Beyers's two brothers-in-law, Kallie and Johannes van der Walt. Brandt said it had been a gruelling hike through thorn and sickle bush so thick that at times they had to crawl under the foliage on hands and knees. He suddenly stopped speaking. I thought the signal had gone dead, then I heard his voice falter. '*Ag nee, man. Nee, man!*' Oh no, man.

My skin crawled. Brandt choked, then said, 'Grant, I can't explain it, man. This is the worst thing I have ever seen. It's like a warzone.'

Voice rasping, he said Beyers had been tusked through his ribs and stomach. His face was unmarked, looking almost tranquil. Death had obviously been instant.

For several seconds I couldn't speak. Beyers was such a vital, exuberant person, it was impossible to imagine him dead. I felt sick to my stomach, still unable to believe it.

'We'll wait here until the police arrive,' Brandt said, and clicked off his phone.

Almost paralysed with dread, I knew I had to get hold of Una. She would soon land in Johannesburg, then would be driving to the family home in Pretoria. That could take some time in rush-hour evening traffic. I did not want to give her the tragic news while she was behind the wheel of a car on a motorway.

As if reading my thoughts, a text from Una flashed on the WhatsApp group: 'Anyone heard from Beyers yet?'

There was silence. None of us replied. We simply couldn't. I knew her mother-in-law, Daniella Coetzee, was with the Coetzee children, Luan (ten) and Lara (five), so Una would have company when she arrived home. Daniella is an incredibly strong woman; a dean at the University of the Free State and highly respected academic. But we also needed someone to be there to break the terrible news in person. Someone to tell a wife, mother and two children that the man they loved would not be coming home. I decided this was not something that could be done over the phone. We needed a strong physical presence.

I called Beyer's cousin, Gaele van der Walt, a giant of a man, and asked him to go to Una's house and wait for her to arrive. 'You're the only person who can tell her and the kids,' I said.

Gaele agreed, saying he would phone me later. I felt terrible for him as he first had to break the news to Daniella, who had also recently lost her husband. Now her son was gone as well.

I waited for his call as the minutes inexorably ticked past. It seemed a long, long time. In the interim, I phoned the police and tried to get a helicopter to fly out to the death scene, but the bush was too thick for it to land. Also, it was too dark. Evacuation could only be done on foot.

Eventually Gaele phoned. Una was home. His voice was heavy with sorrow. He said the family's grief and anguish were beyond heart-wrenching. Breaking the awful news was something that will live with him for the rest of his life.

Meanwhile, deep in the bush, Kallie, Johannes, Brandt and Hendrik kept vigil as they waited for the police to arrive. They covered the body and put a hat over Beyers's face. Our biggest fear now was that the elephants would return. If they did, there would be the added misery of them trampling the body – while the four men would have to run for their lives, just as Hendrik and Thobani had earlier.

The police arrived with body bags at about 11 p.m., nine hours after the attack. That's how remote the valley is. With them was Alec van Heerden, a family friend from Vryheid, who proved to be an absolute stalwart in handling the official paperwork and media enquiries that the family were too distraught to deal with.

They hauled the body through the rough terrain and dense bush, arriving at the mortuary early the next morning. Alec officially identified the body on behalf of the distressed Van der Walt and Coetzee families.

The next day I drove to Mawana. Hendrik was still in shock, understandably, and to get a first-hand account, I spoke to the other survivor, Thobani.

He told me the main herd of elephants had not attacked them, as we had first thought. Instead, it was two teenage males, known as askaris. This, sadly, did not surprise me. We knew the askaris were a potential problem as seven of the fully grown bulls had previously been killed by trophy hunters, creating a huge sociological void in the Mawana herd. In healthy elephant communities, rowdy juveniles are kept in line by mature bulls, pretty much like human society. Consequently, without mature guidance askaris are not taught 'manners'. This is further aggravated when they are in musth, as these two youngsters almost certainly were, and become extremely aggressive.

It seems that while Beyers, Thobani and Hendrik were concentrating on the main herd, unbeknown to them the askaris had doubled back. The attack must have been lightning fast for a man as capable as Beyers not to have fired at least one shot.

Thobani, who has worked at Mawana for years, said they only knew they were in mortal danger when the enraged askaris trumpeted, almost screaming, as they attacked. The bush was so thick that the fleeing men had to squeeze through a narrow gap among the trees. Hendrik, who fired his gun over his head in a desperate bid to scare off the animals, was first out, followed by Thobani. Beyers had to let the others through. That fraction of an instant cost him his life.

'The elephant was right on us,' said Thobani. 'I heard a thump as its head hit Beyers. It tusked him as he fell, then trumpeted again.'

Thobani and Hendrik continued scrambling through the bush for their lives, but became separated in the dense growth. Both fled for higher ground and, after about an hour, Hendrik paused to pull out his cellphone. Panting like a locomotive, he phoned his father, calling urgently for help.

Reaction to the death of a person so prominent and well-liked in the area was swift. Within days, there were demands to have the elephants destroyed. Some communities bordering Mawana wanted the entire herd shot; others just the two askaris.

The calls were not echoed by Una and the Van der Walt family. On the contrary, Una stressed unequivocally that the last thing she wanted was revenge. As she repeatedly said, it's certainly not something Beyers would have wanted either.

However, the tragedy was compounded by the fact that the herd was already under threat until the Mawana fences were made elephant-proof. In fact, the only reason the animals were still alive was because Beyers, almost singlehandedly, had persuaded nine out of the ten neighbouring farmers to sign an agreement indemnifying Ezemvelo KZN Wildlife from any culpability. Now that Beyers had been killed by the elephants he so loved, all bets were off.

That was the supreme irony. Beyers had sacrificed his own life in his bid to save the Mawana herd. And it may have been in vain.

At the time of writing, a final decision on what to do with the herd has yet to be reached. Some neighbouring communities are uneasy, and Ezemvelo is still debating whether the askaris should be shot, although off the record they have said they are almost certain to spare the rest of the herd. The animals are living under a suspended sentence – the last thing Beyers and his family would have wanted.

Beyers's loss to his family, his numerous friends and our entire Loziba rewilding project is immeasurable. The anguish of those he left behind is incalculable. They say no one is irreplaceable, but Beyers came as close as dammit to the definition of the word. If any of the animals are destroyed, everything Beyers worked for in conservation could go up in smoke.

Africa is beautiful beyond belief. It can also be cruel beyond comprehension. But we will never stop loving her.

That is something that Beyers, who gave his life for the wild ones of this land, understood most of all.

CHAPTER TWO

Poaching and Pathogens

Sibonelo Zulu peered through the iron sights of his rifle.
The weapon was an outdated Lee Enfield .303 with four 7.7 mm rounds in the magazine and one in the breech. This particular bolt-action model had seen action in the First World War, more than a century ago. Most poaching gangs had fully automatic AK-47s as well as telescopic-sighted hunting rifles so, in any firefight, Sibonelo and his men would be seriously outgunned.

That didn't stop him. What he and his fellow game rangers lacked in firepower, they more than made up for in raw guts and grit.

Sibonelo could see the vague outlines of men in the night, backlit by a full moon. A poacher's moon, so-called as such nights are favoured by wildlife traffickers. He and his team had been stalking this gang for the past hour, and Sibonelo – who is as tough as they come – knew this was going to end one way or another. He had on numerous occasions warned the vicious rhino-horn syndicates, which had turned his beloved Hluhluwe-iMfolozi game reserve into a warzone, that he was after them. 'Come into my park, and you're dead.'

He could see that the man in his V-sights carried a weapon, a heavy-calibre hunting rifle. Perhaps a .338 – or more likely a .375 H&H Magnum. In other words, a weapon capable of stopping a charging 6-ton elephant, let alone a rhino, dead in its tracks.

Sibonelo lay as still as a gecko. The radiant moon, which had led his patrol to this gang, could just as easily work against him. If he could see them, they could see him. That's why rangers call it a poacher's moon, as bright skies nullify the use of torches that give away positions. Such nights almost without fail mean trouble for Sibonelo and his team of battle-scarred rangers.

Sibonelo's face hardened as he thought of the worst two nights of his life: a poacher's moon in May 2017, when nine rhinos were killed and dehorned, and a blood moon in September 2015 when eight were slaughtered. Blood moons are full moons on steroids; a total eclipse where the lunar orb turns a reddish tinge, like plasma. It's an eerily appropriate description, as on such nights blood is invariably spilt in the beleaguered wildlife parks of Africa.

Sibonelo's grip on his rifle tightened as he remembered kneeling beside the fresh carcasses of the mutilated rhinos and vowing vengeance. He would fight fire with fire. No mercy. No retreat. No surrender. Since that day, he has been doing exactly that.

That night, 6 March 2020, history was repeating itself. He was in the same area, under the same poacher's moon, possibly even tracking the same gang. Just before the nine-rhino massacre three years ago, a group of men had been caught attempting to cross the Swaziland border with a rhino horn that DNA proved to be from Sibonelo's reserve. The ringleader, a man called Leon Stoltz, was arrested. Mysteriously, all charges against Stoltz were withdrawn and he walked free. Two weeks later, the nine rhinos were killed. Most rangers believed that was no coincidence. The anger was still raw.

Sibonelo crawled forward, rifle at the ready. He has been chasing poachers for most of his adult life, a veteran of many fierce shootouts. These are usually sharp, short and brutal, fought at extreme close quarters in bush so dense that visibility is measured in feet and inches. They can seldom see who they are shooting at, firing instead at muzzle flashes while bullets zing like hornets off rocks and trees. These firefights are far more terrifying than most military battles as, in the bush, there are no foxholes, artillery backup or helicopter gunships strafing the enemy from above. Instead, game rangers fight alone or with a handful of equally desperate brothers-in-arms, using ancient bolt-action rifles against state-of-the-art assault weapons. They are, in my opinion, the planet's super-heroes. The debt we owe them is unpayable.

Sibonelo gently squeezed the trigger, holding his breath to keep the rifle rocksteady. He had been in hot pursuit for the past hour. His heart was pounding from extreme exertion and pumping adrenaline. Snipers need glacial calmness, especially at night in dense bush. There was ice in his veins as the gun fired.

The first man went down. Then Sibonelo noticed a second, just a few yards to the left. He fired again. Another hit.

Sibonelo and his patrol waited for a full minute, expecting the night to erupt in a maelstrom of lead. Instead he heard crashing through the sickle bush. The remaining poachers were fleeing.

The Hluhluwe-iMfolozi Park, ironically where the white rhinos of Africa were once saved from extinction, had for the past few years been at the forefront of the most severe poaching spike ever experienced in KwaZulu-Natal. Sibonelo's informants told him this was largely due to poaching gangs moving south from Mpumalanga, home to Kruger National Park and several other world-renowned reserves. The poachers considered KwaZulu-Natal rangers to be less formidable than the vastly better-equipped anti-poaching patrols of Kruger, South Africa's flagship park, which is almost the size of Wales.

Sibonelo smiled mirthlessly. Two corpses in the bush 20 yards or so ahead would disabuse them of that notion.

He stood and with his men walked towards the first body lying sprawled in the dirt. Sibonelo flipped the corpse over with his boot.

He gasped, shocked to his core. Although the skull had been shattered by the bullet, the expressionless, wide-eyed face staring back at him was instantly recognisable.

'*Hau!*' Every man in the unit uttered the word simultaneously. It is the highly expressive Zulu exclamation of extreme surprise.

'Baas Leon,' Sibonelo whispered, almost reverently.

It was indeed Leon Stoltz, at the time the most wanted poacher in South Africa. Baas Leon was the 'baas' – boss – of the most notorious rhino-horn syndicate, a millionaire playboy, head of a biker gang, and responsible for the death of hundreds of rhinos. The same man against whom all charges had been 'mysteriously' dropped after being caught red-handed – literally – with a Hluhluwe-iMfolozi horn at the Swaziland border in 2017.

Sibonelo clicked on his radio, calling the reserve's headquarters. Staff there had heard the shots.

'What happened?' the radio operator asked.

'*Ngimbulele,*' he said. 'I've killed him.'

'Who?'

'Baas Leon.'

There was silence. Then another collective '*Hau!*' staccatoed over the airwaves from everyone in the radio room.

'Are you sure?'

'*Yebbo.*'

Sibonelo could sense their incredulity. Baas Leon had evaded the authorities for so long that some of the more superstitious game guards believed he was protected by *thakathi*, the local word for witchcraft. This was without question the most prominent felon in the poaching hierarchy.

'He is dead,' Sibonelo repeated. He was surprised at how unemotional he felt. He was merely doing his job. If he hadn't have fired first, it would have been him instead of Baas Leon lying motionless on the ground.

Sibonelo and his men then rolled over the corpse of the other man. He too was known to the authorities – Bhekumuzi Matonse, Baas Leon's right-hand man. Next to the bodies was the high-calibre hunting rifle that Sibonelo had seen glinting in the moonlight. There were also several well-honed machetes, which would have been used to dehorn any dead rhinos that the fleeing gang had shot. There was no doubt of the dead men's intentions.

I heard the news the next day. Sibonelo is one of my closest friends. Our bond was forged in fire, working together in building a crack equestrian anti-poaching unit in Nqumeni, the most isolated and vulnerable section of Hluhluwe-iMfolozi. Even though I knew that if anyone could have outgunned the country's most notorious poacher it would be Sibonelo, I was still surprised. I obviously didn't believe in *thakathi* but, even so, Baas Leon had seemed invincible. He had evaded arrest with almost contemptuous ease and he obviously had friends in high places. The only way to stop him would have been an ounce of lead fired deep in the bush. And that's exactly what had happened.

I was also surprised that there was no press release describing the gunfight. This was a massive win for wildlife, but the only statement came from the police. Even that was a bland few paragraphs stating that 'suspected poachers' Stoltz and Matonse had been killed in a game reserve.

'Why isn't this victory being highlighted?' I asked Sibonelo.

He laughed. 'My bosses think my life may be in danger.'

I laughed with him. Whoever wanted to take out Sibonelo would need an army.

'Seriously though,' the tough ranger continued, 'Baas Leon was very popular in Hazyview, so there may be some people out for revenge. I'm told he's getting a celebrity funeral there.'

Sibonelo's information was correct. Hazyview is a town bordering the Kruger National Park, where Stoltz had cut his poaching teeth. His motorbike club, Sun Riders MCC, was preparing a Harley-Davidson guard-of-honour parade through the town centre, and members were asked 'out of respect for the family' not to excessively rev their bikes as the body of Baas Leon was lowered into his grave. However, the bikers were promised that they would later be given the chance 'to properly celebrate Baas Leon's life'.

In conservation circles, the effect of Baas Leon's demise was instantaneous. Almost overnight, rhino-poaching incidents plummeted in KwaZulu-Natal, with the death toll dropping for the first time in years. How long that would last, we did not know. But what was abundantly clear was that gangs from Mpumalanga now knew that KwaZulu-Natal had serious men at the frontline who would not only shoot to kill, but were good at it.

So the momentum shifted, but wildlife trafficking can be a bit like playing whack-a-mole. You stomp it out in one area, and it pops up in another.

In this case it was the North West province, bordering Botswana.

At the same time another deadly threat loomed. Something that could change the face of conservation forever.

COVID-19. The Coronavirus.

CHAPTER THREE

COVID and the New World

The North West is a fascinating chunk of real estate with some of the most impressive wilderness in southern Africa.

One of the reasons for this is that it verges on the southern tip of the Kalahari Desert, a vast semi-arid treasure trove of wildlife that includes the Okavango delta across the border in Botswana and the Etosha pan in Namibia.

It is also one of the more remote regions in South Africa. So when COVID-19 ignited like a bushfire, a perfect poaching storm erupted. With Baas Leon's gang routed from KwaZulu-Natal and horn cartels curtailed in the Kruger National Park due to increasingly efficient technology, wildlife traffickers converged on the province that was most vulnerable and with the least wildlife protection. In other words, the North West.

Added to that, there was chaos in the towns as news of the pandemic spread and residents went on a frenzied spending spree. The government only gave three days' warning before enforcing a countrywide lockdown, resulting in traffic-jammed streets as panicked shoppers stacked their cars with everything from crates of whisky to mountains of toilet paper.

Consequently, the North West administration was in serious disarray and rhino poachers used this turmoil to mount an unprecedented butchering spree. In one incident, seven rhinos were slaughtered in twenty-four hours. It was so bad that the Pilanesberg National Park, which borders the five-star casino resort Sun City, had to dehorn all its rhinos in a desperate effort to halt further carnage. It is to date the largest dehorning operation in the world, and completely safe as a surgically removed rhino horn grows back like a fingernail.

As luck would have it, myself and my colleagues were already active in the North West area discussing range expansion for future ventures as the biodiverse, semi-desert habitat system is prime rhino country. Project Rhino, an NGO of which I am an ambassador, had dispatched me to the Botswana border a month previously to meet Kalahari game rancher Dr David Griesel, who had a sizeable rhino herd on his reserve Nuutbegin (New Beginnings). However, Nuutbegin was also a magnet for horn poachers and Doc, as we called David, had lost thirty-three animals in less than three years. It is still one of the biggest losses suffered by a private owner in the country.

Now, with COVID-19 flaring, he had lost another prime black rhino cow to poachers the day before lockdown. She had previously been dehorned, so the rustlers had butchered a critically endangered animal for a measly inch or two of medically worthless keratin. They had also, for some bizarre reason, disembowelled her. Perhaps they were angry that she had been dehorned. Equally disconcerting was that her twelve-month-old calf was missing.

Doc texted me, 'I need help.'

I contacted the Aspinall Foundation, which had assisted in financing Project Rhino operations, and we swung into action, mobilising a tracking team to rescue the defenceless young rhino. We had to get to it fast as not only was the orphan at risk from other territorial rhino males, there were also several large Kalahari lions roaming the reserve that were more than capable of taking it down. And, of course, the marauding poaching gangs who had killed its mother were still active.

Also on standby was Rhino 911, a non-profit outfit that provides emergency helicopter response for rhinos at risk. But thanks to incomprehensible COVID-19 red tape, even with Rhino 911's assistance we were severely hamstrung. Social distancing rules resulted in the authorities only granting clearance for one person to fly, which meant a pilot was unable to take a vet with him. Equally bizarre was that, even though the pilot was flying solo, he could only do so if he tested negative for the virus – something that took five days to process in the initial days of the pandemic. Consequently, the only unit capable of rapid aerial response was effectively grounded.

To give them their due, the authorities relented after the Pilanesberg massacre and allowed Rhino 911 to fly again, so some sanity was restored. The surgical dehorning of scores of North West rhinos in record time during that early lockdown period is largely due to the incredible work of Rhino 911's founders, Nico Jacobs and Dr Gerhardus Scheepers.

But choppers are insatiably thirsty beasts, and fuel and maintenance cost money – lots of it. It was money we didn't have so, unless we got help fast, Rhino 911 would be stranded even without COVID bureaucracy.

In desperation, I phoned Joe Pietersen, a top professional rugby player who now lives in the USA. Joe is not only a committed conservationist, he is the prototype action man – so if you want something done fast, he's your first point of call.

I met Joe when he was one of our celebrity cyclists in the annual uBhejane Xtreme mountain bike challenge, which raises money for Project Rhino. I knew about him, of course, as he was previously an ace fly-half with the team I support, the KwaZulu-Natal Sharks, before moving to Japan and then America. He now captains the San Diego Legion and so far is the most successful skipper they've had. He's also the humblest celebrity I've ever met, a solid feet-on-the-ground guy who loves the outdoors and rhinos with as much passion as he plays rugby. So it was no great surprise when he formed Nkombe Rhino, a non-profit organisation to help fight the poaching wars.

Without fanfare or fuss, Joe's Nkombe Rhino charity donated fuel money for the Rhino 911 chopper, ensuring this crucial service was again fully operational. As it was the off-season for northern hemisphere rugby, Joe was in South Africa so I invited him to come to the Kalahari with me to see where his money was going. In pre-COVID-19 days, we would have simply got into a car and driven to Doc Griesel's reserve. But now with lockdown, we had to get emergency service permits to travel outside KwaZulu-Natal. This required the usual paper-pushing bureaucracy, so while waiting I took Joe to Loziba Wilderness to show him my flagship project.

It was there that we witnessed an incident that radically changed both of our COVID-19 perspectives. Two men came out of the bush towards us, one wearing yellow dayglow rubber boots so it was impossible to miss him. But what was even more conspicuous was that they were carrying the largest python I have seen. It was almost 20 feet long, which meant it was about thirty years old, with a beautiful gold and tan skin. It was also dead, its head pummelled to pulp by hardwood sticks.

The men stopped and smiled as I took a photo on my cell-phone. Pythons are a listed vulnerable species in South Africa and strictly protected by law. That didn't concern these two guys.

'Why did you kill it?' I asked, hiding my anger.

'We are hungry.'

They walked off. I suppose a python that size and venerable age could feed up to twenty people and, with the current lockdown, rural communities had little or no access to fresh meat. With food scarcely on the table, who could blame them for regarding a giant snake as nothing more than much-needed protein?

Not long afterwards, we watched a group of men with a pack of scrawny hunting dogs coming down the hill. One man had a dead duiker slung over his shoulders. A duiker is the smallest and most timid buck in the bush. The dogs had ripped out its throat.

Both sights infinitely saddened me. Joe as well. We could have told them what they were doing was wrong. We could have berated them for killing a protected creature. But then, what do lofty conservation slogans mean to those with growling bellies? As my friend John Kahekwa, a world-renowned conservationist who took me on my first gorilla safari in the Democratic Republic of the Congo (DRC), often repeats, 'Empty stomachs have no ears.'

The thought of John, who's spent his life battling overwhelming odds from genocide to Ebola in the DRC, gave me some inspiration. He, more than anyone else, knows how to turn awful situations around.

That sparked off an idea. We would feed these starving people ourselves. But only if they pledged not to kill wildlife. No more pythons or duikers would die because of empty stomachs.

At least not on Project Rhino's watch. That would be the message emerging from the wreckage of the COVID-19 crisis.

Joe and I then met up with Chris Small and Steve Mulholland at the Mziki game reserve, north-west of Loziba, where we recounted the python and duiker story. Chris and Steve said the wildlife communities surrounding their reserves were also starving and asking for food. But the problem was so massive that no one seemed to know how to handle it. For a start, where would we get the food?

'We could buy maize meal from agricultural depots and then drop sacks off at the neediest villages,' I suggested. 'That would be a start.'

'Who'll pay for it?' asked Chris.

Good question. We would need sponsors. Who could I ask? I got my answer instantly.

'I'm in,' said Chris. Joe and Steve nodded. All three said they would chip in to cover initial costs to get the project going. The deal was sealed with a handshake and little did I know that it would become one of the country's most successful rural feeding schemes during the pandemic, eventually providing 1.2 million highly nutritious meals.

I had met Chris Small about fifteen years ago and we played squash together, but soon afterwards he disappeared out of my life to start his own company called Savuka Telecoms. It was visionary, but at one stage, Chris says, he was so poor he 'couldn't even pay attention'. Fortunately, he persevered and today Savuka is a major force in African telecommunications. Chris also used to own a white-water rafting company in Uganda, and his chief guide was the legendary Hendri Coetzee, who was killed by a crocodile on the Congo River. Hendri was dubbed 'the greatest explorer you've never heard of', but in kayaking circles he was an absolute legend. Chris's brother Bingo was on Hendri's famous river voyage from the Nile's source to mouth in 2005.

But most important to me is that Chris is an ardent conservationist and one of the most generous men I know, happy to drop everything and fly me out in his Robinson 44 helicopter to far-flung places that I could not otherwise access.

As we were about to leave for the Kalahari to see Doc Griesel, I arranged to pick up a load of maize meal at an agricultural depot in Potchefstroom on our return. This involved applying for yet another batch of endless COVID permits authorising us to distribute food. To do this, we had to give the name of our organisation, which was a problem. We didn't have one. On the spur of the moment, I scribbled 'Feeding the Wildlife Community' on the application form.

That soon became a catchphrase for many starving rural villages, and while we will never know how many pythons and duikers were saved by the project, we certainly made a significant contribution in easing the horrific burden imposed on the pandemic's most vulnerable victims.

To give some background of how hard the coronavirus hit South Africa, when full lockdown came into force on 26 March 2020 – barely a month after we had buried Beyers – everything ground to a complete, shuddering standstill. Almost overnight, the entire country was turned into a ghost town. Even alcohol and cigarettes were banned. Essential shops were allowed to remain open, but people could only leave their homes at stipulated times for medical emergencies or to buy food.

All businesses and all workplaces shut their doors. For many Third World South Africans who lived hand to mouth at the best of times, this was a potential death knell. They desperately needed money for food, but were not allowed to work. They had nothing to fall back on except government grants and food parcels, and delivering that to millions in the rural areas required logistical skills the state simply did not possess. I knew we would soon be facing a hunger crisis of biblical proportions with a corresponding explosion in poaching. Communities living near game parks had little option but to hunt bushmeat. As there were no tourist vehicles or anti-poaching patrols acting as deterrents, with all game reserves closed, illegal access for subsistence poachers had never been easier. Snaring of small game such as impala, duikers and warthog – even aardvarks and porcupines – went through the roof as this became a primary food source. In fact, subsistence hunting rivalled the virus as a pandemic. Which was why our Feeding the Wildlife Community project was so vital.

However, there was at least one ray of light in the bleak wasteland. Rhino poaching across the country ceased almost overnight, although, as mentioned, it lagged for about another week in the North West.

Why did this happen? And why so suddenly? Thinking back, the reason was obvious and shows what can be done with political will. There were simply so many police and army patrols enforcing lockdown regulations that big-game poachers were unable to move freely. It just wasn't worth running the gauntlet of roadblocks with a freshly hacked rhino horn in the boot of a vehicle. So imagine what could be achieved if these blockades around highly poached parks were rolled out on a full-time basis?

However, that was the only benefit to emerge in those awful times. Everything else crashed and burned. My work with Rhino Art – a conservation project targeting youth – instantly ground to a halt as schools shut down. In fact, the last school that Rhino

Art ambassador Richard Mabanga and I visited started to close while we were still on the premises and we literally had to sprint out as the gates shut. Our target of reaching a million schoolchildren in 2020, probably the most ambitious youth conservation project ever created, went up in smoke.

However, this provided another opportunity. Rhino Art had been in operation for seven years and had an extensive strategic, social and cultural network. Seeing as it was now mothballed until schools reopened, why not use that setup to feed wildlife communities?

That's exactly what we did. Exploiting Rhino Art's structures, we launched a roadshow with food substituted for drawing competitions. The thrust was providing emergency meals, mainly Africa's staple diet of maize meal porridge, to settlements on the fringes of game reserves, but it went deeper than that. Delivering bulk food not only physically demonstrated that we could provide in times of crisis but, in return, wildlife communities pledged not to poach. The message was clear: 'Wildlife Cares'.

Pilot projects kicked off in Zululand but soon escalated beyond all expectations. Within weeks, Feeding the Wildlife Community became a lifeline to thousands of hungry people around the country. We could barely keep up. Kingsley Holgate, the charismatic African explorer and my mentor in many rhino conservation projects, joined us with his partner Sheelagh Antrobus, as did sculptor Andries Botha and cricketer Kyle Abbott, a South African quick bowler playing for Hampshire in England. Without question, their generosity saved many lives.

These roadshows brought us face-to-face with the shattering devastation inflicted on those hamstrung by a locked-down economy. It was heart-breaking, depressing and soul destroying in equal measure. Above all, it hammered home how critically reliant some of the most destitute communities are on eco-tourism. Every game park in the country had closed down, and if anyone wanted irrefutable evidence of how much we depend on a healthy planet, COVID-19 provided ringside seats. It also graphically confirmed to those with most skin in the game – wildlife communities – that without eco-tourism the quality of life plummets for everyone.

Consequently, no matter who our donors were, we always stressed that we were distributing food on behalf of the nearby game reserves. The essential message was that the rural communities should not break into the neighbouring parks to poach as these wildlife havens were providing for them in this dire time of need.

In keeping with the wildlife brand, we used our mobile Rhino Art rig for the roadshows, changing the banner from 'Let Our Children's Voices Be Heard' to 'Feeding the Wildlife Community'. The fact that we got the message out loud and clear is in no small measure thanks to my colleague Richard Mabanga, who is a world-class showman.

Standing under a billboard with a photo of instant porridge and logos of nearby game reserves, Richard would plead with communities not to hunt bushmeat as the food we were providing was replacing it.

'When tourists come back there will be jobs and money again,' he said, his megaphone echoing across the countryside. 'But if you kill the animals, there will be no jobs or money, because the tourists will not come back.'

Richard is an incredibly animated orator and takes half an hour to say something that would take anyone else five minutes. But that was the whole point; for the community this was entertainment mixed with a serious environmental message.

He would then introduce us individually, telling the crowd that I was his brother but, unfortunately, I had been put in the fridge on a hot day and had turned white with cold.

He then would introduce Joe, asking if anyone knew of a game called 'rugby'. Despite South Africa having won the Rugby World Cup three times, football predominates in rural areas so only a few in the crowd would raise their hands. Richard would shake his head in mock amazement, saying it's a very strange sport as the ball is 'shaped like an egg' so didn't bounce properly. Even worse, players could only pass it backwards. The crowd laughed uproariously at such absurdity.

He then introduced Kyle, asking if anyone had heard of cricket. This is even less well-known than rugby, and Richard would say it involves a small ball, 'red like an apple', which is flung at a man with a stick who hits it out of the stadium. Then another man in a floppy white hat puts both hands in the air to signal 'six'. Sometimes the game lasts five days, and still no one wins. The crowds invariably found that even crazier.

Although highly effective, roadshows take time, especially with Richard's unique storytelling talents. Consequently, in more urgent situations we would simply drive the food directly to the village for a quick drop-off.

On one occasion I was with Ian Gourley, an adventurer who accompanies Kingsley on his Africa expeditions, and on approaching a village in the Black iMfolozi River valley we heard cheering and shouting.

I phoned the *induna* – headman – and asked what was happening.

'We're watching a football game,' he said. 'Just drive in. You'll see the big crowd.'

This was highly illegal under lockdown rules and instantly set off alarm bells in my head. A large number of people huddled together watching a sports match was exactly what COVID-19 legislation was designed to prevent. Besides that, whenever we distributed food, we were mandated to strictly observe social distance protocols and wear face masks at all times.

'OK,' I replied. 'We'll be there soon, but make sure you are alone on the side of the road with a list of the neediest families.'

The *induna* agreed but, as we entered the village, he rushed out, furiously flagging us down.

'Stop here!' he barked. 'The police have arrived to break up the soccer match.'

Before I could reply, Ian slammed on brakes and said, 'There's no way I'm going in. The cops will confiscate my Land Rover.'

Ian was correct. Even though we had permits, if the police deemed we were breaking lockdown laws they would seize his brand-new vehicle and probably never return it. I still thought we might be able to drop off the food in time, but as Ian had a lot more to lose than me, I said to the *induna*, 'We're out of here.'

'Whoa!' he replied, shaking his head. 'You can't leave. These people have been promised food and are waiting. They're starving.'

Ian and I looked at each other. Apart from the risk of vehicle confiscation, if the police prevented us from distributing food it was highly likely that the hungry crowd would go on the rampage. Food riots had already erupted in other townships around the country.

We had to act fast. Arms pumping frantically, we hauled out the maize-meal sacks and tossed them under a tree. This was also breaking protocol as we were handing over all the food to one person with no guarantee it would be distributed equitably. But as far as I was concerned, that was the lesser of two evils.

I hurriedly took a 'selfie' of myself and the *induna* posing with the food as proof of delivery while Ian did a wheel-spinning U-turn. We sped off in a cloud of dust, and it was with much relief as I looked back to see that the police were not in hot pursuit.

Just another day in Africa . . . but one thing was certain: COVID-19 was a global turning point, socially, economically – and environmentally. The world would not be the same again.

The key question was: what would replace it?

CHAPTER FOUR

A Force of Nature

As the world now knows to its incalculable cost, 'wet' (as in blood-soaked) wildlife markets are a Petri dish of possibly the most virulent pathogens known to humans. They are perfect storms for incubating plagues.

COVID-19 is believed to be a prime example, but Ebola, SARS, Zika and West Nile virus are said to have similar origins. When acutely stressed wild animals are crammed into small cages to be butchered on fly-infested slabs covered in guts and gore – well, what could possibly go wrong?

I have visited wildlife markets in Asia and Africa, and apart from being bacterial cesspits, they are disturbing beyond description.

In Vietnam, I visited several in Hanoi, while my wife Angela visited another in the infamous informal markets of Sa Pa, close to the Vietnamese–Chinese border. So when COVID-19 exploded from what is widely believed to have been a wet market, killing millions and crippling the global economy, I was not overly surprised. What did surprise me was how surprised everyone not involved in conservation was. I mean, how much of a rocket scientist does one have to be to understand that abusing wildlife and obliterating ecosystems are a root cause of zoonotic pandemics? How many more warnings does the planet need to give?

However, the word 'wet' in the case of the Asian markets can sometimes be misleading. It refers more to the constant hosing down of fruit and vegetables about to rot in the sub-tropical sun rather than rivers of animal blood.

But that is mere semantics. Most wet markets are soaked in gore as well as water. Customers point to an animal and it is killed and quartered before them. Although chickens and ducks are also stuffed like sardines into the death cages, most of the meat is wild, ranging from badgers, foxes and pangolins to snakes, lizards, turtles and, of course, bats, the suspected carriers of COVID-19. The reason the animals are alive, crawling on top of each other in bamboo crates, is because that is the only way to keep their flesh fresh without refrigeration. Anyone who cares for other creatures on this planet will feel physically ill.

Not only that, among the blood, guts and bone chips, the rough cement floors heave with flies and faeces. People walk through the gore in flipflops, handling bleeding slabs of meat with bare hands. A machete used to kill a snake is not wiped when it kills a monkey. The bloody debris is swept away with grass brooms, which act as paint brushes spreading more germs.

Meat not sold 'live' is barbecued on charcoal braziers, and to determine whether it's pork or pangolin requires a wild guess. I doubt whether most want to know the answer.

Unbelievable as that is, it's worse in African markets where even more types of bushmeat are on sale. This includes trauma-tised monkeys, trussed-up baby crocodiles, monitor lizards and civet cats. 'Fast food' is often barbecued bat, tinier than chicken wings and grilled to a crisp. It's unclear whether the bats have been gutted.

But before we rightly condemn these markets, we have to realise that for many this is the only protein they can afford. As with most of today's problems, there is no soft solution. But one thing is certain: post-COVID-19 will demand hard decisions to combat future outbreaks. The question is whether global leaders have the steel to make them.

Ironically, COVID-19 erupted like a Frankenstein monster in South Africa just as we were celebrating the most successful six months of my conservation life. And that was largely due to a man who stumbled into my world one night while sitting around a campfire in the Loziba bush with Beyers Coetzee.

'His name's Chris Holcroft,' said Beyers, throwing a log on to the flames as we waited for the mystery man. 'He's from America, but he's a real character.'

Beyers said Holcroft was apparently financing some 'elephant stuff' and wanted to see what we were doing with the Loziba herd. I shrugged. Probably just another eco-dabbler who flies into the country, poses for some feelgood photos, then flies out never to be seen again. We know the breed well.

This was in May 2019, nine months before Beyers's tragic death. After an hour or so wait, a car pulled up in a cloud of dust. The door opened and a figure emerged from the murk swearing like a trooper. He put out his hand as Beyers introduced us. In the light of the fire, I saw his arm was covered in tattoos.

'Sorry I'm late. Got bloody lost,' he said, although admitting that he had probably been driving too fast to read his satnav properly. Then he asked, 'What's happening?'

It was a routine question, but a good one as we soon discovered that, in Chris Holcroft's world, everything happened at lightning speed.

The evening was a blur of high-voltage discussion. Beyers had said Chris was an American, but he was actually born in Wales before moving to California. Several years ago he sold his hugely successful recruitment company for a seven-figure sum to concentrate on his other passion, photography. This led to an even greater passion. Conservation.

Every fibre of his body radiated with vigour and vitality, something often lacking in today's increasingly jaded world. He was one of the most excitable and vibrant people I had met, laughing constantly, and his dive into conservation was done with all-consuming energy. The questions he asked were intelligent and probing. More importantly, he listened to the replies.

The following morning, we went looking for the Loziba elephants and climbed Mawana Mountain for a better view. Mawana, close to where Africa's revered warrior-king Mzilikazi grew up, is sacred to the local tribes. It is a focal point for our proposed wilderness project, so much so that Loziba is named after Mzilikazi's favourite wife.

It was not a good morning for game viewing. A heavy mist smothered the slopes and visibility was next to nothing. Despite that, Chris was dead keen to go ahead as I don't think he'd ever seen a large elephant herd before. But neither Beyers nor I held out much hope, especially on Mawana. Holy or not, on all my numerous trips, I had never encountered any elephants on this revered mountain. Nor had Beyers, whose wife's family owned the land in the shadow of the craggy peak.

Chris sent a camera drone into the sky and, to our amazement, the sun suddenly burned off the mist below. Not only that, the entire herd was coming out of the haze. We crowded around the drone's viewfinder, absolutely entranced, watching as the animals majestically weaved through the acacias and sickle bush.

Chris stayed with us for three days and he loved every second of them. Loziba was primal Africa – action, elephants, thorns, dust, smoky campfires, haunting hyena calls . . . and the beauty of the bush that drills into one's marrow. It was a world he had never experienced.

As we said goodbye, I remarked that we probably would not meet again.

'Maybe. Maybe not,' he said. 'I'm coming back here after an elephant thing next week in Limpopo.'

I stopped in my tracks. I was also doing an 'elephant thing' in Limpopo, South Africa's northernmost province.

'It wouldn't be the Atherstone elephants would it?' I asked.

He looked at me curiously. 'How do you know?'

'Because I started that whole project – and it's taken three years of my life. I'll also be there next week, and you must be the anonymous donor I've been hearing about.'

He was indeed. In wildlife charity circles, donors are never disclosed if recipients can help it. No fundraiser mentions who they are getting money from in case someone else leaps on the bandwagon. And when money is tight, as it always is in conservation, anonymity is even more prized. Chris had come to Africa thanks to the charity Elephants, Rhinos & People, and even though I have close links with ERP, there had been no mention that Chris was a donor.

Luckily, Chris's substantial contribution had been ringfenced for Atherstone so could not be diverted elsewhere. He also had no desire to be a celebrity centre of attraction. As far as he was concerned, he was out here as a photographer rather than a donor. Photo sales would be ploughed back into wildlife charities.

I scratched my head in wonder. The coincidence that a relocation project I had initiated was now being sponsored by someone from America who I met somewhere so deep in the African bush that he'd barely found it on his GPS was simply staggering.

The Atherstone Nature Reserve elephant saga was covered in my previous book, *Saving the Last Rhinos*. In a nutshell, the reserve has too many elephants and the authorities urgently needed to relocate close on half of them. This has resulted in the usual bureaucratic nightmare regarding permits, sponsorships and enough red tape to gift-wrap Atherstone's entire herd, but the biggest headache continues to be finding the animals new homes.

Elephants are not easy to accommodate for the obvious reason that they are big. They devour several hundred pounds of foliage and drink a decent-sized pond of water dry every day of their lives. Small reserves are soon depleted of brush and even fast-growing red grass, not to mention fully grown trees being headbutted to the ground so the pachyderms can get at the canopy leaves.

But that's in South Africa. The rest of Africa is crying out for these magnificent creatures to come home after a century and a half of slaughter for their ivory and habitat degradation by loggers. Africa has many shortages, but wild land is not one of them. Managed, safe relocation and zero tolerance towards poaching are the keys to regenerating the continent's ancient great herds. They do not need to go the way of the American bison.

That is part of my grand vision for the continent, but at that moment we didn't have the funds or political clout for trans-border relocation. That would come later.

In the interim, we had to look locally. With ERP, I managed to secure homes for some of the Atherstone animals at Mount Camdeboo in the Karoo, and also at Buffalo Kloof, a reserve in the Eastern Cape owned by my cousin Warne Rippon and his wife Wendy. We needed substantial funds to do this, and people like Chris Holcroft were not only vital, they were guardian angels.

I flew out to Atherstone on 14 May 2019 and met up with the capture teams and Chris. It was a happy reunion, and I marvelled at how this crazy, tattoo-covered Californian wowed everyone wherever he went. He was one of those madcap eccentrics with whom people cannot help falling in love.

Transporting elephants is no easy feat, but our capture team led by Kester Vickery has perfected it to an art form. Using helicopters to scare the animals into clustering naturally as a family for safety, Kester then chooses which group to dart as a single unit. The family is loaded into trucks with a crane, using ropes to keep the sedated animals upright.

The first batch left on the twenty-hour journey to Mount Camdeboo, while Chris and I tagged along with the second group to Buffalo Kloof. Even though he and I had got on well at Loziba, I initially thought I had drawn the short straw, playing smiley-faced nursemaid to a donor rather than being with the main capture team.

I could not have been more wrong. The journey was one of the most stimulating of my life. Chris was the perfect travelling companion – when not about to kill us, that is. His cruising speed was a hundred miles an hour.

He told me he had met a lot of phonies in both business and conservation, but on this trip he had come into contact with 'real people' – hands-on eco-warriors whose prime focus was animals rather than media exposure or celebrity status. Without actually realising it, he said, this was what he had been searching for all his life.

He said mainstream conservation had done a terrible job explaining core issues facing wildlife in general, and rhinos and elephants in particular. Animals died while jobsworths niggled about which permit to sign and petulant celebrities squabbled over whose turn it was to be in front of a TV camera.

The end result was that in some reserves rhinos and elephants lived their entire lives just one breakout away from being killed. But even if they did break out, they had nowhere to go. That was what galled him most. He wanted to find these wonderful beasts, who once roamed with dinosaurs, somewhere to go. Somewhere safe with abundant forage and water. Somewhere they could call home, despite the fact that fences now strangled their eons-old migration routes.

His sentiments dovetailed with mine, and we spoke of forming an NGO that would pledge to move any animal at risk without hesitation and, equally importantly, without any ego-politics or media grandstanding. We would, to paraphrase Chris, 'just effing do it!'

He said he would take care of finances and media coverage while others handled the logistics, pooling the skills of various organisations such as ERP and Project Rhino. It was exactly the type of charity that I had in mind, although at that stage I had no idea how to bring it to fruition. But Chris did – as I was soon to find out.

We arrived at Buffalo Kloof after talking and driving around the clock, and I introduced Chris to Warne and Wendy Rippon.

If truth be known, Warne was doing me a family favour by accepting elephants from Atherstone, as he already had a herd on his land. So, not to put too fine a point to it, he was not overly ecstatic with the new arrivals.

That changed the instant the Atherstone matriarch lumbered out of the truck with a grace so simultaneously awkward and beautiful that only an elephant can pull it off. She is massive, one of the biggest cows in the country, weighing close on 3.5 tons and standing just under 10 feet at the shoulder. Every step that forced the thick brush aside was like an earth tremor. Warne fell in love like a besotted teenager. He was almost crying he was so happy.

Warne himself is a giant – over 6-foot-6 barefoot – but he's an even larger character. He plays the guitar like Johnny Cash, parties like a rock star, flies a helicopter like a Top Gun, and is an avid cricketer. He was selected for the South Africa Over 50s World Cup team in 2020, but sadly the event was cancelled after the third round due to COVID-19.

Suffice it to say that Warne lives at full throttle. As did Chris, so I was not surprised that they got on like a house on fire. That night the party was memorable even by their high standards, ending close to sunrise with Warne still strumming the guitar.

Warne and Wendy hit it off so well with Chris that Buffalo Kloof became his African home. He said that when he died, he wanted his ashes scattered at Spekboom, one of the lodges.

A couple of months after the elephant relocation, the Rippons invited Chris to film the release of black rhinos at Buffalo Kloof. This was a joint venture with the Yendella community, who own land bordering Buffalo Kloof that is too wild for farming, but perfect rhino habitat. The villagers would lease this to Warne and other private landowners, with the rent ploughed back into sustainable agriculture.

This type of project is close to my heart as the conservation wars can only be won by partnering with communities that live cheek-by-jowl with wildlife. It was also a world first as critically endangered black rhinos had never been moved from the Fish River to other parts of the Eastern Cape before.

Chris filmed the historic event and flew back to California a changed man. Africa was now in his arteries, pumping with burning intensity that crystallised in the formation of Wild911, the wildlife vision we had discussed during the epic trip from Atherstone to Buffalo Kloof. I had nothing to do with the actual founding of Wild911 but was honoured to be appointed the African director.

Chris put his vision succinctly into a text to me from California: 'The plan is simple enough – to raise enough money to go back and start moving at-risk animals and sending them to the areas that have vegetation in abundance where they'll be welcome, protected and they can add significant positive impact to worldwide conservation. We'll see who really gives a shit.'

The last sentence was, in essence, the distillation of Chris's philosophy of life.

Wild911 was instantly called into action. It happened when a giant bull elephant called Harry broke out of the Blaauwbosch reserve in the Eastern Cape, not far from the Amakhala Game Reserve where I grew up.

The authorities decreed that Harry was a danger and must be destroyed. It would not be the first time that an escaped Blaauwbosch elephant had been given a death sentence. In 2017 a bull on the run was shot out of hand, so Harry's future looked short, sharp and brutal.

I phoned Chris to say we needed money to save Harry – and quickly. He uttered his usual four-lettered tirade about murdering animals, then asked, 'How much?'

'Half a million rand.'

'I'm in.' He added there was no way Harry was going to die. 'They'll have to kill me first. I'll stand in front of the shooters.'

I had no doubt he would.

A day or two later he was in South Africa with the money and we started the legal process to save Harry's life. The clock was spring-loaded it was ticking so fast, but fortunately Harry had broken out on to a farm called Mon Desir, and the owner Sandra Skinner bought us time by refusing to allow the animal to be killed on her land. She told the authorities that Harry had battered through Blaauwbosch's dilapidated fence for the simple reason that there was no water on the reserve. His only other option was to die of thirst. The previous Blaauwbosch bull had broken out and been killed for the exact same reason.

Through the newly formed Wild911 and the Aspinall Foundation, Chris Holcroft broke a world record. In less than twelve hours, he spearheaded a team that overturned a 'shoot to kill' order and had it amended to 'relocate'. I don't think that record will ever be broken. And it's amazing what a difference a single word can make. In Harry's case, it was the difference between life and death.

Harry was moved to Mount Camdeboo, where owner Iain Buchanan already had Atherstone elephants on his reserve. Relocation expert Kester Vickery and my brother William, a vet who pioneered healing rhinos mutilated by poachers, supervised the operation. It was a big win for us.

But it didn't end there. Blaauwbosch was a running sore on the credibility of private conservation parks. It was a seriously rundown reserve with sparse water and inadequate forage, but it should have had everything going for it, particularly as the owner Sheikh Khalaf Ahmed Khalaf Al Otaiba from the United

Arab Emirates is said to be among the richest men in the world. Keeping Blaauwbosch viable, it could be presumed, should have been chump change for him.

After the Harry saga, conservationists vowed that the reserve had to face consequences, and the environmental authorities agreed. A warrant was issued authorising the Society for the Protection of Cruelty to Animals (SPCA) to move all animals off Blaauwbosch.

Unfortunately, this was far easier said than done. It was a gargantuan task, logistically and financially, involving relocating eleven more elephants as well as other big game such as giraffe and buffalo. It was, with the best will in the world, something far beyond the resources of the SPCA.

After what Wild911 and the Aspinall Foundation had achieved with Harry, we were the natural go-to people. We were among the few who could do it and the SPCA and conservation authorities knew this. The question was, would we do it?

Chris's response was typical: damn right we would. Although he used more colourful language. We swung into action, ready to move every single living mammal, apart from rodents and hares, off a once-thriving reserve.

The reaction was immediate. Just as we were getting ready, Blaauwbosch's lawyers handed our team an interdict preventing us from entering the reserve.

No problem, said Chris. We'll see you in court. Again, he said that in more colourful language.

We won the case. But unless we moved the animals faster than Noah loaded his ark, it would turn out to be a pyrrhic victory. Without new homes, the creatures would perish.

The biggest problem was the eleven elephants. Where could we put them? I had already used whatever influence I had in finding homes for the Atherstone animals, so I was at a bit of a loss to relocate yet another herd.

Once again, I hadn't bargained on Chris's dogged powers of persuasion. He was staying at Buffalo Kloof and pointed out to Warne and Wendy that the 'happy ending' of Blaauwbosch was not so happy. We had nowhere to place the massive creatures.

Chris then put his arm around Warne – he almost had to stand on a barstool to do so – and said, 'Dude, why don't you take the whole herd?'

Warne was not keen, and with good reason. He already had two elephant herds on his land. As mentioned, he also had just taken on black rhinos. What was he going to do with another eleven pachyderms?

'Please, dude. Otherwise they'll die.' Chris smiled that irresistible Holcroft grin as he verbally twisted Warne's arm to breaking point.

Warne slammed down his beer mug. 'Bring them,' he instructed. 'The whole bloody lot.'

With those words, the Blaauwbosch elephants got a new lease of life. The rest of the animals, including giraffes, buffaloes and antelopes, went to other parks designated by the provincial environmental department.

Ominously, while staying at Buffalo Kloof, Chris said he was suffering from chest pains. He went to see a doctor, who said it was probably exhaustion from all the hours of flying he was doing.

We all shrugged it off as a minor scare. Chris was an indestructible human dynamo. Nothing could stop him. He was a force of nature.

Or so we thought.

CHAPTER FIVE

War and Peace

I was in Angola when the Blaauwbosch elephants were relocated to Buffalo Kloof, which was appropriately symbolic. What Wild911 was doing at Warne's game park was a microcosm of what we wanted to do throughout Africa.

But instead of only moving threatened animals to other private reserves, we wanted to repopulate the vast savannahs and forests of the continent. I'm the first to admit that is an ambitious aspiration, perhaps even a pipedream. But no one could accuse us at Wild911 of not thinking big.

Angola is a key country in our plans as most of its once-abundant wildlife was shot out in a brutal twenty-seven-year civil war that killed 800,000 and displaced 4 million.

But the country has intrinsic, almost mystical, significance for many South Africans. It is where the war of my generation, referred to as the Border War or *Grensoorlog* in Afrikaans, was fought. A war waged in a time of bitter, ancient, unyielding hatreds. The animosities seemed so deep-rooted that many thought them to be irreconcilable.

And yet . . . Africa heals wounds like no other physician. Scratch under the crust of Angola's scorched earth and you will discover an astonishing story of reconciliation and outreach that flies in the face of implacable acrimony. The battlefields, still seeded with landmines, are now sprouting tentative roots of reconciliation between formerly intractable foes.

To some extent, the fact that this extraordinary peace pipe was lit, let alone smoked, is thanks to two remarkable men: a former South African soldier called Johan Booysen and General Fernando Mateus, the former Angolan chief of army.

Johan was just eighteen in 1987 when he, like almost all white youths, was conscripted into the military. He was one of the unlucky ones: he was sent to the frontline and saw intense action with 61 Mechanised Battalion along the Namibian–Angola border; 61 Mech, as it was known, was a lethal rapid-reaction force that spearheaded much of the hostilities during the Border War. It affected Johan profoundly, as it did many South Africans ordered to fight in a conflict they knew little about except that it was 'against communism'.

Angola had been in flames for twelve years before Johan arrived in uniform. The moment the Portuguese colonisers left in 1975, the oil-rich country exploded in a conflict that became the most vicious Cold War flashpoint since Vietnam. FAPLA (People's Armed Forces of Liberation of Angola), the army of the Angolan government, was supported by the Soviet Union and Cuba, while the USA and South Africa supported the pro-West guerrilla forces of UNITA (National Union for the Total Independence of Angola).

This came to a head in 1987–8 at the Battle of Cuito Cuanavale, which is now entrenched in African folklore. To date, it's the biggest set-piece brawl on the continent since El Alamein in the Second World War. To give an idea of the ferocity of the fighting, twelve Honoris Crux medals were awarded on a single day, 25 August 1987. By military standards, the Honoris Crux was two notches below the Victoria Cross, and was the old South African army's highest decoration for courage under fire.

The end result was a stalemate, with FAPLA/Cuban forces claiming victory as they had held on to the village of Cuito Cuanavale, while the South Africans said they had achieved their objective by obliterating FAPLA's advance into UNITA territory.

Be that as it may, the true losers – infinitely so – were the rural people of southern Angola. The South Africans and Cubans have gone home, the Soviet Union has collapsed, and FAPLA and UNITA have put down their guns. But among the dirt-poor peasants who remain, eking out a hardscrabble existence among the deadly detritus of war, casualties still mount. At least 70,000 civilians have suffered severed limbs from landmines, which continue to explode to this day. The number of those killed, or orphaned, is unknown.

Back in civvy street, Johan had to deal with the lingering demons of conflict. As a frontline *troepie*, South African slang for 'conscripted soldier', he had been ordered to do stuff he wanted to forget. He lived with those ghosts for twenty-seven years.

Eventually, he decided to visit the battlefields that still haunted him. With him were three other former soldiers, Cobus Botes, Steve Prinsloo and Wayne Laatz, as well as Johan's spirited daughter Tammy. They got on motorbikes and rode the thousand miles to Angola.

It wasn't just a journey of redemption. Hearing about the dire plight of schoolchildren, ten of whom might have to share one ballpoint pen, the group collected basic education equipment to distribute at local schools. A simple spiralbound notebook for a barefoot kid in a dusty class under a baobab is more precious than any iPad.

In May 2015, Johan Booysen entered Angola for the first time without a rifle in his hands. Instead he had a passport stamp.

There he, his daughter and three brothers-in-arms met Fernando Mateus. For the Angolan general, it was probably the first time he had seen a white South African without a weapon.

Unbelievably, the former foes had a rapport. It is difficult to imagine the galaxy-wide chasm they faced – not just militarily, but ideologically, culturally, racially and, above all, stereotypically. All preconceived notions and presumptions had to be cast into the wind. Pared down to the bones, it was simply old soldiers bonding. As a result, Tammy said they decided to make it their 'life's mission to bring more ex-soldiers to Angola to make more friendships and encourage more reconciliation'.

This sparked off further visits, organised by the 61 Mechanised Battalion Veterans Association, of which Johan is the convenor. Three years later, in May 2018, a convoy of twenty-six vehicles and eighty-three people, mainly grizzled soldiers in their late fifties, crossed the Angolan border. Again, for almost all, it was the first time they had done so without a weapon. Their banner was 'Unidade de Amizade/Unity in Friendship', and the trip was coordinated with General Mateus, now a family friend of the Booysens. The core concept, according to Greg de Ricquebourg, a former lieutenant colonel in 61 Mech, was to 'pay homage to all our lost comrades'. Greg, who is the brother of Bully de Ricquebourg, one of my closest friends, stressed that 'comrades' included Angolans, Cubans and Russians.

This cannot be emphasised strongly enough. For many ex-soldiers, this was not a mere trip. It was a pilgrimage.

Soon afterwards, Angolan veterans led by General Mateus visited 61 Mech's memorial in Johannesburg, where they laid a wreath for fallen comrades of both sides.

However, Johan, a deeply religious man, wanted to do more than just combat reconciliation to heal the wounds of war. He wanted to help those most affected by the destruction. He started talking to General Mateus and the Angolan government about other issues, development projects related to farming, job creation and education, and an overall upliftment of life for those living in the previous battlefields.

Key to this was wildlife. Southern Angola has potentially some of the best bushveld and wildlife habitat in the world. The problem, though, is that there is little wildlife left. Before the Angolan Civil War, which kicked off in 1975 and finally ended with the death of UNITA leader Jonas Savimbi twenty-seven years later, 200,000 elephants roamed these vast mopane woodlands, marshes and savannahs. Today, an estimated 3,500 are left. The rest were massacred for their ivory by Savimbi's guerrillas to buy weapons. Perhaps more than anywhere else in Africa, the sands of Cuito Cuanavale are saturated with both human and elephant blood.

Equally tragic is the demise of the giant sable, an antelope found only in Angola, which is the country's national emblem. In Angolan mythology these graceful animals symbolise energy, speed and beauty. They were also slaughtered on an industrial scale to feed soldiers. They are now on the verge of extinction, with only a few pockets believed to be surviving deep in the densest thickets.

The Angolan government wanted Johan and Tammy, who is an honours graduate in development economics, to look at future tourism projects. As the global price of oil was plummeting, sub-Saharan Africa's second largest producer urgently needed alternative foreign revenue, and tourism was an immensely viable option. So the Booysens invited me along as an environmentalist and elephant consultant.

I jumped at the opportunity. With Chris Holcroft and the newly formed Wild911 prepared to take on the world, this was exactly the type of project we were looking for. Not only could Angola be a potentially feasible location to settle more of the surplus Atherstone elephants, it could be the first step in restoring the country's once enormous elephant herds.

Like Johan Booysen, I was also conscripted into the military – in my case the air force – but I never saw action in Angola. I was based in Hoedspruit on the other side of the country, close to the Kruger National Park. But many of my friends fought in Cuito Cuanavale, and I knew that much of what I would be seeing on this trip would be the same as they had viewed through bombsights or red-hot rifle barrels.

We arrived in Luanda and in the airport lounge met the Angolan minister of environment Paula Coelho and Pedro Mutindi, the former hotel and tourism minister who is still active in Angolan politics.

Almost straight off, Minister Coelho promised us 1.5 million hectares of park land and said a further 12 million hectares, or 6 per cent of the entire country, was designated for environmental and wildlife development. The government wanted eventually to double that.

I whistled. This seemed a dream come true. I just hoped the land promised would match expectations, but that was something I would find out first-hand in the next few days.

We were then whisked off in an official Land Cruiser to the house of Pedro Mutindi, who had previously been governor of the Cunene province on the Namibian border for twenty-five years. Pedro had been a top-ranking FAPLA commander during the Battle of Cuito Cuanavale; he could swear in basic Afrikaans as he said the foulest expletives were the only words he understood when eavesdropping on the South African army's radio comms. Despite my sketchy Portuguese, picked up while marketing Amakhala Game Reserve in Brazil, I soon grasped that this man was a natural-born leader with a lively sense of humour. He was also hard as nails. Just before the end of the war, his leg was blown off by a landmine and he now limped around with great dexterity on a prosthetic limb. It was ironic to think that, almost four decades ago, he and Johan had been intent on killing each other. Now all they were doing was 'murdering' a bottle of red wine – and with huge enjoyment. To me, that is a salutary lesson on the therapy of Africa.

Without even seeing the wildlife reserves, I thought Angola had plenty going for it as far as tourism was concerned. Luanda is a stunning city, almost like Durban, with a lovely clean promenade lined with nightclubs and beautiful beach bars. It's true that, a few streets behind the city centre, Luanda does revert somewhat starkly to the Third World, similar to Rio de Janeiro with *favelas* sprawling behind five-star hotels. But that certainly doesn't do one of South America's most vibrant cities' tourist trade much harm, so I'm sure Luanda won't have problems. Also, Angola has staggering natural resources such as diamonds, iron ore, manganese and, of course, oil. So the country does have a lot going for it, despite being one of the least developed nations of the world.

The plan was to have another meeting with Pedro Mutindi and Paula Coelho, then go and inspect three national parks. The logistics were immense as Angola is Africa's seventh largest country, but Pedro assured us that an army helicopter had been specifically assigned to ferry us around.

Unfortunately, despite the excellent hospitality, I discovered that Angola was no different from the rest of Africa in terms of time management. After three days in Luanda, we had not put foot outside the city, let alone seen a wild animal. And we still had a million and a half acres of game parks to inspect.

We thus had no option but to split up. Johan and Tammy drove 600 miles to the Benguela province with General Mateus to see the Chimilavera Natural and Regional Park, while I would fly south with Pedro on a fact-finding mission in the Mupa and Bicauri National Parks.

Pedro promised to fetch me at 9 a.m. the next day and an army helicopter would take us to the parks. I knew something was wrong the moment he arrived at the hotel.

'*Um problema, senhor*,' he said. A problem.

Our military transport had been assigned elsewhere, so we would have to fly commercially to Ondjiva, the capital of Cunene province, and then drive to the reserves. With a flourish, he handed me a boarding pass. Not only were we in business class, but our seats were A1 and A2.

A moment later, a black limousine pulled up to take us to the airport. We were then escorted into the presidential lounge where at least a dozen cabinet ministers were waiting for planes. They were all dressed immaculately, the men in Savile Row-style suits and the women in designer dresses. I looked like a gate-crashing hobo in my bush khakis.

Unconcerned, Pedro introduced me as the man who was going to bring conservation to Angola, which created a bustle of interest. Despite my sartorial defects, everyone was suddenly pressing business cards into my hand and I made more contacts in a minute than the previous three days combined. They wanted to know what I could do for their country, so I told them about my work in South Africa, largely with rhinos and elephants, and that my family were joint owners of Amakhala, a Big Five game reserve in the Eastern Cape. We got on famously. Networking is absolutely essential anywhere in the world, and Africa is no exception, but I knew from previous experience to moderate expectations when rubbing shoulders with the high and mighty. However, it was certainly a promising framework for future ventures, and a fistful of cabinet ministers' business cards would not do me harm.

If I had any doubts about Pedro's influence, they were dispelled with a vengeance the moment the plane landed at Ondjiva. We were first off the aircraft and escorted with VIP reverence into the terminal, then ushered through another door where a chauffeur-driven black limousine waited. Best of all, its air-conditioning was ratcheted up to arctic levels to blunt the tropical heat.

We didn't even collect our luggage; that would be picked up by Pedro's staff and brought to his house or, more correctly, his mansion. It was like a palace, positioned right next to the airport, and he steered me into a room with a long wooden table that could seat about thirty people. On the walls were numerous framed photos of him meeting various presidents and others from the political elite.

For some reason, Pedro's beautiful mansion seemed to be only half-built, while outside was a large empty swimming pool. But there was nothing half-hearted about the hospitality as Pedro opened a bottle of robust red wine, and the fun started. That night he took me out to the nearby village, where we met other former generals from the civil war, now businessmen eager to see their country flourish. After several hours of wining and dining, Pedro took me back to his house, promising we would visit the reserves the next day.

We were up early and I was raring to go as I had now been in Angola for five days without having seen an inch of the million-plus acres I needed to inspect. It seemed Pedro's chauffeur knew this as he drove on the dirt tracks at over a hundred miles an hour, giving even wannabe-racer Chris Holcroft a run for his money.

It is a trip etched in my mind, veering from adrenalin-fuelled invigoration to bleak sadness. Invigorating because it was some of the most spectacular landscape I have seen, with glorious, massive-trunked baobabs rooted in white sand backlit by vivid red sunsets; and depressing because much of the pristine habitat was ruined by rows of human shanties and overgrazing. Trees are logged at an alarming rate to make charcoal, and as honey is almost a local currency, I saw beehives everywhere.

Over the next two days we inspected both national parks by plane and car, and to my intense disappointment it was clear that at least 10 per cent of what was supposed to be wilderness was totally degraded. In fact, it was almost impossible to tell where the parks started and human settlements ended. The only indication was that the deeper one went, the more scattered the mud-and-thatch villages with scrawny livestock became. I shook my head. There was no hope of regenerating this.

But I was thinking as a South African. These villagers and cows and donkeys with protruding ribcages were temporary sojourners in this potential Garden of Eden. My hosts told me in no uncertain terms that all settlements would be relocated once the regeneration process of Angola's national parks began in earnest.

I was shocked. If that happened in South Africa, there would be a global outcry and enough land-claim prosecutions to keep lawyers cashing cheques well into the next century. But as Angola doesn't have the historical baggage of apartheid, it seems the villagers accept that they are merely squatters on state land.

The wildlife itself was also disappointing, consisting mainly of meat-eating scavengers. Strangely enough, wild dogs, which are threatened or extinct elsewhere, are thriving here, as are hyenas, surviving on a diet of rodents, hares and small antelope. This is because their main competitors, the big cats, have all vanished, either killed or simply dying out with the slaughter of zebras and buck, their natural food.

There is still a handful of elephants, survivors of the civil war, so as far as Wild911 was concerned this was obvious country to revive. With proper security we could also consider bringing in rhinos. But that was unlikely in the short term.

On the border of the Mupa reserve, I came across a small beacon of hope: an old Portuguese colonial government farm called Chavemba. It was owned by Pedro and, with a generator, irrigation pumps, maize milling machine and even an abattoir, it was the only self-sufficient settlement in the area. Lucerne (alfalfa), onions and carrots grow, and a herd of gaunt cattle survives on the sparse grazing and maize husks. Rudimentary in the extreme, it was nevertheless a veritable oasis compared to anything else I had seen. It was glaringly obvious that more projects like this were needed.

To my astonishment, the manager was a South African called Buks Kruger. He has an Angolan wife and children, and had managed the farm for eleven years. Buks knows the area intimately and told me that the Mupa reserve, a stone's throw from the experimental farm, is home to the rare Angolan giraffe, which is much lighter in colour than other giraffes. I didn't see any but knew that the preservation of that, combined with possible intensive giant sable-breeding programmes and the reintroduction of elephant, meant that this was a project worth undertaking.

I then learned that the village of Mupa, after which the reserve is named, had almost as much significance for former South African soldiers as Cuito Cuanavale. During the Unity in Friendship reconciliation trip, 61 Mech veterans returned a beautiful wooden crucifix to a local church that had been looted in the conflict. A remorseful South African *troepie* who had stolen the cross gave it to the Veterans Association for safekeeping until it could be returned to its rightful owners. This was done during a poignant ceremony at the packed church – a touchingly symbolic act of rapprochement between old enemies.

I lay on my bed that night in Pedro's mansion, lost deep in thought. Few lands have such turbulent ghosts stalking the apocalypse as this. From dead soldiers and limbless landmine victims to the departed tuskers and giant sable, blood has been relentlessly spilt.

I decided then and there that it didn't have to be that way, if I could help it. Despite the massive problems, there were many opportunities. The key one was, of course, bringing prosperity to an area that has never recovered from a war staggering in its brutality.

It could be done. Neighbouring Namibia, now one of Africa's most stable countries, has an established tourist industry, and the globally famous Etosha pan was a mere hundred miles from Mupa and Bicauri. In fact, it's part of the same ecosystem. That market and adventure tourism, along the lines of the motorbike rally Johan and Tammy organised with war veterans, were extremely viable propositions. And of course, international tourism. But for that we would need to get the iconic animals back. The Big Five. And that was where I came in. I could picture in my mind's eye elephants stretching to the horizon as they had just fifty years ago.

It was now time to go home. I couldn't wait to tell Chris Holcroft about the trip. The Angolans had promised us 1.5 million hectares, an unbelievable pledge. They had the land; South Africa had the elephants. We just had make sure it was safe for the great pachyderms to return to the ancient migration routes of West Africa. To do that, we would have to finance security by hiring an army of skilled and dedicated game rangers who were prepared to defend the animals with their lives. It was a bold vision, but one thing Chris believed in with a passion was that you go big, or go home.

Going home for me, however, was easier said than done. Pedro was scheduled to pick me up in the morning as we had to drive to Ondangwa in Namibia, about 40 miles south, to catch a plane to Windhoek. True to form, he was late, but promised to get me through the border post at Santa Clara in record time. Despite 'encouraging' the border officials with some choice Afrikaans swearwords, we didn't get through quickly enough. By the time we arrived at Ondangwa's airport, the plane to Windhoek was airborne. If this had happened in Angola, one word from Pedro would have had the pilot returning, but, in Namibia, his authority didn't have the same sway.

He still had immense clout, and after phoning a contact from his war days when Namibian guerrillas fought alongside FAPLA, a brand new vehicle and driver were provided to speed me to the Namibian capital 430 miles away. Pedro even phoned a friend who had a restaurant in the city and booked me a table.

The driver averaged a hundred miles an hour, and this time I got on the plane at Windhoek airport.

I arrived home exhausted. It had been intense week visiting lands where phantoms of slaughtered elephants still trumpet in anguish, and where the reconciliation of former implacable foes defies the word 'miracle'.

Southern Angola is inspirational beyond description. In my opinion, men like Johan Booysen and General Mateus are candidates for the Nobel Peace Prize. No question about it.

Anyone not surprised by Africa is simply not paying attention.

CHAPTER SIX

Death of a Legend

It was nudging midnight when my phone rang. I am used to receiving calls at all hours, especially as many people I work with live in vastly different time zones.

The caller-ID flashed. It was from a Wild911 colleague who lived in the same time zone as me. Why was he phoning so late?

'What's up?' I asked.

The voice at the other end was barely coherent. The caller was sobbing uncontrollably.

'Chris is dead.'

I know a lot of people called Chris. It is a common name.

'Chris who?' But I knew the answer as I spoke. Chris Holcroft. 'How did it happen?' I asked.

No one seemed to be sure. All we knew was that Jac Holcroft had found his father lying motionless on the floor of his bedroom at the family's home in Encinitas, a beach city about 95 miles south of Los Angeles. He frantically tried to rouse him, but Chris was no longer with us. The family suspected heart failure.

Shocked rigid, I put down the phone. Prior to the call, I had been enjoying an exceptionally pleasant evening in Cape Town with Gary Wright, a literary agent, and his partner Heather. We had just returned from a promotion of *Saving the Last Rhinos*, and the response had been positive. I had been feeling good until this sucker punch lurched out of the blue.

We knew Chris had suffered a health scare when he complained of chest pains a few months earlier at Buffalo Kloof, but doctors diagnosed that as exhaustion. We also knew he had been living on the edge, dealing with business problems from his former company, as well as struggling with Californian bureaucrats on the registration of Wild911 as a charity. The constant jetlag from transatlantic flights between the USA and Africa was also taking its toll. He lived at full-throttle, and we watched in awe as he never backed down while confronting the myriad obstacles that dogged us every step of the way in relocating animals. Wildlife was a passion that consumed him to the core. The past six months alone had seen a staggering eighty at-risk animals – including twenty-nine elephants – being relocated to safe havens. Chris had been at the forefront of each one, moving mountains of red tape through sheer indomitable will.

But even so, surely that was not enough to fell someone as on top of his game as Chris? He was only fifty-five, bursting with passion and energy. It was true that he liked a good party, but he had recently moderated his lifestyle and had even taken up mountain biking. Africa had given him fresh vision and he had everything to live for.

My shock intensified when I realised I had seen him barely four weeks ago in KwaZulu-Natal and he had been peaking with vitality. Everything was at last going our way. Wild911 was soaring with multiple new projects – such as my Angolan trip – and the time he and I spent together flew past in a blur of activity. We were talking about relocating the last remaining tuskers – elephants with ivory longer than 5 feet and weighing more than 100 pounds – to safe havens. There are only thirteen left in South Africa, and we planned to move four young bulls from the Tembe Elephant Park on the Mozambique border to new homes to spread the gene pool. This was also vital as tuskers that literally trip over their ivory are magnets for poachers.

Equally exciting was that Chris had been talking to Netflix about screening Wild911's work, including absolutely stunning footage of our Atherstone elephant relocations. We were on the cusp of a massive publicity blaze and becoming a global conservation brand. The proposed Wild911 series would be as much about the people and gritty determination it takes to do frontline conservation work as it would be about animals. It would be brash, full of personalities, robust campfire chats and poaching wars, as well as covering the risky, high-adrenaline operations where blunders are often fatal. Chris had been adamant that this would be no gimmicky made-for-TV reality show – it would be an unflinchingly authentic portrayal of what's at stake in the battle for the planet. Handling the live video footage was top-rated cameraman Andy Malcolm and, with Chris as the wingman, Netflix directors were excited.

However, despite the upbeat tone of our last weekend together, Chris did mention that all was not well on the home front. He and his wife were in the throes of separating, which caused some family strain, but I gathered it was being handled as amicably as possible under the circumstances. He had been determined that this would not affect his work in Africa, and none of us involved with Wild911 had reason to doubt that.

That trip ended in the usual Holcroft way with exuberant, back-thumping bear hugs. Chris was the most tactile person I knew, and social distancing, which thanks to COVID-19 is the new normal, would have been an alien world to him. That final massive hug is something I will forever cherish.

It took me several hours to recover my composure after hearing of his death. The next day I phoned Jac Holcroft to express my condolences. Jac was in obvious grief as he and Chris had been particularly close, but he did say he was aware of how much Africa meant to his father and how important it was for the legacy to continue. I asked what would happen next, and he said that as it took up to ninety days for a post-mortem to be undertaken in the USA, the burial service would be held the following month. I told him we would also be having a memorial service for him in Africa, as he had a lot of friends here.

I then contacted Chris's lawyer in California, Diana Rabbani, who was involved in the legalities of setting up Wild911. She had more bad news as Chris's application to register as a tax-exempt NGO had not been completed at the time of his death. Even worse, it would take at least another nine months for the registration to be validated under Californian law. Until that was done, Wild911 was effectively sidelined.

That was a disaster. We were already moving animals at risk every week, often paid for personally by Chris, and could not put everything on hold for three-quarters of a year. Hundreds of animals could die. We would have to find other ways around that, but an issue that needed equally urgent clarification was the Holcroft family's seal of approval. Without that, Wild911 might not survive.

The big question was, would we get it?

On the face of it, Jac had said he wanted his father's legacy to continue, but I was not sure whether that was the majority family consensus. I started to fear the worst, especially when no one from Africa was formally invited by the Holcrofts to Chris's memorial service in California. It was not exactly a snub, and I'm sure we would have been welcomed if we had arrived, but it did seem a little odd at the time. We could not help thinking that Chris's African connection was, perhaps, not considered that important by the rest of his family.

The official post-mortem confirmed that Chris had died from heart failure. Once that information was released, we held a memorial service for him at a boma – an enclosure – in Pretoria, attended by the people who had worked most closely with him. Messages of goodwill and love poured in from throughout South Africa. I don't think Chris knew how much he affected so many lives. Sadly, conspicuous by their absence, was the Holcroft family, which again seemed to indicate that the African link was peripheral.

I gave the eulogy at the service, with the key theme being that even though Chris was only in Africa for a short period, he did more good than most of us in a lifetime. Later, around a large fire, I used the Zulu 'talking stick' tradition of passing a beaded stick to various people who wanted to recount stories or anecdotes of Chris's life. The Zulu term is *induku zophefumula*, and whoever holds the stick holds the floor, giving everyone an equal opportunity to speak. A beautifully filmed video of Chris's work and his love for Africa, compiled by Andy Malcolm, was then screened. There was not a dry eye in the boma.

I had hoped that the service would bring some closure to those left behind, but I was wrong. The tragedy seemed too big to grasp. One moment we were on the brink of doing great work, and now, in the blink of an eye, Wild911 was brought to its knees. The simple reality was that, without Chris, no one had the global network, the financial contacts, the astute business acumen, the resources, the ideas, the razor-sharp vision and sheer *joie de vivre* to make it all happen at the highest level. Chris had absolutely dominated the conservation scene for the past six months. In that time, he had spearheaded the rescue of twenty-eight elephants, nineteen buffalo, twenty-nine wildebeest and four giraffes. It was absolutely phenomenal. A superhuman achievement.

But could it last?

Chris's death had been too sudden, and without a concrete succession plan in place, it could be the death knell of this NGO that had held so much promise. He had been keen to bring Jac on board as a business partner, but it was unfair in the extreme to expect a twenty-three-year-old to follow in the footsteps of his iconic father. On top of that, the family now appeared to be sidelining Andy Malcolm, who was crucial to our setup. The Netflix deal alone could only happen with Andy handling Wild911's film rights. When he tried to explain that to the Holcroft family, it seemed they had other ideas.

As the Africa director of Wild911, I desperately wanted to keep the charity going. I also had to accept the reality that, in the midst of all this confusion, we still had crucial work to do as soon as possible. For example, we still needed homes for more than thirty Atherstone elephants, who could not wait for boardroom politics to be resolved thousands of miles away in California. If Wild911 suspended operations until its charity status and family approval were sorted, elephant relocation expert Kester Vickery and I would have little option but to continue independently.

Sadly, the first casualty was Angola. We not only needed to move elephants to the 1.5-million hectares we had been promised, but also to guarantee their safety. This would cost money – loads of it. And without Chris Holcroft at the helm, it seemed unlikely that we would raise such a vast sum.

I then heard of a *National Geographic* Exploration grant of US$50,000 that was up for grabs. Andy Malcolm and I immediately set about drawing up an application, and were optimistic as ours was a noble cause by any yardstick. I was not aware of any other venture that was attempting to bring animals back to a land that had been drenched in blood. If we got the money, we planned to do a documentary to raise the profile of the operation. I titled our application 'Hope is the last thing to die', a line from the book *Wildlife at War* by Brian Huntley. Huntley had lived in the Angolan bush for fifty years and the minister of environment, Paula Coelho, kept referring me to his epic work. Hope would indeed be the last thing to die, and I stressed that with the *National Geographic* grant, herds that had been wiped out in an inhuman conflict would return to this potential Eden. Sadly, *National Geographic* did not agree. They didn't give a reason for their rejection.

A month later we lost Beyers, gored by an elephant at Loziba, and then COVID-19 struck. I know conservation is not for the faint-hearted, but what else could go wrong?

I was soon to find out.

CHAPTER SEVEN

Whisky and Wildebeest

No single authority has emerged from the COVID-19 crisis without its reputation in shreds.

From China, where most experts agree it first flourished, to the World Health Organization that initially refused to label it as a pandemic, to the life-threatening action or inaction of Western governments, it has been a debacle from the start.

But perhaps the most incomprehensible reaction of all came from my government. Random rules, many of which defied logic, were introduced with astonishing inefficiency. For example, alcohol and cigarettes, which were not considered causes of COVID-19 by even the wildest of conspiracy theorists, were banned in South Africa. The result? Industries that were two of the country's biggest sources of tax revenue, and therefore desperately needed income, were driven underground.

The insanity continued. People were jailed for surfing on deserted beaches, but allowed to cram into sardine-tin taxis where a single sneeze could spray a cluster-bomb of pathogens. Farmworkers were packed cheek-by-jowl into trucks to go and cut sugarcane, but a stone's throw away visitors were forbidden to enter game parks with only wildlife, the bush and sky for company.

To the surprise of no one, except perhaps bureaucrats, the country's hospitality industry collapsed, with wildlife tourism at the forefront. South African tourism generates R425.8 billion (about £21.29 billion at the time) and 1.5 million jobs a year, accounting for almost 9 per cent of all economic activity. To cripple this golden goose was absurd beyond description.

We were at the coalface of it all. Leeuwenbosch, my family's land which is part of the Big Five Amakhala Game Reserve, did not see a single tourist for almost all of 2020. Our income dried up, yet we still had to pay game guards, rangers, maintenance and lodge staff, as well as continuing our charity work in the surrounding communities as best we could. With heavy hearts, reserve management ordered the selected culling of wild animals to feed our people and pay for security. Equally awful for me personally was that I could not visit my parents. My mother Rose is a cancer survivor, thus topping the vulnerable COVID-19 checklist. My eighty-four-year-old father, Bill – or Tick Bird as he is often called – was also in the most susceptible age category, and I suppose the fact that he smokes a pipe and drinks like a fish didn't help. But my father is as tough as a sneezewood pole, and so far has survived most vices known to humanity.

But now, with COVID-19, Tick Bird was suffering from a malaise hitherto unknown in his life – boredom. He loves company and is what is politely known as a 'colourful character'. In his case, this is code for swearing like a trooper and calling a spade a bulldozer. His name derives from his cricket-playing days when he captained Eastern Province Districts for twenty years, a record yet to be equalled. He was a canny off-spin bowler and, as he has abnormally large hands, he could hide the ball from the batsman until it was whirring in mid-flight. Also, with those bucket-sized mitts, he seldom dropped a catch.

During one memorable game at Port Alfred he was setting a field and behind him was a cattle egret pecking away at ticks in the grass.

'Stand in line with that tick bird,' Bill instructed the fielder at extra cover.

It was a miserable autumn day. Bill's shoulders were hunched against the cold and with his long, beaked nose he looked exactly like the egret in profile behind him.

'Bloody hell, Bill,' replied the fielder, 'that tick bird's the spitting image of you.'

The entire team, as well as the two batsmen, collapsed laughing and the name stuck.

Although it happened half a century ago, Bill still tells that story to this day. In fact, as many people visit our lodge on Amakhala to hear Tick Bird's vast repertoire of colourful yarns as they do to see the animals. In happier times, he would hold court every night at our pub, appropriately called Tick's Bar. It's a century-old cellar constructed from stone and hewn wooden beams, part of the original farm built by Dutch settlers in 1832, and has been in my family for five generations. It's where Tick Bird, pipe in one massive hand and a tumbler of whisky in the other, played host to Prince Harry in one of the most gloriously undiplomatic visits British royalty has ever encountered. While doing wildlife volunteer work in 2015, Prince Harry met my brother William Fowlds, who has pioneered surgery on rhinos mutilated by horn poachers. Harry was invited to Amakhala, and William begged my father to be on his best behaviour. This took wishful thinking to new heights. Within an hour of being introduced, Tick Bird had offered to find Harry a wife (this was pre-Meghan Markle days) but said it would help if the

Prince was a little more handsome. Harry loved it, and we later heard he mentioned the visit as a highlight to his brother Prince William.

Tick Bird's stories all have one thing in common. They are peppered with colourful language and vivid descriptions that you will not hear anywhere else. But with his bar closed during COVID, instead of regaling guests, Tick Bird was reduced to counting cars on the motorway that forms the north-west border of Amakhala. Even that produced slim pickings during lockdown. Eventually he took to phoning old friends but, unfortunately, most are dead. When one widow asked the reason for Tick's call, he replied that he was trying to get hold of her deceased husband but 'he won't answer the bloody phone'. She repeated that to her friends, and everyone in the Eastern Cape outbacks had a good chuckle. I suppose it's appropriate that COVID humour is dark humour.

The only daily chore Tick Bird had during lockdown was to check the water levels on our section of the reserve. As he has bad knees from seven decades of hard farming and three of competitive cricket, he would drive his old Mercedes the 800 yards to the reservoir. Without fail, he would then stop at William's house for a socially distant sundowner. As the trip was so short, he never checked his petrol gauge. I think it was on day eighty-eight of lockdown when he finally ran out of gas and had to walk home on his rickety legs. Once again, the Eastern Cape outbacks had a good chuckle. Only Tick Bird could run a car dry on a trip lasting a minute.

More problematic was when Tick Bird started running dry of whisky. In his opinion, this was far more serious than COVID-19, so eventually Amakhala's managers Steve and Kerry Maartens sent out an SOS. Seven bottles arrived at my parents' house the next day, and Tick Bird declared that he would now survive the pandemic.

When lockdown was eased, my folks left the reserve for the first time in many months and Tick Bird was promptly flagged down by traffic police asking for his licence. By extreme coincidence, I phoned at that exact moment. My mother answered saying, 'Dad can't take the phone as a policeman wants to see his licence. And we all know it's expired.' Unfortunately, she thought she was whispering but, as an octogenarian, nothing is done in a whisper.

This was of some interest to the policeman, particularly as Tick Bird was explaining at length how he had 'mislaid the bloody document' but would find it soon. The cop just looked at this crazy old man and shook his head. Laughing, he said, 'Thank you for being honest. Enjoy your day,' and waved them on.

While Tick Bird's antics provided some light-hearted relief for the Fowlds family desperately wanting to visit each other again, another COVID-19 problem arose in my world that threatened to shatter five years of intricate community negotiations. It also proved to be one of the weirdest poaching incidents I have come across, which in conservation circles is saying something.

It happened at Loziba in early June 2020, a time when everyone involved in the project was still mourning the death of Beyers Coetzee. Sitting on the veranda of the Mawana homestead overlooking miles of pristine bushveld, Kallie van der Walt – Beyers's brother-in-law – heard a volley of rifle shots echoing up the valley. Gunfire is not uncommon in that Wild West part of the world, and possibly could have been nothing more than cattle rustlers settling scores. More often, though, it is poachers. Kallie immediately phoned Alec van Heerden, the friend in Vryheid who had been such a stalwart for the family when Beyers died. I was about three hours' away in Pongola, a town in the far north of the province, so Alec could not get hold of me in time. Instead, he sped out to the Mawana farm lodge with his son Xander and an aerial drone fitted with a camera.

Alec launched the drone close to where Kallie had heard the shots and almost immediately homed in on the suspected poachers. It was instantly obvious that this was not a case of some locals wielding antiquated shotguns and shooting for the cooking pot. Instead, it was a full-scale illegal hunting expedition on private land. The drone's display screen clearly showed three Indian men armed with five medium-bore rifles and sophisticated telescopic sights, accompanied by a small group of what Alec assumed to be local villagers. Alec zoomed in closer to see there had been three kills: a kudu antelope, a warthog and – bizarrely – a critically endangered vulture.

Vultures are inedible as the carrion-feeders have the distinctly antisocial habit of vomiting up rancid food when threatened, so the bird had been shot either as target practice or, more likely, for traditional medicine. *Sangomas*, or witchdoctors, believe the bird possesses extraordinarily strong healing powers, while various body parts are also extensively used as *tagati* – the local word for sorcery. That is one reason they are being hunted to extinction.

Kallie radioed two neighbouring farmers, S. P. Olivier and Izak Uys, who had also heard the shots. Both men are involved in our greater Loziba vision. They grabbed rifles and joined Kallie and Xander, tracking the suspected poachers on foot while Alec followed them with his drone. Xander, who is twenty-one years old and Olympic fit, led the way at a cracking pace, following his father's drone directions by radio.

The drone was the crucial factor, ensuring Xander knew exactly where the suspected poachers were at any given time. On top of that, he, Kallie, S. P. and Izak were completely at home in the bush, whereas the three gunmen appeared to be townsfolk crashing clumsily through the thickets.

The hot pursuit then cut through a particularly wild and dangerous section of Loziba called Hollandia, where several squatters lived. By now, realising they were being tracked, the Zulu locals melted into the bush while the Indians discarded their surplus rifles as well as the animal carcasses and started fleeing in earnest. With Xander literally breathing down their necks, they sprinted up a hill towards a well-known landmark called Poacher's Tree, a large paperbark thorn that illegal hunters sometimes used as a makeshift camp.

Xander soon overtook them, cocking his rifle and ordering them to stop. A few minutes later, Kallie, S.P. and Izak arrived, also cocking their weapons as Xander disarmed the suspects.

Just behind Poacher's Tree, an area strewn with litter and plastic water bottles, were three pickup trucks belonging to the suspects. Our team had caught them in the nick of time. A few minutes later and they would have sped off.

Xander then pointed to the drone directly overhead, saying everything was being recorded and the police were on their way. The men stared into the sky, then started pleading pitifully, almost wailing, as they begged Xander to call off the cops. We soon discovered why – they were prominent businessmen from Empangeni and KwaDukuza, two of the larger Zululand towns, and their reputations were at stake. They said they believed they were on tribal land and had been asked by local communities to shoot diseased wildebeest that were fatally infecting local cattle. Please, they beseeched, please let them go . . . they were merely doing the poor villagers a favour.

'Yeah, right,' said Kallie. He pointed at the two dead animals and bird. 'So, if the community called you out to shoot wildebeest, why have you killed a kudu and warthog? And a vulture – what's that for? Where's the wildebeest?'

The men had no answers.

'And what's more,' said Kallie, 'this is my land.'

The police arrived, shoved the snivelling suspected poachers into a van, and then threw their weapons into the back of a pickup. Much to our delight, this was done with excessive force, buckling expensive telescopic sights in the process. The men were then driven to the police station and charged with poaching and contravening pandemic restrictions by travelling without a permit.

It seemed an open and shut case. The suspects had been caught red-handed with hunting rifles and dead animals, including a critically endangered bird. That alone should have resulted in the book being thrown at them.

Or so we thought. Kallie was still at the police station giving a statement when his cellphone buzzed.

It was a local political leader, an extremely influential man in the area, who politely but firmly told Kallie that if the three hunters were not released immediately, retaliation would be fast and furious. Not only that, the Loziba project would be targeted. 'This reserve will never start,' were the exact words.

The unspoken threat was equally ominous: community unrest, increased poaching and cattle rustling, and possibly destruction of property.

Suddenly, in the blink of an eye, we faced a vastly different and extremely menacing scenario. It was now obvious that the jailed 'hunters' were telling the truth and they had indeed been summoned by people linked to surrounding communities. Whether they had been called out to shoot bushmeat or disease-carrying wildebeest was no longer the question. The overriding issue was that we were instructed to free them or face far-reaching consequences.

A lot hinged on what we did next. We were acutely aware that the community was legitimately concerned about the possibility of their cattle being infected by wildebeest carrying malignant catarrhal fever. This fatal disease is better known as *snotsiekte* (literally, 'snot sickness') as it causes a thick nasal discharge and originates from the placenta of wildebeest calves. There is no cure and no vaccine. As a result, we were considering moving all wildebeest off Mawana, but it was no simple task to corral these extremely hardy animals as sections of the game fence had been destroyed by elephants. The fact that local cattle illegally grazed extensively on private wildlife land added fuel to the volatile situation. However, local communities were aware that we were tackling the problem. So why had they called in the three hunters?

We now had two options: we either ignored the threats and took the alleged poachers to court; or, in the interests of conservation, we dropped the charges. That sounds like an oxymoron but, in my opinion, we had little choice but to consider the bigger wildlife picture. To alienate a section of local residents for an incident considered minor when compared to rhino-horn or ivory poaching was tantamount to winning a skirmish but losing the war.

Other Loziba stakeholders agreed. This was not the hill for us to die on. Consequently, all poaching charges were withdrawn and the 'hunters' released from custody. There was a tiny measure of satisfaction when the three men were fined for violating COVID-19 regulations.

However, some sections of the community were still not satisfied. Even with the release of the poachers, anti-Loziba tensions continued to run at full throttle with *snotsiekte*, a suspected rogue lion attack, and the elephants that had killed Beyers still at large being the key issues. These three concerns converged like a perfect storm and, unless we proceeded carefully, the project would teeter on the point of collapse.

As the mood became increasingly antagonistic, village leaders demanded an emergency meeting with Loziba's project management. Alec and Kallie agreed, but said I would have to be there as well as Richard Mabanga, as we were the spokespeople. I was still in Pongola holding biosphere talks with an organisation called Space for Elephants, so we had to stall for time. The meeting was eventually set for the following Monday at the Stedham Community Hall on the eastern border of Loziba.

Richard and I arrived expecting some fireworks, but nothing we couldn't handle.

Little did we know.

CHAPTER EIGHT

Showdown at Stedham

The first thing I noticed on entering the dusty Stedham Community Hall was that no women were present.

This is always a bad sign. In fact, the worst. It meant that the meeting was likely to be a 'lively' showdown at best, or a testosterone-fuelled confrontation at worst.

I had learnt this through hard experience. Rural women often have a pacifying effect on volatile situations as they do much of the heavy lifting in outback communities throughout Africa. As many of the men are itinerant labourers, it is left to the women to bring up children, reap harvests and manage the essential *spaza* convenience stores. Even the shebeens, speakeasies with mainly male patrons, are run by women. Consequently, in the communities surrounding Loziba, women generally are far more invested in their societies. Issues such as job creation, education, transport infrastructure, investment and tourism seem to strike greater resonance with them. Conversely, some of the most vociferous critics against the Loziba upliftment project were men who no longer permanently lived in the villages.

Not only were no women present, but the men trooping in carried either spears or cane knives, which are similar to machetes but shorter and shaped like a meat cleaver. Some had vicious looking gut hooks at the end. I was not overly concerned about that as most rural Zulu men carry what are known as 'traditional weapons', rather like Sikhs wearing ceremonial kirpan knives. But it did add an edge to the gathering. Fortunately, the weapons were stored in a corner by the doorway of the sparsely painted hall, so Richard and I would not be facing a phalanx of sharp points when we spoke.

Equally ominous was the absence of the community's most prominent politician, Michael Khumalo, a highly intelligent man who was prepared to listen to all sides of the debate. Instead, the meeting would by chaired by a local *induna* whom Richard and I feared would be out of his depth. We both knew him but, when we entered the hall, he refused to acknowledge us.

Also, Alec and Kallie could not attend. Alec phoned earlier to say a similar meeting the week before had disintegrated into racial mudslinging with Kallie being taunted at every turn. This left me and Richard on our own.

The chairman stood behind a rickety table, calling the meeting to order. There were about fifty in the audience, some sitting on plastic chairs, and the belligerent atmosphere was so thick that you could have cut it with one of the cane knives stashed in the corner. Looking at me and Richard – the first time he acknowledged us – the chairman said we had been summoned as we were the people who wanted to start 'this park', referring to Loziba. Then he waggled a finger in the air, 'There will be no park here until our demands are met!'

So much for impartiality. The chairman then noted, his voice rising to a crescendo, that the community had lost ninety-five cattle due to *snotsiekte*, which, he said, our wildebeest had brought to the area. This prompted a massive commotion from the floor with men standing and shouting out their own personal tolls.

'I've lost twenty,' bellowed one.

'I've lost thirty-five,' yelled another, not to be outdone.

The chairman sat impassively, making no attempt to restore order. Everyone in the room had lost a lot of livestock, if the increasingly exaggerated claims were to be believed. A lot more than the chairman's figure of ninety-five.

Richard and I looked at each other. Richard's Zulu name is *Mahlembehlembe*, meaning 'all over the place', due to his incredible energy, but even he was sitting dead still. We were used to volatile community gatherings, but they almost always calmed down once saner heads prevailed. Not this one.

In fact, it got worse. And the chairman appeared to have little ability – or perhaps inclination – to control it. Eventually he stood and held up a hand. 'You will have to get rid of all wildebeest from Loziba,' he said. 'Or there will be serious consequences.'

I nodded. We had been expecting this. However, I had no serious intention of removing all wildebeest in the area, only the ones bordering the Stedham community as that was the sole reported outbreak of the disease.

From *snotsiekte*, the meeting careered downhill with a vengeance to an old bugbear: Kerneels van der Walt, the former owner of Mawana.

Kerneels had died in 2017 yet, to the detractors of Loziba, he still somehow stalked the land like some malevolent poltergeist. It seemed that all tribal grievances, invented or otherwise, eventually defaulted to something he was supposed to have said or done.

Like most Afrikaners of his generation, Kerneels was a

product of his time and believed that the Black communities surrounding his farm should know their place. Unfortunately, many white farmers in those days of apartheid agreed with him, and we are still reaping that bitter harvest. When Kerneels wanted to transform Mawana from a cattle ranch into a game reserve two decades or so ago, it was largely against community wishes as they believed he would bring in lions and leopards. Leopards have been in the area since time immemorial, but they are so secretive and nocturnal that few villagers ever saw them. Kerneels had no intention of bringing in more, and certainly not lions as all his neighbours, white and black, had cattle herds. The risk was too great, and obviously Kerneels would be financially liable if lions on his property caused damage elsewhere.

But he did bring in another highly effective predator, the spotted hyena. When the communities objected, according to them he responded by saying, 'I've bought hyenas to eat your goats and cattle.'

Obviously he did not mean that literally. Whatever one thought of the difficult old man, he would never deliberately have brought in predators to kill neighbouring livestock. It was just his extremely counterproductive way of saying he was the boss and could do what he liked on his land. In any event, hyenas are far more manageable than lions and would be contained within Mawana's fences.

However, for people who regard cattle as their most valuable possession, Kerneels's sarcastic 'hyenas' comment had been verbal dynamite. It is difficult to imagine saying anything more inflammatory and it has been repeated at almost every community meeting we've had.

This gathering at the Stedham Hall was no different. The mere mention of Kerneels's name had the crowd seething.

I stood, trying to explain that Kerneels was nothing more than a spectre from the past – a dinosaur from an era that is long gone. To harp on about something said perhaps twenty years ago was pointless, and in any event, the hyenas were not attacking their goats or cattle. Nor spreading *snotsiekte*.

I also pointed out that the next generation of Van der Walts, Una and Kallie, had for the past few years consistently extended a genuine olive branch of peace to the communities. Una's husband Beyers had been killed chasing elephants away from community lands – that's how deep the family's commitment was.

I sat down, expecting a further barrage of objections. But surprisingly the chairman agreed with me and instructed the meeting to move on to other more pressing topics.

It was to no avail. The next speaker from the floor started his speech on a different note, but within a minute reverted to Kerneels. 'He brought *impisi* [hyena] to eat our cattle,' he thundered. Once again, the crowd was on its feet shaking fists in anger.

And so it continued. Whoever had the floor started pontificating on some unrelated topic – but within a blink reverted to Kerneels, stoking audience anger to new heights.

Finally, after everyone from the floor – or so it seemed – had vented their spleen on hyenas, we were asked what we were doing about the lions.

Three lions, two males and a female, had wandered into the Loziba area about eighteen months earlier. We weren't sure where the female was from, but the males, whom we believed to be brothers, had escaped from the Hluhluwe-iMfolozi Park. They had been spotted walking along the road by motorists and, within hours, every hick with a gun was giving chase. One of the lions headed west, slaying thirty-two prized Bonsmara cows on S. P. Olivier's ranch before being snared in a fence and killed. The other, it seemed, headed north-west where it apparently attacked Sabelo Masondo, a local villager from Gluckstadt. The story was widely reported in the press, and Mr Masondo told reporters he escaped with his life by jumping over a fence into a macadamia nut farm. He had bite marks on his knee and puncture wounds under his armpit. Now, according to the community, they were too scared to collect their cattle because of marauding lions. And it was all our fault.

Hang on, I said, the lions came from outside the area. They were not ours.

'Yes – but you brought them here,' one man retorted. 'You want this park to be Big Five, so you secretly put lions in your truck and brought them here at midnight.'

This was now getting stupid. I had to nip it in the bud right away. 'If we see the lions, we will shoot them,' I said. 'Much as Richard Mabanga and I love lions, we know that they are trespassers and not welcome here.'

'Then what about the elephants?' asked one man. 'They must also be killed.'

This was a different issue altogether. We knew we had to shoot the marauding lions, but had no intention of destroying the two askaris that attacked Beyers, which in any event were now deep in the Thaka Valley and out of everyone's way. It was not what Una wanted, and certainly not what Beyers would have wanted. But there was no way I could say that to this confrontational gathering. I had to stall for time.

'We have to get permission from the government to kill elephants,' I said. 'There is a lot of paperwork and lots of permits needed.' That was not what they wanted to hear. I continued,

'We only have a permit to kill the lions. But the elephants are not a problem. We have already collared the animals and are following them to make sure they are not causing damage. If they come near your land, we will chase them off, as we have done before.'

'But they are killers,' shouted one man.

'Yes, one askari killed Beyers but these elephants have been here since 2003 and never hurt anyone before that. For seventeen years, there were no problems.'

'But they are now aggressive,' another member of the audience shouted. The crowd noisily agreed.

I was starting to get angry and decided it was time for some inconvenient home truths. I pointed to the crowd before me. 'Everyone here has to accept one thing. If the elephants are becoming aggressive, it is because they are being provoked by hunting dogs used by poachers on Loziba land, and also by cattle being herded illegally. That is the real problem.'

The ruckus from the floor was deafening. They were not poachers, they shouted back. Their cattle grazed on community land, not the park's, they said. And if the land was not theirs yet, it soon would be.

The chairman rose to deliver what he considered to be an ultimatum. Richard and I were told in no uncertain terms that the two askaris and the lions had to be killed, and the wildebeest – every single one – had to be moved out of the area. They were talking about herds tallying perhaps two hundred animals, most of which were in the remoter areas of the game reserve and nowhere near their cattle.

I sighed. It had now come to this. But yet the solution was simple. All of these problems – lions, *snotsiekte* and elephants – could be solved by game-proof fences separating the Loziba

Wilderness from tribal lands. We could easily and legally do this, but without community consent, any fence we erected would be instantly torn down. This was no secret. We had repeatedly been told that the people surrounding Loziba would only consider allowing fences if tribal leaders had the final say where they went.

All previous negotiations we'd had with them about this had not revolved around cut-and-dried legal matters such as title deeds and property rights. Or even whose property a fence was on, as one would expect. Instead we had to consider various locations of ancestral graves, sacred sites, or something as mundane as a tribesman saying his cattle had always drunk from a particular waterhole.

The reality was that if we put any game-proof fence up without community approval, regardless of who owned the land, it would be destroyed. We knew that without doubt. It had happened on countless other game reserves throughout the country.

However, I was now at my wits end. Hoping to at least salvage something out of the disastrous meeting, I decided to raise the issue.

'A fence will fix all of this,' I said.

There was a howl of protest. A chant went up – no fences until all other demands had been met. They would not budge on that. End of discussion. It was a bitter blow as it was now obvious to all interested parties that the entire future of Loziba should hang almost solely on the issue of game-proof barriers. That, in essence, was what this meeting was all about. Fences would solve every problem from *snotsiekte* to prowling lions.

The chairman shook his head. No fences.

He then gave us fourteen days to comply with the three other issues. Otherwise, he said, they would 'solve' these problems themselves by bringing in gunmen to kill all of Loziba's wildebeest as well as the lions and elephants. With the farcical arrest of the three hired poachers three weeks' previously, we knew he meant it.

Then one man in the crowd stood and pointed at me, saying. 'You think you are *Nkunzi ayihlehli* [the bull who never backs down]. That is what some call you. This time we will make you back down.'

Sensing my growing rage, another stood, saying, 'You have a small heart.'

I stared at him for a long moment. In my anger, I interpreted the idiom in the Xhosa rather than Zulu sense. In Xhosa, it means I do not care for others.

I lashed out verbally. 'I've got a whole truck of porridge from Feeding the Wildlife Communities waiting outside. I was going to give it to you, just as I have given to other communities here. But because you say I've got a small heart, I'm taking it back.'

Richard and I walked out.

CHAPTER NINE

Cows, Crooks and Cartels

'*Eish!*' said Richard, yanking the handle of the truck door. 'That went badly.'

We always rated community meetings and conservation presentations out of ten. 'This one is a nought,' Richard continued. 'A fat zero. But I think you misunderstood what that man said about your small heart. In Zulu it means you have no patience.'

Of course! In my anger I overreacted. The Xhosa interpretation that I was heartless was incorrect. I felt terrible about the mistake.

That night despondency hit me like a blow to the head. Although I had despaired at the numerous setbacks over the Loziba project before, I had never considered giving up. This time was different. The obstacles seemed infinite. It was all too much, draining me physically, mentally and emotionally. The costs were simply too high. My stalwart, Beyers Coetzee, had given his life for the work we were doing. So, indirectly, had Chris Holcroft, whose passion and fundraising skills were unmatched. There was little doubt in my mind that his heart attack was to some extent triggered by the enormous burden of fighting conservation causes in Africa. I thought back to the time when the three of us had watched the elephant herd emerging from the mist like a mirage on the mountain at Mawana. It had been magical. We had felt on top of the world, as if we were achieving something considerable. Now I was the only one of the trio left. The thought shook me more than I cared to admit, especially as not that long before, my life had also been threatened – by the anti-Loziba faction.

It happened via an anonymous phone call. The caller, his voice crackling with bad-signal static, said it had taken years for 'his people' to get land back from white farmers – and now, like the evil former apartheid regime, we were trying to steal it again. We suspected the caller was a local taxi driver, who apparently was also a prominent cattle rustler. The precise words of the threat are seared in my mind. Literally translated from Zulu, the caller said, 'You will stop breathing air.'

I didn't tell Angela, my long-suffering wife, as she already had misgivings about Loziba. She said there was 'too much negative stuff' surrounding the project, even disregarding the tragedy of Beyers. Angela does not frighten easily. She has come with me to some of the scariest parts of the Democratic Republic of Congo and Rwanda. But even so, I was afraid that if I told her about the death threat, it would be the tipping point as far as she was concerned.

The most pertinent question was whether Loziba Wilderness was a viable project or merely another eco-pipedream, as some were saying. Did I really think we could build a game reserve in one of the wildest, most poverty-stricken regions of the country? Could I, in all honesty, promise jobs, investment, education and infrastructure in an area where cattle rustling is considered a career move? Could I – or anyone for that matter – persuade bandits, who operated like Mexican drug cartels, that eco-tourism was the future? Or convince their children that Bill Gates was a better role model than Billy the Kid?

It was no secret that the cattle thieves did not want Loziba to succeed. A game reserve with elephant-proof fences would close off strategic routes into the largely inaccessible Thaka and Babanango valleys, where the stolen animals were hidden. Once in the deep ravines of dense thorn thickets, the original owners had little hope of recovering them. Even if farmers by some fluke did find their cattle, they would most likely be driven off by gunmen. Those lawless, desolate gorges rivalled part of Somalia and Afghanistan.

Consequently, as far as cattle rustlers were concerned, the Loziba project bringing prosperity, tourism, jobs, infrastructure and, above all, fences was bad for business. In fact, any progress was counterproductive in their eyes.

The cattle cartels surrounding Loziba spread as much fear locally as Central American drug runners. It's estimated that five thousand stolen animals have been driven into the nearby valleys, where they are simply left to run wild. Then, after two years without being claimed, cartel bosses pay locals to round them up and drive them to their homesteads, where they are corralled and branded with the new 'owner's' mark.

This was a major problem in getting community support for Loziba. Rustlers would pack the village hall during key meetings, vociferously opposing the reserve and shouting down our supporters. As they were hard men, not afraid of physical confrontation, they invariably scared off the more law-abiding villagers who actually wanted growth. The silent majority unfortunately lived up to their name.

However, silent or not, I knew that most people were firmly on our side. I was told that unequivocally by several prominent chiefs. People stopped me in dusty streets to wish me well. Many were mothers worried about the lack of choices for their children. Others were simply fed up with the current stagnant status quo and wanted progress, which they knew only eco-tourism would bring.

The bottom line was that we knew we had overwhelming support, even though it could not be peacefully expressed at community meetings packed with criminals. That was what gave me hope, and we owed it to those courageous and defiant people to keep fighting. I couldn't just give up.

I slept badly that night, but woke with new resolve. This was no time for self-pity. Instead, I had to move fast as we had a mere two weeks to rid the area of *snotsiekte* and save the entire project.

The first task was to get a permit to capture the animals. The problem here was that almost all the wildebeest deemed to be spreading the disease didn't specifically belong to anyone. They had wandered through various holes in fences wrecked by elephants, and then come into contact with village cattle grazing illegally. Most were on the abandoned farm called Hollandia, a stretch of barely penetrable bush where poachers were extremely active. Squatters were also starting to build a shanty town, and by adding *snotsiekte* to the mix, the situation was dynamite waiting for a spark. We had to get a fence up fast to prevent that. However, as the hostile Stedham mob at the previous meeting had stated in no uncertain terms, they would tear down any barrier we erected.

Although Hollandia was designated as part of the Loziba project, to get the wildebeest off the vacated farm required a capture permit signed by the absentee owner, listed in the deeds register as Mr Boetie van Rensburg. We could not legally move animals off his land even though they did not belong to him. But where was he, when the only residents on the land appeared to be squatters and poachers?

I finally tracked Mr Van Rensburg down to Hillcrest, a small town about 200 miles away. He was initially hostile, claiming the animals were his as he had 'bought' them twenty years ago. If we wanted to move them, we would have to buy them off him.

This took chutzpah to new heights and I was fast losing patience, particularly as we didn't have time for games. I slammed the capture permit down on a table before him and said if he refused to sign, he faced a land invasion and all the animals would be slaughtered. Fortunately, he relented and gave us the go-ahead.

I then hired Tracy & Du Plessis, a game capture company, to move the animals. We have a good relationship with them and the costs of the operation would be funded by the sale of the wildebeest. Grant Tracy, the company owner, said he needed at least thirty wildebeest to cover overheads and, as the Stedham community leaders claimed there were 'hundreds', I said that was no problem.

We arrived at Hollandia with a helicopter, two huge articulated lorries, a crane, four vehicles and twenty-five people. It was the last day of the deadline, and it seemed most villagers had expected us to renege on the deal. They arrived in droves to see what we were doing, watching open-mouthed as we offloaded the heavy-duty equipment. They could not believe the effort that went into catching wild animals.

Soon a festive atmosphere developed with people singing and taking selfies next to the helicopter and crane, while others came to me saying we would never get a hundred unruly and agitated wildebeest into the trucks.

I laughed. 'Come here in two hours. The truck will be filled with *nkonkoni*. There will be no more *snotsiekte*.'

On top of that, I also brought a few bags of maize meal for the community. It was part of the same load that I had refused to donate at the previous meeting after being accused of having 'a small heart' and misinterpreting the idiom.

However, once again, problems that had dogged our every move since arresting the 'hunters' continued to plague us. No sooner had the helicopter taken off when it fell out of the sky – literally. A loose bolt on the exhaust manifold shook off and it was only superb pilot skill that converted a certain crash into a controlled emergency landing. The pilot, Harry Hensburg, reacted instinctively as the manifold started rattling and deftly feathered the joystick, touching down with little more than a bump. If the exhaust had shaken off, it could have flipped the chopper and possibly sheared the rotor blades. We were lucky.

Even so, this wrote off the next twelve hours as we had to hoist the chopper back on to a truck and take it back to base camp for repairs.

While mechanics worked feverishly, we spent the rest of the day checking the capture nets, set in a V-formation to funnel the running animals. Bagging wildebeest is basically an adrenaline-fuelled aerial pursuit in which the pilot herds the animals into a netted enclosure. This is a highly skilled operation, and the chase can take hours, spanning many miles. The wildebeest are first pushed on to a trail they are familiar with and herded at a slow gait into the net opening, which is then pulled shut like a giant drawstring. Once encircled, the animals are guided through a corridor into the back of a game truck.

To coerce them into the capture area, pilots have to fly low, often just a few yards off the ground. They sometimes even prod the animals with the chopper skids and use the turbulence from the rotor blades to 'blow' them forward – that's how good they are. However, wildebeest are as fickle as all hell, often turning on a coin and stampeding in the opposite direction. When that happens, the whole operation has to be repeated.

Capture pilots are, in my opinion, the best flyers in the world. Harry, our pilot, was a personal friend of Prince Harry, sixth in line to the British throne. They met in Malawi when Harry (the prince) was doing volunteer conservation work, and Harry (the pilot) was involved in one of the largest translocations of elephants in conservation history. Harry Hensburg was invited to the royal wedding when Prince Harry tied the knot with Meghan Markle in 2018.

Harry rounded up every wildebeest he could find. But even so, the tally was only thirty-eight, far removed from the 'hundreds' of animals spreading the fatal disease as claimed by the community. But at least we had enough to pay the game capture team.

Then, out of the blue, we had our first real break. Harry was flying at several hundred feet, looking for more wildebeest, when to his astonishment saw a lion nonchalantly feeding on a large Brahman cow near Poacher's Tree, the same area where the 'hunters' had been cornered. Alarmingly, it was also the exact spot where we had been the day before, setting up capture nets. The lion must have been watching us at the time, just before making its kill.

It's possible that it was the same big cat that attacked Sabelo Masondo fifteen months earlier. We could not be certain of that, but we could be certain that it was the lion the villagers claimed was scaring them away from herding cattle. There were no others in the area.

As we had pledged to the community, we had to shoot the animal, much as we all hated to do so. We immediately applied for a destruction permit, which was granted overnight due to the danger it posed to the community. Harry said the lion would be sleeping off the effects of its prime-beef meal for at least the next two days, so he knew exactly where to find it.

In the helicopter with Harry was Xander van Heerden, the young man who had led the chase against the suspected poachers. Xander, a deadly accurate shot, took aim as Harry steadied the chopper. A second later, the magnificent creature dropped dead.

Harry landed and Xander took a photo, which I later showed to community leaders. They were ecstatic.

I then told them that the *snotsiekte* wildebeest had also been captured and would be moved far from their lands. I expected them to be doubly ecstatic, as both problems had now been solved. But they were sceptical.

'Have you got them all?' one asked.

'We've got all the ones that were here,' I replied.

'How many?'

'Fourteen that came across the broken fence and another twenty-four that were nearby.'

The men shook their heads. 'That's not enough. There are hundreds out there.'

I repeated, 'All wildebeest causing *snotsiekte* are gone. We've searched everywhere. Maybe the shot killing the lion also scared them back into Mawana, away from your cattle.'

In front of me was a sea of shaking heads. One *induna* wagged a finger at me. 'You are not leaving here until you have loaded over a hundred,' he demanded.

We had no option but to send Harry into the air again. He

came back an hour later, confirming what I had said earlier. There were no more wildebeest.

The community leaders got into a huddle to discuss this. They had seen Harry flying search-grid patterns overhead, and perhaps were now convinced that the problem had been removed. But, true to form, it was replaced by another issue.

'What about the elephants?' the *induna* asked. 'The ones that killed Beyers?'

I thought quickly. There was no way we were going to shoot the Mawana herd.

'As I said at the meeting, we have collared them and are monitoring their movements,' I said. 'We know exactly where they are, and they are far away from you. We're now waiting for Ezemvelo's instructions.'

Luckily, some members of the community had seen us putting a radio collar on the matriarch several weeks previously, so knew this to be true.

'When will Ezemvelo tell you what to do?'

I scratched my head as if deep in thought. This was an ideal opportunity to buy more time. 'It's hard to say. There is lots of paperwork to get a permit to shoot an elephant. Maybe a year.'

To my surprise, the *induna* smiled. 'OK,' he said. 'As long as you're doing something.'

Actually, we were not in the least concerned about the elephants at that particular moment. The tracking collars were working beautifully and we knew the herd was deep in the bush, far from human habitat, and causing no problems whatsoever. The two askaris facing a potential death sentence were also moving contentedly along with the rest of the group. This clearly told us that they were peaceful, and only retaliated when chased.

Any worries that the herd might be 'rogue' were now dispelled, although the suspended death sentence remained.

Then came the biggest breakthrough. As luck would have it, Michael Khumalo, the hugely influential local politician who had not been at the Stedham Community Hall meeting, suddenly pitched up to see what was going on. Michael is not completely sold on the Loziba Wilderness project, but he is pragmatic and someone with whom we can do business. He is also a good friend of Xander's father, Alec van Heerden.

As we watched the trucks drive off with the wildebeest, Alec said, 'Michael, the only thing that will work here is a fence. Cattle on one side, wildebeest on the other. Not only that, building it will create a lot of jobs.'

Michael nodded. 'I agree. The question is where?'

I looked at him, aghast. I couldn't believe what I was hearing. 'You mean the community would agree to a fence?' I asked.

Michael turned to me. 'Depends where it goes.'

At last we had it – an acknowledgement from someone with clout that we should fence off Loziba. This was a massive breakthrough. At the previous raucous meeting in Stedham, I couldn't even mention the word 'fence' without sparking an angry uproar. Now the most powerful local leader in the area had cautiously agreed that good fences could possibly make good neighbours. A dead lion and the capture of thirty-eight wildebeest had achieved more than any community meeting had in the past. I knew this was only the tentative start of some hard haggling, as to build a fence alongside tribal land is one of the most torturous endeavours imaginable. However, I wanted more wild land and the community wanted more cattle grazing, so maybe – just maybe – we could reach a compromise.

From an appalling start, the problems that began with hired gunmen coming on to Loziba lands and ending with a tragic – in our view – lion kill, had to everyone's surprise concluded marginally in our favour. Most important, Loziba was on track again. Despite the powerful rustling cartels, we now had a tacit agreement that a fence should go up. A few weeks ago, that alone would have been more than I dared hope.

Then, finally, came the best news. The national COVID-19 travel restrictions had been eased. That meant I could return to continuing the work we had been doing with Chris Holcroft, and also taking advantage of the poaching hiatus following the death of Baas Leon Stoltz.

I decided to kickstart a project close to my heart – the rescue of one of the most endangered creatures on the planet. So endangered, in fact, that in South Africa you can almost count them on your fingers.

Those animals are the tuskers, the modern-day mammoths with ivory so huge that it shaves the ground. At one stage there were thousands of these goliaths roaming the continent. But now, hunted to virtual extinction first as trophies and then by ivory poachers, the gene pool is almost dry.

The terrifying thought that these majestic icons of ancient Africa would die out on my generation's watch fills me with equal measures of bottomless rage and infinite sadness.

With some like-minded people, I decided to do something about it.

CHAPTER TEN

The Tembe Tuskers

Of the many eco-crimes committed over the centuries, few are as sad as the blood-soaked demise of the original free spirits of Africa – the vast, footloose elephant herds.

They once inhabited every corner of this continent, except the arid empty quarters of the Sahara Desert. They came and went as they wished. They did as they desired, unhampered by borders or human rules.

Today, apart from a few pockets in inaccessible jungles, these free-ranging herds are no more. First they were decimated, then they were fenced.

Except decimation is a misleading word. It's original meaning is the killing of one in ten and was used by the Romans as a form of military discipline. If a cohort of legionaries was mutinous or showed cowardice, a tenth of the group was executed.

In the case of Africa's elephant herds, the figure is reversed. A tenth survived.

Statistics tell the story more starkly than words. In the early 1800s, there were 26 million African elephants. In 1989, thanks largely to the mass slaughter by poachers and hunters, there were barely 400,000. And in that gore-drenched killing spree, the most visually impressive of all, the tuskers, were virtually exterminated.

Tuskers are the legendary 'hundred-pounders'; elephants whose ivory weighs more than a hundred pounds, or 45.5 kilograms, on either side. There are reputed to be perhaps thirty genuine tuskers left in the world today. Yet barely a century ago, these extraordinary creatures with tusks scuffing the soil numbered many thousands and were a common sight roving the savannahs and woods of Africa.

Obviously, the biggest single reason for the industrial-scale massacre was the ivory trade, as in the nineteenth century even a simple hair comb might be carved from an elephant's tusk. The hunters of old were not trophy seekers. For them, a tusker provided more ivory per bullet than a small elephant, and that was their business – getting ivory. Among the best known are Frederick Selous, an aristocratic adventurer, and Scottish soldier Walter 'Karamojo' Bell, who between them shot more than two thousand elephants in the late 1800s and early 1900s. But the most prolific is said to be Roy 'Samaki' Salmon, who lived in Uganda early last century and killed as many as four thousand elephants. That's the equivalent of an elephant being shot every day for almost eleven years – by just one man.

In the wake of people such as Selous, who was the inspiration for H. Rider Haggard's swashbuckling books, the mystique of the big game hunter emerged. It was an overly romanticised image later endorsed by writers such as Ernest Hemingway and Robert Ruark. In that macho mythology, the most prized target was a tusker, inspiring the era of the trophy hunter.

The largest known elephant tusks are stored at the Natural History Museum in London. Interestingly, the shorter of the tusks is heavier, weighing just under 207 pounds. The larger, close on 10½ feet, weighs 196 pounds. Legend has it that an enslaved African shot the animal in 1898 on the slopes of Mount Kilimanjaro on behalf of his Arab 'master', and the tusks were sold in Zanzibar.

One can only weep at such atrocities. Although there is a handful of tuskers in the Kruger National Park, the biggest gene pools are found in two areas: Tsavo in Kenya, and Tembe in South Africa.

Obviously, I'm committed to the latter. But what makes the Tembe elephants even more interesting is that not only are they the world's largest ivory giants, they're also scarred survivors of one of the most ruthless conflicts on the continent; the FRELIMO–RENAMO civil war that raged in Mozambique from 1977 to 1992. The Tembe animals were shot on sight to feed soldiers on both sides.

To escape, the elephants – once the largest unfenced herd in the world – fled across the border to an area known as Maputaland in the north-eastern corner of South Africa.

What follows next is inspirational beyond belief, and shows what committed people can do in defying the insanity of war. Conservationists combined forces with the indigenous Tembe people to erect game-proof fencing to protect the herd, but also left open strategic gaps facing Mozambique to allow in all other pachyderm refugees. In 1989, when most of the herd had escaped across the border, the open sections were snapped closed. The entire area, now fully protected, was named the Tembe Elephant Park, in honour of the tribe that helped save them. This not only kept the animals permanently on the safe side of the border, but determined men stood guard preventing further slaughter from soldiers. The handful of rangers may have been armed with obsolete rifles, but they shot to kill. Both FRELIMO and RENAMO knew it.

It was only several years later that scientists discovered the herd contained what is thought to be the largest concentrated gene pool of tuskers on the continent.

The elephants started arriving in 1983, but the gates of the Tembe Elephant Park were only officially opened in 1991 when conservationists deemed that the traumatised and heavily hunted animals were safe for tourists. Today there are more than 220 elephants in the Elephant Park and at least four bulls have tusks well over 100 pounds, while an increasing number of adolescents is also expected to exceed that magical mark within a few years. There is also a significant number of 'near-tuskers', those in the 80- to 90-pound range. In short, no other single herd has a greater pro rata count of animals sporting such impressive ivory.

The importance of this for African conservation cannot be stressed strongly enough. To put it into context, in Mozambique's Gorongosa National Park – also ravaged by the RENAMO–FRELIMO civil war – a third of all female elephants are now born without any tusks at all. We can only speculate, but it's as if nature has stepped in to protect them and deliberately skipped an evolutionary process that would normally take eons.

The most famous of Tembe's giants was Isilo, who before his death in 2014 was believed to be the biggest living tusker on the planet. *Isilo* means 'king' in Zulu, and is a befitting title as Isilo was truly one of nature's gentle giants. He never seemed to lose his temper or even get annoyed with the scores of humans that came to view and film him. Isilo weighed about seven tons, which is impressive in itself, but his tusks would have challenged even a woolly mammoth. They were more than 9 feet long, with the right tusk weighing 143 pounds and the left one 132 pounds.

This meant that every time he tilted his head, he was 'bench-pressing' 275 pounds.

Although Isilo died of natural causes, poachers found the carcass first and stole both tusks. To think that this wonderful, gentle goliath's ivory is now probably a gimmicky knickknack on some mantelpiece is beyond heart-breaking.

Isilo's rival for largest tusker status was a Kenyan giant called Satao in the Tsavo Conservation Area, whose tusks with a combined weight of 222 pounds were lighter than Isilo's. However, Satao's ivory was so long that it perpetually scraped the sand. He could be tracked by the funnels the tusks made. He was shot by poachers with poisoned arrows in March 2014. His ivory is also probably adorning some unknown mantelpiece.

However, we take our successes where we can and one is that the Tembe herd is now breeding so prolifically that the cows are on contraceptives. The irony is almost farcical – one of the world's most valuable herds on birth control. But the reality is that Tembe Elephant Park is only 35,000 hectares, which might sound big, but not for the planet's largest land mammal. The good news is that there are several corridors linking Tembe to other reserves in an area that also includes Swaziland and the herd's old stamping ground of southern Mozambique, thankfully now peaceful. The obvious next move is to take down those fences, creating a large transnational hub and re-establishing ancient migration routes.

But we have to move fast. Not just because the Tembe herd is getting too big, but because communities spilling over into the corridors are expanding even faster. Soon there will be no room.

I saw this first hand when I flew over the strategic corridors as part of a relocation team darting Tembe bulls in 2020. The rocketing speed of human population growth in the area was mind blowing. Large chunks of bush had already been slashed and burnt for cultivation, while villages and shops were mushrooming like wildflowers. The race for land was on. Consequently, it was now more vital than ever that we not only open all migratory passageways with extreme urgency, but also extend this priceless gene pool to other parts of the country. The most effective way to do that was to relocate surplus bulls.

However, just because an elephant comes from a tusker herd doesn't guarantee it will have big ivory. It's also difficult to tell which young adults will become legendary tuskers until they are between thirty-five and forty years old. So relocating an askari, or young male, and hoping it will grow into a hundred-pounder can be a hit-and-miss affair.

Dr Johan Marais, a tusker expert and founder of the frontline NGO Saving the Survivors, says the reason for this is that tusker ivory only gets a growth spurt when a bull reaches its prime breeding potential. But even so, he believes Tembe has the world's richest tusker gene pool and is already outperforming Tsavo: 'Just do the maths. In Tembe we have four genuine hundred-pounders in a herd of 220 – that's about 2 per cent – whereas Tsavo has seven out of a herd of 1,200, or roughly 0.5 per cent. Statistically, that indicates Tembe elephants are four times more likely to produce hundred-pounders than Tsavo, where most tuskers come from today.'

This was vital information as no one wanted to move the already established hundred-pounders off the Tembe park. Instead, it was a case of selecting teenage bulls with bigger than average tusks and 'guesstimating' that they would grow even bigger. But still, as Johan said, the law of averages is promising.

However, even if the relocated bulls do not grow to be hundred-pounders, we would still be inserting potential big-ivory genes into other bloodlines for future generations. In the fight to save the last remaining tuskers, that is absolutely crucial. But it's not going to be easy as elephants will not just mate at will.

The harsh reality is that once relocated, the Tembe bulls would have to fight other males to get anywhere near any resident elephant cow in season. Logically, it would seem that would not be a problem as a big tusker should easily outfight an animal with smaller 'weapons', but that is not the case. In fact, large ivories can be a disadvantage as the extra weight makes the animal less nimble. On top of that, tuskers are famously placid – just as large humans are often less aggressive – so will not necessarily provoke a challenge. This was very evident with the Tembe herd, which had been severely traumatised by the Mozambican war, yet seldom showed hostility towards humans in the park. In fact, the more belligerent big-ivory animals were almost always ones with broken tusks.

All we could do was move as many surplus bulls as possible and let nature take its course. That's always worked best for me in the past.

But how do you catch a creature with abnormal tusks? The answer is – carefully. The trailer has to have hydraulic stabilisers for the simple reason that, when a juggernaut with a tranquilliser hangover wakes up and starts stomping around, the entire rig is likely to tip over. Only when the animal is stood up and then settled are the stabilisers, which look like derricks on an offshore oil platform, removed.

My main role in these projects is to source a suitable range for any extra bulls. But as I found with moving the Atherstone herd, elephants in South Africa are notoriously difficult to place

as they are so big. We no longer have the vast savannah wildernesses that Angola or Mozambique have.

So the question was where.

The response came in one of the strangest ways imaginable.

CHAPTER ELEVEN

Chávez and Shaka

A flock of scarlet ibis, glinting like rubies in the rising sun, rocketed into the sky as vividly coloured macaws squawked from lofty perches in thickets of moriche palms.

Below, on the sandy beach of a translucent marsh, a rare Orinoco crocodile waited, still as a stone. Its next meal, a capybara, the world's largest rodent, foraged barely 10 yards away.

Also greeting the red-gold dawn were troops of howler monkeys, swinging in the swamp forests fringing the crystal lagoons and waterways that flowed into the immense Orinoco River. On the wetland savannahs that stretched to the horizon, plump Brahman cattle grazed contentedly as *llaneros* – Venezuelan cowboys – saddled their *Criollos*. The steeds, bred for toughness and grit, are descendants of Spanish and Creole horses that have roamed the Orinoco plains since the days of the conquistadors.

In short, 4 April 2009, was just another day on Hato El Frío, the world-renowned ranch run by one of the country's most distinguished families, the Maldonados.

Then the soldiers came.

Assault rifles slung over shoulders, they leapt out of trucks with the letters GNB etched on the doors, confirming – as if anyone doubted – that they were the much-feared Guardia Nacional Bolivariana de Venezuela. Following them, glowering behind wraparound sunglasses, were paramilitary police from Venezuela's largest law enforcement agency, the CICPC (Scientific, Penal and Criminal Investigation Service Corps). And behind them were officials from the Ministry of Agriculture, clutching documents authorised by President Hugo Chávez himself to allow the seizure the 80,000-hectare farm. It was now a 'state unit of socialist production'.

All employees at the ranch, from bosses to cleaners, were rounded up at gunpoint and given two hours to vacate the ranch that had been the crown jewel of the Maldonado dynasty for almost a century. The family's business management team, led by Alexander Degwitz Maldonado along with his cousins Veronica and Samuel Maldonado Degwitz, were in the capital Caracas at the time, but heard about the land invasion as it happened. They scrambled to get to the farm, but their lawyer, Dr Hugo Amaya, stopped them. This would create the exact media circus the Chávez government wanted. There was also the very real risk of being arrested.

The ranch's acclaimed El Frío Biological Station – where scientists and biologists pioneered trail-blazing projects such as breeding Orinoco crocodiles, the world's rarest crocodile, which has been almost exterminated by the fashion industry – was also shut down. The staff's research was ground-breaking, but they also protected highly endangered pink river dolphins, giant otters and anacondas, and healed injured jaguars and marsh deer wounded by poachers.

Like the rest of the Hato staff, the scientists were given two hours to pack and leave.

Chávez's view on the redistribution of wealth was no secret and firmly aligned to the standpoints of Fidel Castro in Cuba, Evo Morales in Bolivia, Rafael Correa in Ecuador and Daniel Ortega in Nicaragua. All were hardline socialists. The Maldonado family knew full well of *El Presidente*'s vendetta against them.

However, what was a massive shock was the heavy-handed and brutally swift eviction edict, particularly as the Maldonados had spent the past year negotiating in good faith to sell the ranch to the Venezuelan government. The price was laughably below market value but the Maldonados knew it was all they were going to get.

But now the president had treacherously reneged even on that ridiculously lopsided deal. He had opted instead for a fully armed, state-mandated land invasion. To this day, the family has received no compensation. Not a single worthless bolívar has been paid into any account for arguably the country's most majestic hacienda.

In a sane world, the Hato El Frío would be considered a model enterprise regardless of ideology. It was a highly productive beef ranch in a country where food was critically scarce, and also an inspirational model of conservation coexisting with agriculture in a beautiful but fragile ecosystem.

An even more puzzling aspect of the land grab was that the hacienda's historical legacy is priceless, cemented into the rich folklore and national psyche of Venezuela. It was founded by the most iconic South American of all time – Simón Bolívar, the man who liberated most of the continent from Spain. We in Africa revere Nelson Mandela, but to South Americans, Bolívar is Mandela on steroids. President Chávez himself referred to Bolívar as his 'idol'.

106

It seems, however, that Chávez had not read history. For if he had, he would have discovered that on 4 February 1824, Bolívar personally donated Hato El Frío to General José Antonio Páez as a reward for his outstanding loyalty. Páez, another South American icon, was not only Bolívar's most successful general, but also one of Venezuela's founding fathers. His El Frío herds fed Bolívar's liberation army, and Páez's original house on the *estancia* still stands.

With its proud heritage intact, Hato El Frío was acquired by Samuel Dario Maldonado in 1911. A doctor, he was the founding director of Venezuela's National Health Office and is credited with eradicating yellow fever from the country. He was also the governor of three separate states and passed laws protecting the rights of indigenous peoples and abolishing slavery. It's difficult today to grasp the extraordinary courage that took as slavery was rife on the fabulously wealthy rubber plantations. Samuel Dario personally had to confront the politically powerful rubber barons, and his life was regularly threatened.

After buying Hato El Frío, Samuel Dario became not only a successful rancher, but also a pioneering conservationist. He was greatly concerned with protecting all creatures in this wetland paradise, from the highly venomous fer-de-lance snake, or *cuaima*, to the most elegant of the big cats, the jaguar. When he died in 1925, his son Ivan Dario Maldonado took over the *estancia* and continued to expand the family business. Like his father, Ivan Dario was an exceptional farmer, eventually owning twelve ranches totalling 110,000 hectares. Again like his father, he was an ardent conservationist and his vision was not only to preserve and expand the land, but to leave an ecologically thriving platform upon which his heirs could build the family business. He and his son Álvaro, together with Spanish biologist Javier Castroviejo, initiated the El Frío Biological Station, which attracted scientists from around the Spanish-speaking world.

Ivan died two years before his beloved hacienda was seized. Realising that they could no longer function freely in their homeland, his heirs – the fourth generation of Hato El Frío Maldonados – with heavy hearts relocated the headquarters of the family business, GEM (Grupo Económico Maldonado), to Miami, Florida. They lost their prized ranch, but due to astute investments, retained their global enterprises.

One of these, to my absolute amazement, was a cattle farm called Ven-Africa Ranches (VAR) in Zululand. And that's where I come into the picture.

I was chatting to a good friend, Ryan O'Connor from Ezemvelo KZN Wildlife's crime department, when he mentioned that a farm in Mkuze owned by a Venezuelan family was planning on moving from beef to eco-tourism. As Ryan knew that my family had rewilded our cattle farm Leeuwenbosch into an integral part of the Big Five game reserve Amakhala, he suggested I get in touch with VAR's management team. I am always on the lookout for wilderness range expansion, and helping commercial farmers rewild is right up there on my bucket list.

But what firmly grabbed my attention was that Ven-Africa was already talking about taking in a couple of the Tembe tuskers, as the Tembe Elephant Park was only about 70 miles away.

Ryan set up a meeting, and I hit it off right away with Grant Norval, Ven-Africa's game reserve manager. Grant, who sports a luxuriant beard like Kingsley Holgate albeit lacking woodsmoke and rum stains, took me to see the area first-hand. I was blown away, first by the beauty, and then by the incredible potential of a rewilded ranch I never even knew existed.

As fate would have it, Ven-Africa bordered a village called Hope Farm, which is where my Rhino Art partner Richard Mabanga lives. When I mentioned this to Richard, he said one of his clearest childhood memories was hearing hyenas maniacally cackling in the night on the nearby ranch. To me, that graphically indicated that this was intrinsically raw, wild country, despite being a cattle farm for several decades.

But it was not only the magnificence of the place – it was also the amazing life story of the Maldonados, who had lost so much in their home country, that grabbed me. Ivan Dario bought Ven-Africa in 1975 on his first visit to Zululand as he wanted to bolster his Venezuelan haciendas with cutting-edge South African expertise. At the time, South Africa was a world leader in cattle management, so it was a sound business investment and Ivan brought in Herman Venter, a local veterinarian, as a partner. When Dr Venter became ill in 2002, Ivan's son Juan moved to South Africa from Venezuela to take over management of Ven-Africa for the next fifteen years. He was succeeded by Tim Machpesh, a South African business strategist and wildlife consultant, who is the current managing director.

Ven-Africa was established nearly five decades ago, but that is effectively light years ago in terms of the political situation the Maldonado family now faces. Today, Venezuela has imploded, and a significant number of foreign investors believe South Africa could go the same way. I think they are wrong. I see endless opportunities, not just problems, on this continent because I am African. The Maldonados are not. Which begs the obvious question: why were the Venezuelans, who had numerous other successful global businesses, continuing to invest in Africa when so many investors had fled in the polar opposite direction?

And particularly when the family had already been severely burnt by the government in their homeland?

That question was eloquently answered when I first met the directors of Ven-Africa's board and foundation, Veronica Maldonado and her brother Sam. Veronica, the great-granddaughter of Samuel Dario, said conservation runs deep in Maldonado blood and the wild land of Ven-Africa uncannily reminded her family of Hato El Frío, where she, Sam, Alex and their cousins had spent their childhood holidays.

'We would be out all day playing among the wild animals – being feral ourselves!' she said. 'My mom would have to fetch us and we'd reluctantly come back covered in scratches, bruises, dirt and dung. We had the most privileged childhood imaginable. Our friends were the kids of the workers. Our pets were wild animals that we rescued as orphans or were injured by poachers. We had snakes, capybaras, deer, crocodiles and caimans, birds of all types, turtles, jaguars . . . we were blessed to have been stewards of such a natural treasure. We'd roam wild in the marshes, gallop horses across the savannahs, get chased by angry bulls, step on crocodile nests, fish for piranhas, get bitten by baby capybaras, ride beside pink dolphins in *curiaras* [wooden boats], laugh at the waterdogs playing in the river, rescue freshwater stingrays stuck in mud, get hit by mangoes thrown by monkeys . . . my heart explodes with love and gratitude just thinking back to those days. We were so happy . . . so lucky to be able to run free in an infinite natural playground filled with possibilities, adventure and pure joy. Today, those feelings come flooding back whenever I am at Ven-Africa. Maybe that's why I love being here.'

Her brother Sam agrees. 'I think this project would not have been possible for my family if we didn't have the support of our

South African team, specially Tim Machpesh. I am proud to be a part of the continuation of our family's legacy of conservation but what has made this project specially inspiring is that there are competent South Africans that are deeply committed and aligned with us on the greater vision of conservation of wildlife and work incredibly hard towards that purpose.'

I was asked to do a promotional overview on the newly rewilded reserve and pointed out that, from a marketing aspect, it was somewhat isolated. Consequently, I drew up a speculative business plan joining up with other nearby private reserves to form a large biosphere, similar to what we had done at Amakhala more than twenty-five years ago. As it happened, I was already having talks with Ven-Africa's neighbours, Amakhosi Safari Lodge and Chamanzi Wilderness, about pulling down common boundary fences. By incredible good luck, Ven-Africa provided the jigsaw puzzle piece necessary to join this exceptional eco-system together in what is now called the Greater Mkuze Valley. The combined three reserves total 50,000 hectares of pristine wilderness and, if we linked up with Ezemvelo's Ithala Game Reserve north-west of Ven-Africa, it would give us 85,000 hectares. This in turn would open up migration corridors for elephants and rhinos as well as being superlative Big Five country.

By why stop there? I envisaged joining up with other reserves, such as Ndumo and the Tembe Elephant Park on the Mozambique border. This would eventually encompass 126,000 hectares of big-sky bush and, crucially, include the Tembe tuskers.

While researching this, I discovered that Ven-Africa is not only a wilderness Eden, it is also a historical treasure trove as rich in legend as it is in wildlife. The main lodge, Makongo Hills, derives its name from the hilltops it overlooks, the scene of perhaps the most pivotal Zulu clash of all time – a bloody showdown that settled irrevocably the question of the nation's royal bloodline.

It's known as Battle of aMaqongqo, fought between King Dingane and his half-brother Mpande. Both were also half-brothers of Zululand's greatest monarch, King Shaka, whom Dingane and another half-brother, Mhlangana, had murdered twelve years previously. Dingane seized the throne, and his first royal act was to execute his siblings – including his co-conspirator Mhlangana – to prevent them from following his own treacherous example. However, Mpande was spared as he was considered a weak man who showed no interest in politics.

After a few years, Dingane had a change of heart and instructed his chief *induna* Ndlela kaSompisi to kill Mpande. Ndlela, a Zulu patriot, baulked at this as Mpande was the only sibling of Shaka's to have children, and Ndlela considered the continuation of the royal bloodline crucial to the stability of the nation. This hesitation gave Mpande and his followers time to escape across the Thukela River into Natal.

Later that year, 1838, the Boer Voortrekkers who had fled British rule in the Cape Colony asked for a meeting with Dingane to discuss forming a neighbouring Boer republic. Dingane agreed and invited the Boer leader Piet Retief to visit the royal Zulu kraal, *uMgungundlovu*.

During the talks, Dingane suddenly stood and shouted '*Bulalani abatagati!*' ('Kill the wizards!') His warriors clubbed the entire party of Boers to death.

This resulted in the Battle of Blood River on 16 December 1838, when 470 Boers armed with rifles and led by Andries Pretorius routed 10,000 assegai-wielding Zulus on the banks of the Ncome River. Legend has it that the waters ran red with blood.

As Dingane's warriors fled, Mpande seized the initiative and asked Pretorius for military support to get rid of the Zulu king once and for all. Still smarting from the treachery of Retief's murder, the Boers agreed and Pretorius said he personally would lead a commando of four hundred men. This was a game changer, as although the Boers were few in number, they were unrivalled marksmen. To bring down a lion while galloping full speed on horseback was not considered unusual, and the alliance was a huge morale boost for Mpande's military.

On 14 January 1840, Mpande's army under General Nongalaza kaNondela crossed into Zululand, advancing up the coast towards Dingane's encampment at the aMaqongqo Hills.

When they arrived, Pretorius's commando unit was still a hundred miles away. However, rather than wait, Nongalaza attacked. Both armies were around five thousand strong; both adopting the traditional Zulu 'bull's horns' formation of advancing and simultaneously encircling the enemy. As the fiercely contested battle raged, according to folklore Nongalaza cunningly fooled Dingane's warriors into believing the Boers had suddenly arrived. Already demoralised after the crushing defeat at Blood River, Dingane's fighters deserted in droves.

Dingane was furious and had his loyal *induna* Ndlela – the same man who had previously spared Mpande – strangled on the spot. Dingane himself was murdered shortly afterwards by a patrol of Swazis and Nyawo tribesmen.

Mpande was now king, ruling from 1840 to 1872, and became the second-longest reigning Zulu monarch. The longest was his great-great-grandson King Goodwill Zwelithini, who reigned from 1968 until 2021, although his role was purely ceremonial.

To have a game reserve nestling on this gem of Africana is absolute gold dust, and I have no doubt the Greater Mkuze

Valley will become a prominent destination, not only for its teeming wildlife but rich heritage.

Sadly, the same was not true of the Maldonado's Venezuelan properties. The story of Hato El Frío does not end well for either people or animals. Not only did the Chávez government run one of the country's most productive farming families off the land, but this jewel of biodiversity and eco-research was converted into a drab, gigantic rice paddy. As the Orinoco valley is flooded for much of the year, Chávez – a soldier not a farmer – decided rice was the miracle food to feed his country's starving people.

Unfortunately, Chávez did not listen to his agriculturists who pointed out that the wetland's infertile soils were fine for marsh-savannah pastures and swamp woodlands, but disastrous for mass commercially cultivated crops. The entire harvest failed.

Hugo Chávez died of cancer in 2013 but his policies persist. Today the Hato El Frío is said to be in rack and ruin. The once grand mansion built for liberation hero Generalissimo Páez looks like something from a squatter camp.

Yet . . . this may not be the end. The Maldonado family has not given up. They still believe sanity will prevail. They hope for the day when they will recover their ranches and continue the pioneering projects started by their forebears. They continue to support local communities, some of whom had lived on Maldonado land for generations, through the family foundation Compañia Humana, which provides education and essential support for low-income families.

To correlate the squabbling siblings of Shaka with the land seizures of Chávez may be considered a leap too far for many. But that, in essence, is what this story is about. From owning a ranch founded by South America's most revered hero to building a model of conservancy in the shadow of the Zulu kingdom's most iconic battle, the Maldonado family straddles legends from two continents.

Not only that, their land had become a vital link in creating elephant migrations that possibly would seed the regeneration of the continent's once-fabled tuskers.

As I keep stressing, in Africa anything is possible.

CHAPTER TWELVE

Jozini Jumbos

Optimism reigned supreme. With the creation of the Greater Mkuze Valley, we now had potential lands and a viable migration corridor for Operation Tusker.

If it worked, it could restore the almost extinct sub-species of iconic elephants. I had no doubt we could pull it off as we already had a blueprint with Operation Rhino, which saved the last-surviving white rhinos from certain eradication in the 1960s. That had been spearheaded by Ian Player and a group of determined rangers, where the white rhino gene pool was distributed not only to other areas of South Africa, but to reserves and even zoos around the world. It is still the most successful relocation project ever undertaken and would be our inspiration.

However, I was aware of the hurdles facing us, not least being the fact that Player's team of absolute heroes had several hundred white rhinos as a gene-pool nucleus. Tiny as that number was, it was still larger that the number of tuskers in Tembe.

With the Greater Mkuze Valley, Angola and Loziba Wilderness, I was now juggling three major range-expansion projects specifically targeting rhinos and elephants. If one worked I would be happy. Two – ecstatic. And all three? Indescribable.

Ostensibly, our work with the Tembe relocations would focus on elephants, but Project Rhino would also be heavily involved. So much so that, with COVID-19 lockdowns being eased, Richard Mabanga and I geared up for a frenzied round of Rhino Art sessions in schools surrounding the Tembe–Mkuze corridors to create more awareness of what we were doing, which now would include the movement of tusker elephants. As Feeding the Wildlife Community had been supplying emergency food to many of these villages during the pandemic, our communication lines were already established. This had also created much goodwill, which was crucial as we needed community cooperation in opening the corridor.

Operation Tusker, for want of a better phrase, was about to get the green light. Or so I thought.

I was driving home after a meeting at Ven-Africa when my phone bleeped. It was an urgent call to arms from fellow conservationists as three elephants from a herd barely 30 miles from Tembe were about to be executed for the 'heinous' crime of eating sugarcane.

The mayday came from the Space for Elephants Foundation (SEF) NGO, which was formed in 1997 with the noble aim of reopening ancient migration routes. The mission was global, but the main focus was on a local herd now numbering about 135 elephants in the Pongola Biosphere, some 40 miles east of Ven-Africa. The animals had been introduced in the 1990s and SEF's founding members, Dr Heinz Kohrs, a Pongola veterinarian, and the late Digs Pascoe, a Zululand community conservationist, were concerned that their freedom of movement would be curtailed as the biosphere was run by three vastly different administrations.

SEF's chosen battleground has immense significance as the Pongola Biosphere is the oldest game park in Africa. Named after the Pongola River, the Zulu word for 'trough', it was proclaimed on 13 June 1894 by the president of the Transvaal Republic, Paul Kruger. This makes it a couple of years older than the Hluhluwe-iMfolozi Park, which Wikipedia erroneously lists as Africa's oldest reserve.

Today it consists of three game parks; the Pongola Nature Reserve run by Ezemvelo KZN Wildlife; the Pongola Game Reserve, owned by a bloc of nine private landowners; and the Royal Jozini Big Six (the usual elephant, rhino, lion, leopard and buffalo, plus the tiger fish, Africa's hardest-fighting freshwater fish, as the sixth), a luxury private reserve across the border in Swaziland. It also straddles one of Africa's most beautiful human-made waterways: the Pongolapoort Dam, more commonly known as Lake Jozini. Built in 1972 to irrigate the fertile plains of the Makhathini Flats below, the dam could not be used for many years due to a bitter international dispute as its waters would flood into Swaziland.

There were also concerns from Mozambique that if the dam wall collapsed at full capacity, a 200-foot inland tsunami would sweep down the Makhathini Flats and obliterate everything in its path up to the capital Maputo. So the massive construction stood as yet another monument to political folly.

The dispute was settled elementally rather than politically when Tropical Storm Demoina smashed into Africa's east coast in 1984 with biblical ferocity. The dam not only filled, but overflowed in twenty-four hours. Lake Jozini is 19 miles long and close on 5 miles wide in some places, so one can imagine what an awesome sight that must have been. To the relief of all, the wall held.

With that, a miracle happened. Almost overnight, the area was transformed into one of the most dramatic inland waterfronts in the world. Lake Jozini is now the Kariba of South Africa, and the Lubombo Mountains looming mystically in the east look eerily similar to the Matusadona range fringing Zimbabwe's priceless jewel. Lake Jozini is also home to huge shoals of tiger fish, similar to Kariba; the lake is the southernmost boundary for these ferocious predators which make a piranha's dentistry look average. Like Kariba, when cruising along the shoreline in a fishing boat one sometimes has to swerve to avoid butting into elephants wading out to graze on swamp grasses.

But that carefree image is misleading. These elephants are among the most threatened in South Africa for a variety of reasons. But unlike their big-ivory cousins, the Tembe tuskers, they do not have iconic status. They desperately needed our help.

However, from my point of view, the most pressing issue was the imminent murder of three bulls.

Much of the western bank of the lake is surrounded by the private land collectively called the Pongola Game Reserve, which caters for wildlife tourism and some tightly controlled hunting. The owners have a constitution that protects this wilderness ethos and they have dropped communal fences separating the properties to allow the free migration of wild animals.

Except one owner. Mr Alexis Steenkamp, a Zululand businessman on the southern end of the reserve, has instead converted his land into a sugarcane farm. I'm told he decided this was more profitable than eco-tourism. When, to no one's surprise except perhaps Mr Steenkamp, elephants arrived to eat his cane, he applied for a destruction permit. The animals were going to be killed.

I shook my head in despair. Had we really come to this? Killing elephants for eating sugarcane? Barely six months ago we had tenaciously fended off destruction permits for two elephants that had actually slain Beyers Coetzee, one of my best friends. Now we had to stop a wealthy landowner from shooting animals for eating what in a wildlife area is basically bushveld candy. Equally concerning, in my opinion, was that the destruction permit had been signed by an Ezemvelo District conservation officer – ironically the same man handling the Loziba elephant complications. Not only that, he had done so while his boss was on leave.

We had to act fast. I contacted Ezemvelo and said that the death sentence was, at best, ill-advised and possibly unlawful. We would be taking legal advice.

We then hit the jackpot. The destruction permit contained a glaring error, stipulating that the animals had to be executed with a .303 rifle. When we pointed this out, the professional hunter tasked with the cull was stunned. The correct calibre should be at least .458, and to hunt animals weighing more than six tons with anything less than that was downright dangerous. The hunter agreed to a stay of execution.

That bought us time. We also were getting updates from others in the area who couldn't stomach the proposed killing of innocent animals, letting us know whenever the elephants approached Mr Steenkamp's cane fields. When that happened, Chris Small loaned us his helicopter and Jason Fischer, a local game-capture expert, chased the animals away.

The next win for us was getting hold of Mr Steenkamp's Environment Impact Assessment (EIA), which stipulated he had to erect an elephant-proof fence around the sugarcane. It appeared he had complied with this – but not fully, as a railway line ran through his farm. The elephants had come on to the land through that narrow unfenced gap, which meant that in terms of the EIA, they were not there illegally.

Ezemvelo KZN Wildlife had no choice but to hold off. The bulls dodged the bullet, thanks to Project Rhino working in conjunction with SEF and the Pongola Game Reserve's legal team.

However, my biggest worry was that our success with the sugarcane elephants was merely a flash in the pan. We had saved three animals, but the big picture was far more bleak. The herd was in jeopardy due to an Elephant Management Plan (EMP), commissioned by the Pongola Game Reserve, which concluded that only thirty-seven elephants should be allowed on the biosphere.

This meant that to comply with the report, close on a hundred elephants would either have to be relocated to other reserves or culled. But with the previous global COVID travel restrictions, many of the suitable private reserves, which had not seen a tourist for close on a year, were either bankrupt or facing financial ruin. The last thing they needed was more animals, particularly those as demanding on the environment as elephants.

The one thing in our favour was that by the reserve's own admission the five-year-old EMP was outdated. It had also been drawn up on the premise that the Jozini elephants were 'non-priority', rather than weighing up the ecosystem's actual animal-carrying capacity. We were in the throes of updating it with environmental scientist Vicky Boult and researcher Heike Zitzer to provide a more realistic picture. The general consensus was that plenty of land was available, but only if we opened up the currently blocked migration routes. To do that, three hurdles stood in in our way.

Firstly, the Royal Jozini Big Six was not really a classic game park as it included a luxury resort with an eighteen-hole golf course, gourmet waterfront restaurants and plans for a spa and casino. As a result, they only want about twelve Jozini elephants on the reserve, and have now fenced off the top section of the biosphere to prevent further migration. As this area is in Swaziland, there was little we could do about it.

On the South African side, Ezemvelo KZN Wildlife's Pongola Nature Reserve is naturally separated from the private reserve by the Pongola River, which curbs permanent access.

The third issue was the ongoing Steenkamp dispute. Not only had Mr Steenkamp asked for three elephants to be killed and fenced off most of his land for sugarcane, he had also dug a deep irrigation trench on the banks of the lake that severely restricted animals migrating into the rest of the biosphere. Consequently, his farm was a formidable obstacle to large-scale movement, even though the rest of the private landowners had dropped their communal fences.

With the Swazi border in the north and Mr Steenkamp's farm in the south preventing unrestricted migration, most of the elephants were confined to the eastern shores. There were no fences there as the Lubombo Mountains and ruggedly beautiful Jozini gorge leading to the dam wall form natural barriers, but the risk of contact with humans was increasing. Cattle herders from the Nyawo tribe, whose ancestral home is the Lubombo range, were telling us they feared for their lives as they came down the slopes for fresh grazing. Although the remarkably unaggressive Jozini elephants had not attacked either people or livestock, we had to accept that this could be a potential conflict zone.

Serious as these problems were, they were swamped by one single fact. The east bank of the lake has such thick bush that it would be impossible to dart and relocate the animals in any event. There are no roads on the mountain slope, so it was out of the question to drive cumbersome transport trucks into those solid thorn thickets. As a result, even if we could find other reserves to take the so-called surplus elephants, we could not move them.

With such intractable obstacles jinxing our every move, the only solution in complying with the EMP stipulation appeared to be mass culling. But that was against everything we stood for. We simply couldn't do it. There had to be another way. This was the oldest game reserve in Africa. Surely, on that premise alone, we could come up with something?

It was time to delve into the history books again. Coincidentally or not, one of the most influential private landowners in the Pongola Biosphere is Karel Landman. He is a direct descendant of the revered Voortrekker leader Karel Pieter Landman, who was second in command during the rout of Dingane's army at Blood River in 1838. Equally coincidentally, just across the lake from the Landman property is the Hlatikulu Forest where Dingane was tracked down by Nyawo warriors and stabbed to death. His grave is in a clearing under the shade of a wild fig tree.

So, by a quirk of fate, descendants of people from significantly different cultures who had toppled the treacherous Dingane many years ago and brought some stability to Zululand now lived on either side of the lake. Today, close on two centuries later, we would be asking them to join forces with us at SEF. This time to save threatened elephants.

Maybe I'm being idealistic, but Africa does that to people: it brings unlikely people together in the name of a good cause. I don't know. What I did know is that somehow we had to get out of this stalemate.

CHAPTER THIRTEEN

Space for Elephants

My involvement with the Space for Elephants Foundation (SEF) goes back to my friendship with Digs Pascoe.

Digs, who died in 2018, was one of those wild, unconventional characters that Africa inexplicably seems to concoct out of the ether. He was the founder member of a bunch of eccentrics that we in the sane world dubbed the 'Eshowe Hillbillies', an idiosyncratic group of free thinkers with three common traits: an unquenchable thirst for life; off-the-wall ideas; and a passionate love of wild places. The town of Eshowe is the oldest European settlement in Zululand and its name (pronounced esh-how-wee) is said to have been inspired by the sound of the wind blowing through the nearby Dlinza Forest. That should have been etched on Digs's tombstone, except in his case it was a force-10 wind.

Digs was an unforgettable sight in both Eshowe and the remoter Zululand outbacks. He always wore a leather cowboy hat and drove a mud-encrusted, dented Vauxhall Corsa pickup with elephants sketched on the doors. Also conspicuous were three enamel mugs dangling from brass hooks screwed roughly into the dashboard to hold tots of Captain Morgan rum, his favourite tipple. He called the rum his emergency rations, and with good reason. Once on a trip to visit fellow Hillbillies Barry Leitch and Kingsley Holgate in the nearby town of Melmoth, he ran out of fuel. Under the seat was a jug of rum. He poured half into his fuel tank and the vehicle, spluttering on alcohol fumes, somehow made it to Barry's home. He then proceeded to celebrate his arrival with the balance of the jug.

The only thing constant about Digs was his inconsistency. If he made an appointment, he wouldn't be merely half-an-hour late. He would be half-a-day late. On one notable occasion he told his long-suffering wife Melanie that he was popping out to see Kingsley Holgate. He returned three weeks later and apologetically explained to Melanie that they had got lost somewhere in Tanzania, a few thousand miles away. But as both Kingsley and Digs believe that being lost is a state of mind – it only matters if you care – they didn't consider contacting home.

One thing Digs was deadly serious about, however, was conservation. He also loved elephants more so than anyone else I know. Zulus have a unique art of giving people uncannily accurate nicknames that are an insight to their soul. In Digs's case, it was *wayedlula indlovu* – let the elephants pass. That too should have been engraved on his tombstone.

The Pascoe family had a fine pedigree in conservation activism. Digs's sister, Blythe Loutit, was a legend in Namibian wildlife circles as she took on the might of the South African military as well as influential politicians who were illegally hunting elephants and the critically endangered desert black rhino. This was during the Border War, and the military was the most powerful and feared organisation in the country. To confront colonels and generals was considered borderline treason and took extraordinary courage. Today she is credited with saving the Namibian desert rhino from extinction, and deservedly won the prestigious Survival Award for Conservation of an Endangered Species in 1992.

SEF now owns Blythe's famous 1958 Land Rover that she used to patrol the Namibian deserts tracking down those killing endangered animals. After her death in 2005, Digs went to Namibia and drove the battered old vehicle nearly 1500 miles back to Eshowe. Like its former owner, few vehicles have such an illustrious pedigree and a few years ago it was officially 'retired' from rescuing both Namibian rhinos and Jozini elephants. Aptly named 'Blythe', the sexagenarian Land Rover today is a proud museum exhibit on a reserve in the Pongola Biosphere called White Elephant Safari, owned by pioneering game farmer Karl Kohrs, whose son Heinz is SEF's co-founder.

Pongola veterinarian Dr Heinz Kohrs loves elephants, so it was inevitable he would get together with Digs. His fascination with these hugely intelligent creatures is endless, but he says one special event in his extraordinary wildlife career stands out. It was when Lake Jozini's resident bull named Ingani broke out of the reserve in March 2000 and there was much consternation that he would wander into populated areas. If so, he would have to be killed, but Ingani soon returned. Not only that, he brought with him five orphaned elephants that he had found on the nearby Somkhanda Game Reserve. Mature elephant bulls are largely solitary creatures, and Heinz says this incredible act of compassion in bringing stranded youngsters to a new home was one of the key inspirations for him and Digs forming SEF.

As his name attests, Heinz's forebears were Germans, who came to Africa in 1854. In a moving letter to the then South African president Jacob Zuma on World Elephant Day 2017, Heinz made an eloquent personal plea for Mr Zuma – who is also from Zululand – to personally intervene in the plight of the animals on his doorstep. 'It seems unthinkable that wild elephants should disappear. How can we make sure it does not happen?' he asked.

Equally powerfully, he told Zuma of his love for Africa.

I have a very German name – Heinz Karl Kohrs – but I have often thought of changing my surname to Nkosi and living life under customary law. I feel I must be a Zulu boy at heart, having lived all my life in Zululand. I grew up on a farm at the foot of the Lubombo Mountains near the Golela border at the south eastern side of Swaziland, playing *umlabalala* [a Zulu board game] with my friends, herding sheep and cattle, and hunting birds with a *isiklingi* [catapult] and *unogwaja* [hares] with a *isagila* [club]. I decided that when I grew up I would be a rural livestock veterinarian and look after the land and its animals.

That's exactly what Heinz has spent his life doing. However, he has an extremely busy practice to run and, when Digs died, SEF teetered on collapse. Digs was the 'face' of the organisation, and few would dispute that he had successfully run it on sheer force of personality and not much else. As a result, SEF's records and documents, as Digs would have been first to admit, gave new meaning to the word 'shambles'. If Digs liked someone, he or she ended up as a trustee. Sometimes this would include people he had just met. To somehow untangle this bookkeeping quagmire, Heinz and Digs's daughter Dulcie asked me, as ambassador for Project Rhino, to take over the organisation.

Much as we all loved Digs, I wasn't sure about doing that as just sorting out the mountain of random paperwork would be horrendously time-consuming. But the more I heard about the plight of the Jozini elephants, the more I realised Digs's administrative 'skills' were the least of our problems. Then when I heard that elephants were about to be executed for eating sugarcane, refusal was no longer an option. I had to get involved. In any event, Project Rhino was doing a lot of similar work to SEF in other areas, so it made sense to combine forces.

However, even in my more optimistic moments, I thought the situation looked bleak. There was no way around the fact that to comply with the Pongola Game Reserve's EMP and also minimise the increasing amount of elephant–human contact, we had to move some of the animals off the eastern bank. But to do so meant filling in irrigation trenches and pulling down fences in the rest of the biosphere, something neither Swaziland nor Mr Steenkamp agreed upon. Granted, the EMP was being updated, but even so it was unlikely that all 135 elephants would be permitted to stay in the area.

The stalemate seemed insurmountable.

Then the answer dawned. It was staring us in the face. If the current biosphere corridor was blocked, we needed to open up another one. And not only was there another potential migration passage available, thanks to previous SEF researchers we had a blueprint for where it should go.

It was tentatively called the Lubombo Spine. And it had already been accepted in principle by the main players in the area, including hugely influential people such as Karel Landman.

So why hadn't this been done before?

Broadly speaking, there were two reasons. Firstly, when first drawn up by SEF and other stakeholders, it was wildly ambitious, envisaging a corridor stretching eastwards to the Maputaland coast and south towards the iSimangaliso Wetland Park, a

World Heritage Site. This would also include a Trans Frontier Conservation Area with Swaziland and Mozambique, an agreement that could take decades to hammer out due to political ramifications. In short, it was cumbersome whereas, to sort out the existing Jozini elephant stalemate, we had to be nimble. We had to radically scale down the blueprint to more manageable proportions.

The next reason was the enormous amount of legwork needed to consult the myriad communities living on the peripheries of the proposed Lubombo Spine, starting with Dingane's historic arch-enemy, the Nyawo tribe. Most people simply didn't have the time to do that.

I then thought of elephants being shot for eating sugarcane. I thought of elephants being culled due to fences or irrigation trenches in the way of their God-given migration routes. I thought of the fact that these animals in an economy stricken by COVID would never find another home. A simplified version of the Lubombo Spine was their last chance.

I would find the time and do the legwork.

I contacted Heinz as well as environmental scientists Vicky Boult, Heike Zitzer and Suzette Boshoff, and using the original Lubombo Spine outline we focused solely on opening a single corridor to ease the elephant numbers. It would run south through the Ubombo Mountain Nature Reserve in the Nyawo tribal area, and then through the Mkuze Gorge, one of the most stunning tracts of land I've ever seen.

The next step was to persuade the various other communities involved to come on board. We had to convince them that a corridor joining up major reserves of northern Zululand could lead to a substantial growth spurt. Not only would it bring more tourists, there would be other potential microbusinesses such as bird-guiding safaris, natural history field trips, cultural tours and river rafting along the Mkuze River. Or fishing trips on Lake Jozini itself, where we could arrange finance for local fishermen to buy boats and take tourists tiger fishing for a fraction of the costs charged by five-star resorts.

The beauty of the Lubombo Spine was that it was not just about elephants, although they were the cornerstone of the project. It could snowball into something far bigger, kickstarting eco-businesses that would take poachers out of the killing fields, feed hungry families and give hope to hundreds of thousands living on the edge of society.

It was a big call, and at times I wondered if I could do it. But if I couldn't, I wasn't sure who could. Through circumstance more than anything else, I had inhaled the soul of Africa as a small boy, running wild in the bush on my family's farm with Xhosa boys. They were my first real friends. As a result, in later life I was as much at ease talking to grizzled elders in a mud hut as I was in a boardroom giving a PowerPoint presentation. Often more so. I love this continent, its peoples, its vibrant cultures and, of course, its superlative wildlife. It is all I know.

This is no great achievement on my part. It is pure accident of birth. I went to an excellent school, St Andrew's College in Grahamstown, but my main education was undeniably in the bush and my inspirational teachers were those who lived with the land. From as far back as I can remember, I have spoken Zulu or Xhosa as often as I have spoken English. So while I have no scientific or academic certificates hanging on my study wall, I can talk to people in the most remote outback, in the idiom and using imagery to which they relate. I am blessed to have a foot in two cultures. It's the simple reality of my life in Africa. I have learnt as much from illiterate tribespeople in the so-called developing world as I have from multimillion-dollar fundraisers in designer suits. This project was what I was born for.

I also had the good luck of having two incredible partners who would guide me financially and logistically on this mission: Francois du Toit, CEO of African Conservation Trust, which is the umbrella body for Project Rhino, and conservationist land developer James Arnott. Also with me would be Richard Mabanga, my longstanding Rhino Art colleague, and Abednigo 'Abe' Nzuza.

Abe had been a wildlife manager at Ezemvelo KZN Wildlife for twenty-six years but now worked as a tour operator in the town of Jozini. However, with COVID, Jozini tourism was an oxymoron, so Abe was technically unemployed. I brought him on board as my aide-de-camp, and he more than proved his worth with his priceless network of contacts. Apart from being eloquent and polite, there seemed to be no one in the area whom he did not know.

Abe, Richard and I started talking to the communities right away. First stop was the Nyawo tribe. They were the closest to the elephants on the east bank of the lake and it was imperative they came on board.

The Nyawo don't want elephants as they are almost exclusively cattle herders. However, they were amenable to the idea of a corridor, as that would enable elephants to migrate south off their land.

Next was the Gumbi tribe. These negotiations were initially complicated as the tribe has two leaders, twin brothers Myeni and Ngwenya, who don't always agree. The Gumbi twins own land on the lake shores immediately north and south of the gorge, so their agreement was critical.

The meetings with the Gumbi brothers and Nyawo leaders involved the usual five stages of progression I always encounter when talking to communities: initial hostility (thanks to historical apartheid baggage), followed by suspicion, then reservation, tentative acceptance and finally enthusiasm. This can take several years, and we did not have the luxury of time not only to save the elephants but because, in the crippled post-pandemic economy, many of these communities faced grim futures. Much of their ancestral land was only suitable for wildlife and to link up with viable game reserves in a corridor that one day could extend all the way to the coast offered a definitive opportunity. They realised they had to seize it.

Perhaps the most impressive section of the first stage of the Lubombo Spine is the Mkuze Gorge, through which the Mkuze River meanders like a lazy python. The valley floor is rich savannah that turns gold-red as the sun sets and is studded with the glossy-leafed wild fig and pale-yellow fever trees that are synonymous with the area. But then it suddenly sheers steeply upwards into the beautiful wildflower crags and flinty cliffs of the Lubombo Mountains. Silhouetted on the skyline are two spectacular features, the summits of the Gaza and Ghost Mountains where ancient kings are buried in a taboo cave.

The Gaza dynasty ruled the area for centuries, with the Lubombo Mountains being an impregnable fortress. Well . . . almost impregnable. When they were eventually conquered by Shaka in 1819, their leader Soshangane fled into Mozambique and formed the Shangaan clan incorporating scattered remnants of the Tsonga and Tembe peoples. Soshangane adapted Shaka's military tactics, welding the Shangaans into a formidable fighting force, often overrunning Portuguese colonial settlements in southern Mozambique.

Soshongane died in 1856 and, as was custom, his warriors wrapped his mummified body in black cattle skins and carried their king to the royal graveyard at the top of Ghost Mountain. They had to hide during daylight to avoid Zulu patrols, so only travelled at night.

To this day, local tribesmen say the mountain is haunted, claiming to hear eerie shrieks and see 'fires and strange lights' flickering like phantoms from the fissures and cliffs of the summit.

True or not, the legend gained such traction that even H. Rider Haggard, author of *King Solomon's Mines*, told of the mystic mountain in his 1892 book *Nada the Lily*: 'It is a great and strange mountain. It is haunted also and named the Ghost Mountain, and on top of it is a grey peak rudely shaped like the head of an old woman.'

With the Lubombo Spine, I had unwittingly linked three different eco-projects with the most defining offshoots of Shaka's Zulu nation. First was Loziba where Mzilikazi, the Zulu general who founded the Ndebele tribe, grew up; then Ven-Africa, the battleground that re-established the Zulu nation after Shaka's assassination; and now the Lubombo Spine, the burial site of the legendary leader Soshongane. I couldn't believe the rich vein of history that was unfolding before me. These reserves and corridors were lynchpins tying together the incredible story of one of Africa's most iconic peoples.

Then we got the best news of all. A crucial stretch of private land belonging to the Senekal family, the largest private landowner along the proposed spine, opened up to us. Dreyer Senekal agreed to grant us access along his eastern boundary, which meant the corridor could be routed down to the valley below Ghost Mountain. That breakthrough was the key to unlocking the entire project. Without it, the migration route along the Lubombo Spine would be forever blocked. Like Karel Landman, a driving force on the board of the Pongola Game Reserve, the Senekals are descendants of Voortrekkers. All the historic groups in this north-east corner of the country, regardless of age-old feuds, bitter battles and shifting alliances, were now coming to our aid. It was a true modern-day South African wildlife story of hope.

We also had to get permission from Ezemvelo KZN Wildlife, so Abe booked a meeting with the CEO, Ntsiki Dlulane, in Pietermaritzburg. Francois, Abe and I arrived with detailed topographical maps of the area pinpointing exactly what we wanted to do, which we spread over Mr Dlulane's desk like a giant tablecloth. He seemed impressed, and asked for a detailed business plan. The meeting ended well, and the Lubombo Spine was tentatively now on.

With invaluable support from Richard and Abe Nzuza, the opinions of local communities started to shift our way and fences slowly began falling along the corridor. We weren't out of the woods but, come hell or high water, the first phase of the Lubombo Spine was going to open. The elephants would be saved.

Then I got another SOS. This time it came from nearly 2,500-miles away.

The Democratic Republic of the Congo.

(above) Grant and John Kahekwa.
(Marcio Lisa)

(right) Peter Eastwood, Ben Wallace, Marcio Lisa.

Nunu Jobe, Paul Dutton, Dennis Gumede, Sarah Cobden-Ramsay. *(Grant Fowlds)*

(right) Richard Mabanga and pupils of Mphakema Primary school. *(Grant Fowlds)*

(below) Great Kei valley, landscape.

(right) Jack Brotherton and Ken Collins, Greater Kuduland.
(Grant Fowlds)

(below) Grant Fowlds, Sbu Jiyane, Beyers Coetzee, James Glancy.

Elephant x 10, Loziba.

Neil Potter, Mlungisi Bushula, John Rance, Dr. Jacques Flamand, Anton Hagerman, Craig Middleton, Ben Middleton. *(Grant Fowlds)*

(right) Grant and Kingsley Holgate rhino walk in Hluhluwe park.
(Angela Fowlds)

(below) Grant, Robyn Dougans, Tarryn Hunt, Luzaan Preston, Lyn Reeves.

(above) Pete Dunning,
Darren Gough, Kevin
Pieterson, James Glancy,
Grant Fowlds. *(Laura Glancy)*

(left) Alice Fowlds, Angela
and Grant with masks in
Kahuzi Biega NP. *(Alice Steyn)*

(right) John and Grant planting trees at Miti, DRC.

(below) Adidas gifts to a school boy at Hlomo Hloma Primary. *(Grant Fowlds)*

White rhino. *(Marcio Lisa)*

Dad Bill Fowlds, brother William, Joe Cloete (brother-in-law), Dale Paul (brother-in-law), Grant Fowlds, taken 1999.

CHAPTER FOURTEEN

Plagues and Primates

The Kahuzi Biega National Park (KBNP) is a World Heritage Site, which is no small feat in the chaotic conditions of the Democratic Republic of the Congo.

Officially the world's third poorest country, the DRC is a fascinating mixture of inspiration and anarchy, hope and despair. Its allure is almost hypnotic.

The anarchy and despair are the tragic result of more than a century of kleptocratic misrule, genocide and two civil wars that killed or displaced 8 million people. The flipside of the coin is an astonishing story of survival that defies logic. Despite crushing odds, the country remains standing. The flames of hope may have sputtered alarmingly at times, but they have never died. And no one has kept those embers flickering more than a heroic conservationist called John Kahekwa. John has devoted his life to saving the world's largest and most threatened primates, the gorillas of Kahuzi Biega. The debt this planet owes him can never be paid back.

The park is 2,316 square miles of rainforest, bamboo woodland, swamp and peat bog. It's home to a spectacular variety of wildlife, including forest elephants, diverse herds of antelopes and 349 species of birds, some unique to the area. But the undoubted stars are the eastern lowland gorillas, the immensely powerful yet gentle giants that once roved the foothills of the Great Rift Valley in their thousands.

Today, there are perhaps 250 of these magnificent creatures left in Kahuzi Biega. Their survival is not guaranteed.

As a young man, John was a tracker in the park, putting his life on the line countless times as he fought poachers and militia spilling over from the Rwandan genocide across the border. He now runs the Pole Pole Foundation (meaning 'slow and steady' in Swahili), an NGO which provides jobs, food, resources and education to communities surrounding Kahuzi Biega. Through his Herculean efforts, the foundation has brought large-scale rainforest plunder and poaching under some loose semblance of control. Many former poachers now have jobs in KBNP communities.

But all that incredible work was again under threat. The reason this time was not genocide or civil war, but COVID-19, which obliterated the DRC's fledging tourist industry. It also resulted in overseas donors withdrawing in droves.

As in all catastrophes, the most affected were the poorest of the poor. With airlines grounded for much of 2020–21 and the First World in isolation, the DRC basket-case economy ground to a shuddering halt. In the KBNP, rangers who earn a paltry US$48 a week were not paid for almost an entire year. The short-fall was to some extent made up by Western charities, but even those donors had to abandoned ship as pandemic paranoia spread.

The results for conservation in the DRC were catastrophic. In the national parks, there was no food for game rangers and their families, no fuel for vehicles, no medicines for the sick, no schools for children – and no money for anyone.

Security collapsed as, without vehicles, the only alternative was foot patrols in a rainforest that is seven times the size of New York City. Within a month, few of the exhausted rangers had soles on their ragged boots. Fewer still had functional raincoats. They had no bullets for their guns, so if they ran into poaching gangs or militias, any challenge would be suicidal.

With such dire shortages, it is unsurprising that morale hit rock bottom. Even fully supplied and at full strength, the KBNP has only 250 staff to safeguard this sprawling wilderness, less than half the number realistically needed. And when one considers that the UNESCO World Heritage Site is one of the last refuges of the planet's most vulnerable ape, it defies sanity.

I visited John with a group of tourists at the KBNP several months before the COVID outbreak, and I am beyond grateful that I did. It was originally set to be a real 'United Nations' trip with Peter Eastwood and his son Blair from New Zealand; Christina Skytt, her husband Niklas and daughter Lexi from Sweden; wildlife videographer Ben Wallace from England; *National Geographic* photographer Marcio Lisa from Brazil; Silvana Di Lello from Argentina; and the South African contingent, my wife Angela and youngest daughter Alice.

Peter Eastwood is a philanthropist who fell in love with the continent while competing in a car rally called Put Foot, which is more of an African experience than an actual race. He was one of Rhino Art's first donors and has been more than generous, both to John Kahekwa and us. Conservation can be a disheartening battle as there are times you feel the entire world is against you. Fortunately, I rarely have those dark days but, when I do, Peter is always there to put things in perspective. I felt he was vital on this trip, as John faces more struggles and setbacks than anyone else I know.

I first met Christina, a top executive coach, several years ago at Shakaland, a Zulu cultural village in KwaZulu-Natal. She is the author of the top-selling motivational book *Power Goals*, and urged me to write a book about my life in conservation. Not only that, she insisted I wrote down her advice and kept it as a reminder in my wallet. At times, it was the only item in there.

Ben Wallace is a world-class videographer, who worked as an intern cameraman for my brother William's Vets Go Wild projects. He is passionate about Africa and combines that zeal with superb wildlife films. He had cash flow problems at the time and crowdfunded to come along on this trip, which showed the depth of his commitment.

Marcio Lisa works for *National Geographic* and we became friends after a chance meeting on a flight to São Paulo. His skill with a camera is combined by an unflagging optimism, so he's a good man to have on board in any situation.

We needed that optimism as, just as we finished buying tickets and finalising the itinerary, everything went pear-shaped. Not minor problems such as visa or travel hiccups, but actual national disasters. Firstly, Ebola, which always seems to be lurking somewhere in West Africa, suddenly swept through the interior of the DRC, placing entire villages in quarantine. Next, the Mount Nyiragongo volcano near Goma started rumbling ominously and there were fears of an eruption. Finally, proving bad news travels in triplicate, a game guard was gunned down in the Virunga National Park, either by poachers or one of the murderous ragtag militias. I told everyone not to read the newspapers as these types of incidents regularly flare up in the DRC – and just as suddenly die down. In any event, I pointed out that all of this 'drama' was some distance from the KBNP.

But the damage was done. Christina and her family were first to pull out, deciding not unreasonably that the risks were too great, followed by Blair Eastwood, whose fiancée was a doctor and extremely concerned about the Ebola threat. Peter was also under pressure, but he was adamant he wasn't going to let me down. However, Silvana, his travelling companion, decided to withdraw, whittling our multinational party down to just six hardy souls. With some trepidation, we boarded the plane in Johannesburg, not sure what to expect.

We arrived in Rwanda, which is deservedly getting the reputation of being the Switzerland of Africa despite the genocide where more than a million people were literally hacked to death with machetes in 1994. Although at first glance the blizzard of bicycles and mopeds on the capital Kigali's streets are reminiscent of other cities in the developing world, the modern airport and mushrooming steel and glass high-rises reaching for the sky are the flipside of the coin.

We hired a car and driver, and our first trip was through the Nyungwe Forest, a national reserve run by Africa Parks in the south-west of the country. Billed as the 'best-preserved forest in Africa', it straddles a ridge that separates the vast drainage basins of Africa's largest rivers, the Congo and the Nile. Our destination was an eco-settlement on the outskirts of the forest called Banda Village, run by an innovative NGO called Kageno.

However, we almost didn't make it as our kombi got stuck in the glutinous forest mud and could go no further. Fortunately, I somehow managed to get a faint cellphone signal and contacted the manager of the lodge where we would be staying. It was a situation with which he was more than familiar and he said he would send people to fetch us.

We heard them before we saw them; six beat-up little 125 cc motorbikes buzzing like angry hornets as they slewed along invisible jungle trails. Each bike could only carry a single passenger and overnight bag, so our driver remained with the kombi to continue digging it out of the mud as we set off riding pillion.

What followed next was a helter-skelter scramble through arguably one of the world's most spectacular low-mountain woodlands, swooping down ravines and up escarpments, scattering excitable troops of colobus monkeys and chimpanzees in our path. Slipping and sliding were the norm as we skidded along obscure logging tracks that were little more than mud slurries. Everyone took spills, and Angela suffered a minor burn on her leg from the revving bike's exhaust pipe. However, we all agreed that the tumbles were well worth the experience.

About an hour later we came to a clearing on a crest where, far on the horizon and hazy in the afternoon sun, we could see the jutting western peaks of the Great Rift Valley mountain ranges. Almost directly below us, dwarfed by forest and crags, was Banda village.

At first glance it looked lacklustre and dull amid the luxuriant greenery. The most prominent building was a rectangular mud-brown school built from locally forged bricks and timber hewn from the margins of the forest. What a bleak place, I thought.

I could not have been more wrong. That drabness was a total illusion. Far from being dreary, Banda was a serene haven built on twin pillars of sustainability and tranquillity. I had never come across anything like it before.

That is all thanks to Kageno, an American non-profit charity formed in 2003 to transform poverty-stricken communities into oases of opportunity. The name means 'A Place of Hope' and, in Banda, Kageno has more than achieved that goal.

Soon after arriving, we were invited to a church service where the choir would have topped any gospel music chart. The harmonies were haunting, the voices as pitch perfect as songbirds. We were introduced by name to the congregation, and I think none of us has ever felt more welcome.

Then we were shown around the village, and to this day I still shake my head in astonishment at what can be achieved by little more than sweat, commitment and initiative. The eco-village was completely self-sufficient and everything, apart from the odd sack of cement, was either manufactured on site or painstakingly hauled in on the treacherous, muddy, slip-and-slide roads through the forest. Even cooking gas was produced on-site by mixing dung from the resident Friesland dairy herd with barnyard straw and piping the resulting methane directly into community kitchens. But it didn't end there. The straw-and-poop residue was then compressed into briquettes and used as a charcoal substitute. This meant few, if any, trees had to be logged in the forest.

All food was grown locally, resulting in delicious meals such as freshly ground peanut sauce spread on jacket potatoes plucked from the ground the same day. Our entire group turned vegetarian for this trip after committed vegan Peter Eastwood repeatedly pointed out that gorillas only ate plants – 'and look how strong they are'.

'I'm going to live forever,' he quipped while tucking into yet another plate of greens. I knew first-hand that meat in the DRC, where we would be for the next week, was sometimes of dubious freshness in the tropical climate, so I encouraged the others to follow Pete's example.

Our rooms were in an old mud and brick house with a shower consisting of holes punched in a bucket, but it was that sort of comfortable simplicity that made Banda such a highlight of the trip.

A day later we were on the road to Cyangugu on the DRC–Rwanda border. We travelled along the Rift Valley through tea plantations, the fluorescent jade-green fields shimmering in the mountain sunshine. Many say it's one of the most scenic areas of Africa, but equally impressive is that the beauty highlights the innate energy and unflagging vitality of this booming country.

Crossing the bridge over the River Rusizi into the grime and chaos of the DRC brought everything back into perspective.

It was another world altogether.

CHAPTER FIFTEEN

Crisis at Kahuzi

As we drove to John's humble home in a shanty town bordering the lakeside city of Bakavu, rain started pelting down in buckets.

Soon the roads were muddy torrents of trash and sewage streaming through the suburbs. Nothing could have been a starker contrast to the beauty, tranquillity and industriousness of the tea plantations and the village of Banda that we had just left.

John and his wife Odette greeted us and we sat down to a simple meal with this extraordinary family. The conversation flowed easily, and John spoke in depth about his country, its wildlife, its beauty and its problems. I could see every member of our party was struck by his humbleness, remarkable charisma and commitment.

The next day we went gorilla trekking. That alone was enough to rekindle my passion for this wonderful yet struggling land. It has so much potential, but one could be forgiven for thinking that the odds against it were stacked worse than a rigged poker hand. Without even taking crushing poverty into account, the logistics alone were overwhelming. For example, the DRC is close to western Europe in size but with little to no infra-structure, so it is hardly surprising that it's basically ungovernable. The socio-economic situation was far too complex and deep-rooted for conservationists to solve, so we had to concentrate solely on situations we could improve. In John's case, the mission was clear: saving the KBNP gorillas and communities that live there.

We left early as trekking was slow going, often having to hack through barriers of thick rainforest. It was also impossible to track the animals in a conventional manner as dense undergrowth covered the ground like a verdant mat. There were no footprints to follow and rangers instead looked for trampled foliage or snapped twigs as a signs of a troop's presence.

The other method was odour. Most trackers smell the animals before actually seeing them in the thick jungle. It's not unpleasant – more wild and musky than pungent. For those who spend much time in the bush, it's the organic smell of life.

John pointed to a shaking tree. He motioned us to stop. We heard a branch snap.

'Gorillas,' he mouthed silently.

A ranger chopped a gap through a section of tangled vines. Then we saw them. Closest was the silverback, massively muscular, crunching a thick bamboo stem as if it was an asparagus stalk.

The ranger, a seasoned gorilla tracker from the local Batwa tribe, made shy eye contact with the silverback, his body language requesting permission to approach. That is the secret of getting close to gorillas; receiving approval from the patriarch. Rangers will not allow anyone in a trekking party to approach females or babies before being accepted by the silverback. Nobody, human or animal, can proceed without the boss's permission. That is either granted with chilled nonchalance, or rejected with an annoyed bark. When that happens, there is only one option – retreat at speed, even if only for a few yards. Fortunately, these gentle titans seldom refuse permission.

John leaned in close, whispering in my ear, 'Bonané.'

I looked at him, astonished. Bonané was the leader of the troop that Angela and I had encountered on a trek with John four years previously. But I would never have recognised either him or his family as the group had grown beyond belief. When we first met Bonané, he had three wives and two children. I leaned forward, peering through the gap in the foliage, and started counting. Behind the gigantic shoulders of the silverback were at least five females camouflaged in the thickly tangled lianas. A movement caught my eye, a juvenile male . . . then another. As I was counting, an explosion ripped through the undergrowth and we looked at one another. John grinned – it was another juvenile that I had not spotted, fast asleep and noisily passing wind while he digested a lunch of shrubs, shoots and leaves. His stomach rumblings did justice to a thunderstorm.

I ended up counting fourteen gorillas. It was phenomenal. Bonané's family had expanded beyond our wildest expectations. I almost wept with gratitude. At last, a success story. A gorilla family not only surviving, but thriving.

Barrel-chest muscles and biceps rippling with every move, Bonané studiously ignored us. He knew John and the trackers well and was quite happy to have us nearby. The most cautious of the troop was a young female with a baby that was barely a few weeks old. Fiercely protective, she refused to allow any of us to see it. When she walked past, she turned her back, holding the infant tightly to her chest. But the inquisitive baby was equally determined to have a peep at these strange creatures ogling her and we got a brief glimpse of wide, chocolate-coloured eyes gawping at us from under the mother's armpit.

We then had another stroke of luck. Ben was filming a documentary on snaring, one of the cruellest forms of poaching, so our group was granted permission to extend the trek to see another huge silverback. His name was Mugaruka and he had been trapped in a wire snare as a four-year-old, losing his right hand in a desperate attempt to free himself. Despite that handicap, he had acquired a harem of twelve females, but this attracted the attention of bachelor silverbacks.

The inevitable had happened. With only one hand, Mugaruka lost a series of fights and his wives in the process. He had then decided to live a solitary life and has been celibate since, making no attempt to find a mate. As a result, the trackers have dubbed him 'the priest'.

The name fits, as Mugaruka exudes an aura of monk-like gravitas. He is still a massively impressive specimen and we met up with him in a nest of vines that he was using as a base. Although good-natured, he obligingly mock-charged us, but I couldn't help feeling that this was more to give his visitors a true gorilla experience rather than aggression. Even though he is in good health and seems to thrive in solitude, it was heart-breaking watching him using his mutilated stump of a hand to feed himself. Ben's video brilliantly captured that, starkly showing the barbarity of wire snares that more often than not slowly garrotte or starve animals to death.

Despite adrenalin pumping, every one of us was emotionally drained after the trek. Ben, who had remarkable footage, said without hesitation that this had been the most phenomenal day of his life. Peter, a veteran of gorilla treks in Uganda, said this close encounter was far more 'elementally rewarding' than the commercial tours he had been on.

Indeed, this was not a mere wilderness hook-up for any of us. It bordered on a spiritual experience. That may sound over the top but John, who has taken thousands of people including billionaire Bill Gates into the jungle, says this life-changing 'rapture' at meeting gorillas is almost universal.

John invited us to take part in a tree-planting project, ensuring that we did not just leave footprints behind on our departure. Through his dogged efforts, the Pole Pole Foundation has now planted an incredible 4 million plus saplings that are distributed to communities around the KBNP. The wood is harvested for building materials and charcoal, which provides the foundation for thriving cottage industries. But equally important is that these trees create a crucial buffer zone between the communities and the rainforest, and having their own wood eliminates the need to chop down gorilla habitat.

On our way back to South Africa, we visited Rwanda's genocide memorial before boarding our plane at Kigali's airport. The memorial is harrowing in the extreme for anyone, but for me it was personalised by what my friend John Kahekwa had faced when the murderous militias who had perpetrated the 1994 slaughter fled across the border into his neighbourhood. Peace has now been restored, but the tragic ripple effects of the conflict in the eastern DRC, where John and his beloved gorilla families call home, have never truly gone away.

So when COVID-19 struck several months later and the trickle of hardy tourists wanting an authentic, no-frills gorilla trek in the DRC dried up, the future of the KBNP looked not only bleak, but potentially doomed. I phoned John from South

Africa for an update. It was one of the most disheartening chats that I can remember.

'We have no food rations and our rangers have not been paid,' he said. 'We have no medical supplies for those injured in gunfights defending the park. We have no medicines for their families. There is no money to pay for their children's schooling.' He paused for a moment. The line crackled with static electricity as John said thunderstorm clouds were gathering over the Kahuzi Biega mountains. But his message was crystal clear. 'What is the future of this World Heritage Site if the world turns its back on us?' he asked. 'What hope is there for us?'

It was a wretchedly sad question. Just to keep marginally operational for the next three months, John said they needed a thousand litres of fuel, four hundred bags of basic foods such as rice and maize flour, twenty gallons of cooking oil, rubber boots and raincoats for rangers patrolling in one of the continent's wettest regions, and lifesaving medicines for the staff.

Total cost? A mere US$23,750 – less than the annual salary of most charity workers in the West. But it was not forthcoming. In fact, the reverse. Donors were backtracking.

Conservation is not solely about fighting poachers, nursing animals and patrolling wildernesses. That's the Hollywood image. The reality is also juggling complex social, economic and cultural issues that are way beyond most of our paygrades. But, above all, any solutions have to include rural communities, their welfare and aspirations. Feeding wildlife communities and raising critically needed funds are as vital a function of frontline conservation as darting sick animals or shootouts against bad people in the bush. Make no mistake, the success or failure of most wildlife causes relies on the people that live on the surrounding lands.

For me it was crystal clear. To save Bonané's family, Mugaruka's solitude and the other beleaguered gorillas of the Kahuzi Biega National Park, we also had to save the people living there.

I got out my phone and started dialling.

CHAPTER SIXTEEN

Requiem for an Eco-warrior

Soon after returning from the DRC, I had the sad task of helping organise a memorial service for my fallen friend and eco-warrior Beyers Coetzee.

The night before he died, I had introduced Beyers to the great sculptor Andries Botha. Beyers's environmentalism, passion for life and love of wild lands had so impressed Andries that he wanted to sculpt a monument as a tribute to an extraordinary man's life. In fact, he wanted to sculpt two monuments: a four-metre, highly visible one that would be placed on Mount Mawana itself, and another smaller one marking the exact spot where Beyers was felled by elephants he was trying to save. The larger statue would be a shrine where people visiting Loziba could pay homage; the second, deep into the bush, would be a pilgrimage for family and close friends.

Beyers had been laid to rest in Pretoria about eight months previously, but we all knew his heart was spiritually in the wilds and we wanted to honour that. Consequently, both statues were to be in the form of a Zulu *isivivane*, a type of cairn, made of rocks and stones, which has been used to revere the dead since time immemorial. In Africa, an *isivivane* is even more evocative as it also is a tribute to a brave warrior, whose body is covered in stones to mark the spot where he fell in battle. It was a fitting tribute as Beyers was a courageous fighter for the land he loved.

Andries is highly sought after and commands top dollar for his superlative work. He and his team did this project for free. It was entirely a labour of love and respect. The *isivivane* stones, all selected on site, were encased in a metal gabion morphing into an elephant head. Radiating out of the top were shafts of light resembling tusks, representing the ivory trade and tragic decimation of wildlife, but also symbolising the innate power of the natural world. The statue would be placed in such a way that visitors paying their respects could add their own stones to the *isivivane*.

Not only that, Andries – a spiritual and philosophical man – wanted both sculptures to be in exact alignment with the Nilotic Meridian, the geographic centre of the Earth's landmass and a mythical axis around which ancient civilisations believed the universe rotated. Consecrated in deep-rooted folklore, the Nilotic Meridian runs horizontally along the 31-degree longitudinal line from the Egyptian pyramids and Great Sphinx through the Great Rift Valley and ending at the Indian Ocean just below Durban. Among African shamans, the meridian is the arterial blood of Mother Earth, a subterranean river of energy mirrored in the cosmos by the Milky Way, hence its alternative name River of Stars. Mythical or not, there are more sacrosanct sites dotted along this revered meridian – including the Giza plateau, Temple of Philae, Great Zimbabwe Ruins and Timbavati, birthplace of the white lions – than anywhere else in the world. It also crosses the source of the Nile, Africa's mightiest river.

The smaller statute was completed first, but to get it to the exact spot where Beyers died was a major mission. With spring approaching, the bush was greening rapidly and choked with sickle bush that slices vehicle tyres as cleanly as a razor. So the first thing we needed to do was bulldoze a rough track to get as close as possible. Even so, the last 3 miles would have to be a footpath hacked with machetes. I liked that. The fact that Beyers's memorial would be a haven of isolation and peace was a fitting elegy.

Andries wanted people who had been close to Beyers to take part in the project, which involved several trips to the site collecting suitable rocks and other indigenous materials. Andries also selected a chunk of pink quartz from Mawana Mountain, which he chiselled into two pieces. The bigger one was in the shape of a heart, which Una placed in the statue, while the second piece was given to Beyers's mother Daniella. She keeps it on her bedside table, its translucent light shining as a permanent candle for her son.

When finished, the statue stood just over 6 feet, Beyers's exact height, with an elephant trunk cradling a human head on top of the gabion facing the meridian. It was magnificent.

While clearing the site and digging foundations, Jess Bothma, Andries's skilled protégé, found what looked like a piece of bone on the rock where Beyers fell. We knew that Beyers's arm had been broken in the attack, and we weren't sure if it was bone or ivory. I sent it off to a laboratory for DNA testing, but we got the confirmation we needed when we later darted the askari that had attacked Beyers in order to fit a tracking collar. While the animal was sedated, we discovered its tusk was chipped and the fragment Jess found matched the break perfectly.

It was a glorious big-sky day when about twenty family members and close friends assembled at the spot where Beyers drew his last breath. Una, her children Luan and Lara and their grandmother Daniella were there, as was Loziba's lawyer Peter Rutsch and Francois du Toit, my financial partner in the wilderness project. Mount Mawana glowed before us in the honey-coloured light of the late autumn sun and one could feel the presence of something powerful. I had no doubt it was Beyers's spirit, pulsing with the energy of the Nilotic Meridian on which we stood. The fact that we had gathered at his last stand made it even more moving.

There were several speeches and, in that small clearing of Africa, the anguish of those who loved this extraordinary man was in plain sight. An emotional moment came when Una walked over and hugged Thobani Masondo, the last man to see Beyers alive. Thobani had not only fled for his own life that fateful day, he faced his own demons to return and help build the statue. As the two embraced, there was not a dry eye in the surrounding bush.

Then Andries stood. Pointing to the ground, he reminded us that this was where a man gave his life to create a vision, and where his blood had soaked into the ground. The monument we had gathered around was built with respect and veneration. Every rock in the *isivivane* had been carried by people who knew and loved Beyers.

'Thank you for giving me the opportunity to speak about a man I knew for only eight hours,' Andries said. 'For him to have made such an impression on me shows what an unbelievable person he was. All of us here were touched by Beyers. Grant and Francois introduced me [to him] for one glorious evening. It was the evening before the day [of Beyers's death]. I was deeply touched, not only by his life, but by the symbol of his life and those who came with him and this particular family to carve out a piece of South African history.'

Addressing Kallie van der Walt, Una's brother who had been among the first in the rescue party to find Beyers, Andries said he could not imagine how he felt that night, coming across the tusked body of his brother-in-law. 'I cannot think of anything more courageous, moving and powerful than to sit with someone you love who had been taken in such a brutal and mythical way. You sat here for six hours guarding Beyers around a fire, and then carried him out over the hills. I simply cannot imagine how you felt.'

There was silence as Kallie and Una hugged each other.

Andries continued, 'I cannot think what it must mean to have your life ended by an elephant. I know it's not a good thing to talk about. But Beyers didn't lie in a sickbed with pipes in every place. He was where his heart and soul were forged – in the land. He was doing what he had to do.

'This land is an unbelievable place . . . we are seeing that at this moment. But you haven't seen what is going to happen. You have no idea what lies in the future of this land . . . this land of unbelievable possibility. And you are all part of that future.'

At that moment I realised that Andries was getting to the heart of his speech, something few had voiced before. Most of us there that afternoon knew that the Loziba project was fraught with problems and quarrels. These ranged from death threats from cattle rustlers to blatantly opportunistic demands for compensation. Not only had I been berated at fiery community meetings by angry residents, as at the Stedham Hall, but we'd had to deal with marauding lions, elephant breakouts, wildebeest disease, community cattle grazing illegally, mass trespassing and endless poaching. To add to our woes, one suspected poacher had recently died after being bitten by a puff adder, and some were trying to pin his death on us.

But even more debilitating was an escalating feud among the Van der Walt family on the future of the project. I did my best to steer clear of that as it was something they had to sort out internally, but it could kill the Loziba dream stone dead. This we all knew, but dared not say.

Except Andries. He knew that if anything needed to be said, now was the time. He paused, seeming to look at us one by one. He spoke slowly and clearly so we all heard perfectly. He wanted no confusion of his message. 'In spite of everything, in spite of the history of this land . . . it is gone and a man has lost his life. Just there,' he said pointing to the statue, 'is where he fell. We marked this piece of land to say that the past is in the darkness and the future stands in the light. We are all now in another time.

'This piece of land is a symbol of possibility – of what can happen in the future, and you are all part of it. It won't help you to sit and chew on the negativity. That will slowly but surely kill you. You need to move towards the light. Each and every one of us has to do just that and you have to work out exactly how you will do it.'

That simple speech, delivered from the heart without notes or dramatics, was exceptionally powerful. Without dwelling on the 'darkness' of past problems, Andries stressed that the symbolism of the statue standing where Beyers had shed his blood was far more potent than any petty squabble. His allusion to that was infinitely more effective than dwelling on the past bitterness. Obviously, all our problems were not going to magically disappear, but Andries was telling us that we had reached a critical juncture; that Loziba Wilderness would emerge like a beacon from the ground zero of the past. His conviction that was going to happen was like granite.

I desperately wanted to share his unshakeable optimism, but it was hard going as at times the family feuds and the community resistance – to something that most agreed was a powerful force for progress – seemed too deep to defuse.

Not only that, another bitter reality was that the elephants had killed Beyers on neighbouring property, so we didn't even own the land where the monument stood. Technically speaking, the annual pilgrimage that we would do each year on the anniversary of his death would be trespassing.

So, was Andries's prophecy just a mantra to comfort grieving people? Would we soon forget his fine words and allow the petty disputes to resurface?

I had my answer a couple of months later. It came electronically out of the blue via an email from across the world. In a few brief lines Nevvar Hickmet, the manager of truWild which had been established as part of the Chris Holcroft legacy fund in California, told us that US$40,000 had been wired to our conservation account. That translated to R615,252 in local currency. A massive amount, thanks to the exchange rate.

The project's precarious financial situation changed overnight. With that windfall we bought the land where Beyers fell. His resting place is now part of Loziba Wilderness; the dream he gave his life for.

Andries had been right after all. We had turned a corner, both symbolically and financially.

I was alone on Loziba when I read that pivotal email. I looked at the sky above Mount Mawana and silently thanked Chris Holcroft. Just a year before, he and Beyers had been with me as we watched the Mawana elephant herd magically emerge from the mist on the sacred mountain.

Still looking at the sky, I tried to thank both men, acknowledging out loud what they had done to make this planet a better place. The words caught in my throat.

My brothers, my friends . . . you will never be forgotten.

CHAPTER SEVENTEEN

Keepers of the Flame

The cavalry arrived not only for Loziba but also, to my delight, for John Kahekwa in the DRC. My desperate phone calls to donors after our last trip to Kahuzi Biega were answered.

The lifeline, for that's exactly what it was, came via close friends, New Zealanders Pete Eastwood and Rebecca Hunt. Rebecca's apt Congolese nickname is 'Msaada' meaning 'help', while Pete had been with us on the previous gorilla trek. His team from the Tanglewood Foundation, a charity that he founded, swung into action and sent over a massive donation of food, fuel and equipment to the Kahuzi Biega National Park.

Equally impressive was that when the vital supplies arrived, two DRC army generals as well as the chief military commander of South Kivu personally escorted John's Pole Pole crew to the park, providing a VIP welcome not accorded to any other charity in the area. This was truly a turn up for the books. Unfortunately, due to COVID lockdown, neither Pete nor Rebecca, who were in New Zealand, could attend.

The truckloads of rations included bags of beans, rice, maize and cassava flour and gallons of vegetable cooking oil. Equally important was that there were enough raincoats and rubber boots to equip all the park's rangers, and the delivery of 340 litres of fuel would see anti-poaching vehicle patrols running again. Finally, the German development bank KfW, in conjunction with the Congolese Institute for Nature Conservation (ICCN), agreed to pay all Kahuzi Biega staff ten months' salary. They could buy clothes and schoolbooks for their children again.

Obviously all of this was short term but, in Africa, if you are standing at the end of the day, you are winning. In the DRC we were still on our feet. Which in effect meant that so were the gorillas.

I have spoken of John at length as both a friend and an eco-muse. He is, in my opinion, a prophet of the planet, but here in my own country I have equally inspirational conservation friends and mentors. Even more profound for me is that this unique group, to whom I speak individually at least once every week, are founts of natural wisdom that bridge the rhythms of ancient Africa and new Africa. While people like me often swap sweat-stained khakis for suits and ties when dealing with global institutions and big-name donors, these men are the grassroots guardians. They are the true keepers of the flame – the future of conservation.

I have mentioned my colleague Richard Mabanga, whose work with Rhino Art is immeasurable, as well as Abe Nzuza, my guiding light in addressing often suspicious rural communities. But another amazing inspiration is a remarkable eighty-eight-year-old man called Mdiceni Gumede – or plain 'Gumede', as we refer to him with absolute reverence.

I first met Gumede through Paul Dutton, himself a legendary ranger with the former Natal Parks Board. The charismatic old man instantly captivated me, but the pleasure of meeting him was tinged with sadness knowing that his priceless knowledge of bush lore would die with him. I wanted to absorb every crumb of that incalculable gift he generously bestowed on those who listened.

As a young man, Gumede worked with conservation icon Ian Player and was with him when Player learnt, by his own admittance, the most crucial lesson of the bush – respect, or what the Zulus call *hlonipha*. It's a story Gumede has told around countless campfires, and still tells to this day.

Player and his Zulu mentor Magqubu Ntombela were hiking in the iMfolozi Game Reserve when they passed an *isivivane*, the type of cairn sacred to the Zulus that formed the basis of the sculptures in memory to Beyers Coetzee. It is customary for anyone passing one to spit on a stone, make a wish, then place it on the cairn.

Both Magqubu and Gumede did this instinctively, but Player carried on walking.

'Hey, *Madolo*,' Magqubu shouted after him (*Madolo*, meaning 'knee', was Player's Zulu name as he limped from a leg injury). 'Pick up a stone as you are walking past a sacred Zulu place.'

Player curtly replied that it didn't affect him as a white man and continued walking with his dog. In essence, he was saying he didn't believe in mumbo-jumbo.

Magqubu was outraged. 'I'm telling you, this is a Zulu custom. You will do it!'

The men glared at each other. Player was not used to being ordered around by a subordinate. He also saw no point in taking part in what he considered a Zulu superstition. A stand-off ensued. It was stifling hot and flies were buzzing around the two angry men, drinking their sweat. It was a clash of wills, and the sheer force of Magqubu's personality finally broke Player. Grumpily, he picked up a stone and in a sulk placed it on the cairn.

A few steps later, a giant black mamba reared out of the tall grass, hissing like a punctured tyre. According to Player, the reptile's satanic eyes barely a yard away were level with his own. If it attacked, they and the dog would be dead. The strike of Africa's deadliest snake takes only fifty milliseconds and its neurotoxic venom would kill them long before they could trek out of the valley. The situation was intensified by Player's dog, a type of small terrier, which was barking ferociously.

But the snake – inexplicably, considering a mamba's innate aggression – didn't strike. After a long moment the giant reptile sank down and slithered off, vanishing in the long grass.

There was an eerie silence, the men staring in shock as the snake disappeared. Magqubu spoke first, staring directly at Ian, his voice throbbing with anger.

'That was the spirit of this place. Had you not honoured it, we would be dead.'

Ian nodded. He knew it was true.

On the walk back to camp, Magqubu gave Ian the lecture of his life. Without *hlonipha*, Magqubu said Player would learn nothing. *Hlonipha* honoured the land, the rivers, animals, birds, insects – even deadly snakes. Magqubu explained that the hills and trees lived. The animals and birds were his spiritual siblings. That 'spirit' could never be disrespected. Those who did not understand that, perished in the wild, as they nearly had.

'If you don't listen to Zulu customs you will die in the bush.'

Ian understood. He later said he did so at an elemental level far deeper than he ever imagined. He never made that mistake again. He also never again disobeyed a command from Magqubu.

We will never know how many people that rangers in tune with the planet, such as Magqubu and Gumede, have saved, either through *hlonipha* or their finely honed bush skills. Some of their life-saving actions are obscure and unable to be scientifically proven, such as Magqubu's telepathy with the mamba at the *isivivane*. But one of the more obvious ones is the saga of an actual snake catcher, which Gumede told me one day while trekking the bush.

It happened at iSimangaliso Wetland Park when a herpetologist – a zoologist who specialises in amphibians and reptiles, including snakes – from the Johannesburg Zoo arrived with a permit to catch a trophy python. In those days – the 1970s – scores of these impressively large constrictors regularly sunned themselves on the rocks scattered along Lake St Lucia's shores, and head ranger Paul Dutton told Gumede to show the snake catcher the reptile's favourite spot.

Gumede initially declined. Nothing frightens him in the bush. Except snakes. And pythons are the biggest.

'But Paul insisted, saying I didn't have to get close to the snakes,' said Gumede. 'All I had to do was take my rifle, go to the rocks and point them out. The white man would then grab the python he wanted.'

Gumede reluctantly escorted the snake catcher to the shoreline and pointed out a python basking about 50 yards away. He then said he was going no further.

'No problem,' said the herpetologist. 'I've caught thousands. I'm an expert.'

He went on to the rocks, but instead of bagging the reptile that Gumede had pointed out, decided to go for a bigger trophy.

Gumede sat down, minding his own business, when something made him look up.

'I then saw with some surprise that the white man was not catching the snake. The snake was catching him.'

Indeed, the giant python had at least four coils around the man's body. More alarmingly, the snake catcher's head, poking above the writhing black-and-gold scales, was turning blue.

Despite his fear of slithery creatures, Gumede ran to help, jumping over several other basking pythons in the way. He couldn't shoot the snake as the bullet would almost certainly also kill the snake catcher, who was being rapidly asphyxiated.

'I grabbed the python's head, drew my knife and pressed the point beneath its bottom jaw, twisting it sideways but not stabbing it. The snake instantly relaxed its coils as a reflex action and fell to the ground. I let go of its head and it shot off into the bush. The white man was gasping for air and almost fainting with shock, but was alive.'

Gumede helped the herpetologist back to camp. Legend has it that he was on the next flight to Johannesburg and was not seen darkening the shores of Lake St Lucia again.

That was not the only time that Gumede learnt not to place too much store on city slickers' expertise in the bush. For many years he was also a iMfolozi Wilderness Trails guide, and on one of the more memorable trips his charges included a honeymoon couple who could have been the inspiration for the phrase 'get a room'.

'They were kissing and holding hands all the time,' Gumede said. 'Then a black rhino charged us. Everyone remembered my instructions either to hide behind a tree or climb it. But the man in love took this one step further. He jumped up on his wife's shoulders to get up the tree faster, leaving her on the ground. Funny, they didn't hold hands much after that.'

Sadly, the conservation authorities had not been good to Gumede. They had not renewed his trail guide licence, saying he was too old and could no longer shoot straight in an emergency. This is arrant nonsense as, even at eighty-eight, Gumede can out-hike people half his age and he says he could shoot a matchbox off my head. I believe him, although hopefully he will never have to put that to the test. But the bottom line is that today he has to survive on a ranger's pension of the equivalent of US$25 a month. I use him as much as I can, paying him to talk to our donors around campfires, and also bring out groups of schoolkids to learn from his vast knowledge of the bush. It's magnificent to watch his craggy, weather-beaten face light up like a sunrise as he recounts adventures most of us can barely imagine.

We finally got him some recognition when Paul Dutton nominated Gumede for a Wildlife and Environment Society of South Africa (WESSA) Lifetime Achievement Award. It was a prestigious gathering and among the winners were the producers of the courageous 2018 documentary *Stroop: Journey into the Rhino Horn War*, for which filmmakers Bonné de Bod and Susan Scott infiltrated the Asian wildlife mafia.

As Gumede can't speak English – in fact, he never went to school – I was asked to be his interpreter. I flew with him to Midrand, a town north of Johannesburg, and also decided to give him a few tips on public speaking. Gumede is no stranger to addressing gatherings, but only at fireside chats, light years removed from the air-conditioned auditorium we walked into. I suggested he should be his normal, humble self but, as he was a consummate mimic, he should also do his impression of a tick-infested rhino scratching itself on a tree stump. The squeals of ecstasy were something to behold, and I don't think the WESSA audience had ever witnessed anything like it. Dignified luminaries fell off their chairs laughing. That night, Gumede was the only person in the hugely impressive line-up to get a standing ovation.

If Gumede personifies the courage, stoicism and ancient wisdom of the older generation, Nunu Jobe is the charismatic new breed. The press has dubbed him the 'rhino whisperer', and although that sort of phrase is now jaded, with Nunu it is apt.

He grew up in KwaJobe, a settlement nestling in the fever trees and indigenous fig forests on the Makhathini Flats near the Mkuze Game Reserve. As an adult rite of passage, all village youths had to sneak into the reserve and kill an animal. It was similar to the Maasai ritual of a boy only becoming a man after he had killed his first lion. In Nunu's case, he tracked and illegally killed a nyala buck, and so today he is the personification of a poacher turned gamekeeper. He is able to tell other youths from first-hand experience that poaching steals from all of us.

He spent nine years as a guide with iMfolozi Wilderness Trails, following in the footsteps of bushveld legends such as Gumede, and today he is a partner in a company called Isibindi Africa Trails, which offers guided walking safaris.

He also does sterling work for Project Rhino and loves teaching kids and working with wildlife communities. In short, he is a major inspiration to the younger generation and his message is essentially that Africans are sitting on a gold mine – but they 'don't know how to mine'.

'We have to show what conservation really is and not just take wildlife tourists walking into the bush. We have to bring them into our homes, let them eat our food, learn about our medicine plants and the ways of nature. They have to experience, not just see, how we live in harmony with the land.'

He also looks the part of the new breed with a wide grin, flowing dreadlocks, and says he identifies with the 'peace and love' ethos of Rastafarians.

However, he is probably best known as the ranger who never wears shoes. This is no affectation; for Nunu it is a deep-rooted belief that bare feet keep humans in touch with the earth. The soles of his feet are like leather and he says thorns are therapeutic, like acupuncture. He can walk without flinching through sickle bush that could slash a car tyre. Standing on a snake is not something that enters his mind, but his one unbreakable ritual is that no matter how tired or dirty he is after a day in the bush, he never goes to sleep without washing his feet.

To understand Nunu, there is no better story than that of his holiday trip to Sri Lanka some years ago. He was sponsored by one of our clients, but Nunu decided he wanted to do it the 'Zulu way', which meant physically experiencing every aspect of the journey. He has his own car, but decided that was too 'citified' so caught a traditional minibus taxi packed to the roof and blaring *maskandi* Zulu folk music. He then instructed the driver to drop him off on the highway several miles from King Shaka International Airport. From there, dreadlocks blowing in the wind, he walked barefoot to the departures hall, pulling his two-wheel suitcase behind him like a tramp. Other passengers, many of whom had passed him in their cars, watched amazed as he checked in. Still barefoot, he smiled and told them he was flying to Colombo via Dubai and won them over with his easy, unaffected charm. When he said the journey made no sense if one just drove up and parked in the airport garage, somehow they understood.

On many occasions I have hiked with both Nunu and Gumede in the wilderness, and it is mind-blowing. It's tantamount to a getting a master's degree in bush education in a single walk; a ringside seat watching the baton pass from one generation to the next.

Another of my heroes is Thulani Thusi, with whom I worked on wildlife community food projects during COVID-19. Yet Thulani almost had his exemplary career in conservation abruptly terminated through a gross travesty of justice that has yet to be corrected.

It happened in 2007 when Thulani, a wilderness guide, was leading a party of German tourists in the Bhekabantu corridor that links Tembe Elephant Park to the Ndumo Game Reserve. One of the tourists, completely captivated by the unique wilderness experience, asked to visit his home and family. She was flabbergasted when he took her to a simple wood and iron structure in the white sand forest adjacent to the Tembe reserve. The shocked tourist said that instead of giving him a tip as was customary, she would deposit money into his bank account as long as he promised to use it for home improvements. That he did, and when he discovered there was still some money left over, he founded a community crèche.

It was all done innocently and in the open but, even so, the fact he had a new house sparked such jealousy and suspicion that he was accused of accepting bribes from rhino poaching syndicates. Head-office bean counters then initiated a 'lifestyle audit' and he was fired.

Fortunately, Ernest Robbertse of the Tembe Tusker Foundation heard of Thulani's plight and knew right away that something was radically wrong. Thulani was as honest as the day was long – everyone in the community knew that. Ernest subsequently managed to get access to Thulani's bank records proving that the donation to improve his extremely humble abode was absolutely above board.

Despite that, Thulani's former employers refused to reinstate him, so Ernest hired him as a community liaison officer for the trust. His work is invaluable and, like Gumede and Nunu, he is another wonderful example of a humble man who gives back to the community.

His story is also vitally important in the context of the overall conservation situation in Africa. We nearly lost Thulani through nasty conjecture and gross misinformation that should never have been allowed to fester. The loss would have been incalculable, and it's a salutary lesson that if we cannot nurture future indigenous conservationists, there is little hope.

People such as Gumede, Richard, Abe, Nunu and Thulani are vital to my work, as I know I am to theirs. I help them in getting sponsorships, rewilding land, uplifting wildlife communities and securing range expansion. Even securing food in pandemics.

But in return, I get something you cannot buy. A grassroots connection with Mother Africa unsurpassed anywhere else on the planet.

CHAPTER EIGHTEEN

Arabian Nights

Sometimes getting your face, telegenic or otherwise, on TV helps.

As I found out after being interviewed on Sky News in London by Emma Crosby when my cellphone buzzed. It was a text from my neighbour back home, Ahmed Kassam, who had seen the news clip 6000 miles away. He said he was 'proud of what I was doing'.

I call him a neighbour, which is not strictly true as he owns but does not live in a property next to me on the KwaZulu-Natal north coast. When not travelling, Ahmed lives in Johannesburg, but I was soon to find out that he's extremely well-connected and an advisor to heads of government throughout Africa and the Middle East. He told me he had a 'big conservation thing' happening on the Arabian Peninsula and asked me to send him my résumé.

Intrigued, I emailed it off, and a week or so afterwards Ahmed phoned. 'I have some guys who want to talk to you. It's about rewilding a game reserve in Saudi Arabia.'

Saudi Arabia? I knew there was a growing market for African wildlife in Middle Eastern zoos and theme parks. But rewilding specifically means reverting to natural, not exotic, origins. It was my speciality, but so far solely in Africa. I told Ahmed I was certainly interested.

Ahmed is extremely charismatic and has more politicians and decision makers on speed-dial than anyone else I know. Among various other business interests, he is a strategic negotiator for the South African-based Paramount Group, a leading global corporation involved in defence and aerospace innovation. To say he merely knows people in high places is understating the case.

In this instance the client was the Royal Commission for AlUla, a Saudi government-sponsored conservation organisation, and the project was a mass rewilding of the 1500-square-mile AlUla Sharaan Nature Reserve. I was told that it was a favourite retreat of Saudi Crown Prince Mohammed bin Salman Al Saud.

But there were unique problems. The main one, of course, was that this was in February 2020, and the world was locking down like a maximum-security prison as the COVID-19 pandemic exploded. Consequently, everything from introductions, résumé exchanges to project ideas and proposals had to be done via internet conference calls. For me, it was surreal as every eco-venture in my previous life had involved hands-on field trips where I sniffed the clear wilderness air, touched the trees and shrubs, and talked to people on the ground. I had to get an intimate feel for something before I was comfortable with taking it further. Obviously that was now impossible. We had no choice but to negotiate via soulless computer screens with potential partners many thousands of miles away. The irony did not escape me; here we were using the most sophisticated electronic communications on the planet to brainstorm on how to revert ancient desert to primordial landscape.

I soon discovered the AlUla area has huge historical significance for Saudi Arabia. The town itself is directly on the legendary spice route, which linked Mediterranean traders with the Far East, and for centuries was also a key stopover for pilgrims on their way to the holy city of Medina.

The reserve is dramatically crisscrossed with red-rock canyons, steep-sided ravines, and wide valleys levelling out into open desert with scattered rocky outcrops that once teemed with wildlife. Sadly, that is no longer the case as wandering Bedouins, nomadic herdsmen and subsistence hunters have encroached to such an extent that a once-thriving desert is in the final spasms of death. Wildlife, notably the Arabian leopard and white oryx, has been shot out, while voracious domestic livestock herds and centuries of camel-train travel has trampled and grazed the fragile arid vegetation to the nub. The Saudis now wanted to reverse that, regenerating the land to its ancient splendour, and they had the political will and a bottomless pit of money to do so.

We spoke at length via conference calls with a high-powered consulting team led by Mutasem Khashouq of FMC (Future Management Company) pulling everything together on behalf of the Saudis. I soon realised that Saudi Arabia faced many of the same debilitating environmental issues that we did in South Africa, such as poaching, habitat destruction and human invasion. The main difference was that the Saudis had oil money to spend. Tons of it. They could suck water up from the deepest artesian wells, they could re-green the entire desert – hell, they could tow icebergs from Antarctica if they wanted to – and they could buy any animal from any zoo or theme park, no matter how high the price. Also, as the Sharaan was already a proclaimed reserve, there would be no messy, highly emotive relocation of local people.

I gave examples of what we had done in Africa, from Amakhala where we had successfully rewilded destroyed cattle land, to our current developments at Ven-Africa and Loziba. These were living, breathing prototypes of modern rewilding.

I could see I was making progress. The Saudis liked the South African model and they liked the way we included communities and spin-off commercial projects for local employment in our vision. They liked the idea of 4 x 4s going off road for game viewing, common on most South African reserves. They also liked the way we managed the land, restoring and restocking with only indigenous animals and plants. As a result, they tentatively offered me a job as general manager of the AlUla project.

Despite the lucrative proposal, this meant that I would have to move to Saudi Arabia, something I couldn't do at the time as I had ongoing projects in Africa. However, I said that if I got the contract, I would find them the right person to manage it on site.

The figure bandied about for a six-month consultation was many millions of dollars. When told this, I gasped out loud. For me, out in the sticks of Africa, it was a telephone number. But for the Saudis, it was a mere book entry. Their keywords were 'deliverability', 'competency' and 'ideas' – something I think the Western world would do well to heed. Suddenly, after a lifetime of working on shoestring budgets, I was talking to people where money was no object, but ideas were. The overriding issue was that under the grand economic vision of the crown prince, the Saudis were no longer content to be solely oil producers. They wanted their country to be a major tourist destination by 2030, and AlUla featured prominently in that strategy.

The biggest challenge facing us was that the Sharaan Nature Reserve not only had little nature left, it had no wild animals.

Every blade of edible vegetation had been chewed to the roots, which meant that once the desert had been restored, almost every living creature needed to turn this into a viable wildlife reserve would have to be sourced elsewhere. In other words, few indigenous Arabian wild animals were actually in Arabia. But there were pockets scattered around the world in zoos and theme parks, and we would have to bring them home.

To me, this would be the most interesting aspect of the project. This was a true Noah's Ark project where animals caged in foreign cities would return to the deserts their ancestors had roamed since time immemorial.

I then contacted people at the Aspinall Foundation, who are world leaders in repatriating caged animals, and they provided a list we should be interested in. If we got the contract, the Aspinall Foundation would be our main partner in sourcing the animals.

I was shocked rigid when I saw how many species that had once ranged these arid lands now lived in cages or small enclaves behind fences, albeit in humane conditions. Apart from the better-known Arabian oryx and leopard there were sand gazelles, dromedary camels, tahirs, fennec and red foxes, caracals, hamadryas baboons – considered sacred by Ancient Egyptians – and the rare Arabian wolf. Sadly, now not even found in zoos were Arabian striped hyenas, golden jackals and Middle East mountain gazelles.

For me, the most distressing story of all is that of the Arabian leopard. The smallest of all leopard subspecies with males averaging 66 pounds and females just 44, this gorgeous desert creature is on the run like none other. There are fewer than two hundred individuals in the wild. Not only has its habitat been degraded to wasteland, but its natural prey of ibex and hyrax, or dassies as we call them in South Africa, are also being hunted to extinction, forcing leopards to kill livestock or starve. This has led to ferocious reaction from villagers and this graceful feline is poisoned or shot on sight in most areas. Thankfully, there are a few in captivity, and these would be our main gene pool for rewilding. Even so, it would require extensive rehabilitation programmes to teach these beautiful cats how to hunt again, but we are already doing that at Amakhala with semi-wild African leopards and cheetahs. In fact, our rehabilitation programme was watched on TV by several million people in 2021 when the UK's *MasterChef* presenter Gregg Wallace visited Amakhala and was shown our work by my brother William.

The Arabian or white oryx is also fundamental to the AlUla project. Declared extinct in the wild in the early 1970s, this regal antelope was only saved from total annihilation through a captive breeding programme. It took more than ten years for their numbers to be considered viable enough to attempt a reintroduction to the wild, and what followed was a truly heart-warming success story. So much so that in 2011 the Arabian oryx was the first animal in history to have its status officially reverted from 'extinct in the wild' to 'vulnerable'. There are now an estimated 1,220 individuals in the deserts and about 7,000 in captivity worldwide.

The Arabian oryx is closely related to the South African gemsbok, a slightly larger animal with the same wickedly sharp horns that have been known to kill lions. Sadly, these majestic horns have resulted in oryxs becoming one of the most highly prized hunting trophies and they have been shot out in much of Africa.

Another extremely vulnerable species on our list was the Nubian ibex, a big-horned desert-dwelling mountain goat.

The wild population is estimated at 1,200 individuals but declining alarmingly through hunting and habitat destruction. Like the leopard and oryx, we would have to source these once prolific creatures from zoos and theme parks.

Despite everything being done electronically, we were making good progress. In fact, we were all but assured of getting the contract. It even got to the point when the Saudis offered to plough funds into one of our wildlife education bursaries, bringing vital conservation money into South Africa. However, the project by now was too big for me to handle alone from our side, so I brought in my partners Francois du Toit and James Arnott from Communal Wild Conservancies (CWC Africa) as well as consulting with Dr John O'Brien, a renowned conservationist who has worked in the Middle East before. In turn, the Saudis brought in two Jordanian ecologists, Dr Maen Al Smadi and Yehya Khaled, who had done a similar project at Petra, the archaeological World Heritage Site village near the Dead Sea in southern Jordan.

All we needed was a signed document. Without that, we could not subcontract the Aspinall Foundation to locate the rare species, nor could we start drawing up a plan of action and recruit other external experts.

Then, three months later, everything went quite. Almost overnight the flurry of invites to Zoom conference calls ceased. Communication died like a snuffed flame. James, Francois and I thought it was because the Saudis had decided to hire the Jordanians as they spoke Arabic, but Dr Al Smadi assured me that was not the case. He said he had not heard from the Saudis either.

Word slowly filtered through that there might have been some political interference from the Saudi government, but more likely it was the general chaos caused by global COVID-19 lockdowns. Saudi Arabia was one of the most affected countries as they had to radically restrict the annual Hajj, which attracts up to three million pilgrims to the holy city of Mecca every year. The religious, cultural and economic upheavals of that were tectonic, and it appeared that the AlUla project was simply put on the backburner. No one seemed to know.

But for me, the lessons learnt from those intense few months were profound. It showed me more than anything else that we Africans have a priceless gift to give to the world. Our knowledge and experience of rewilding the planet were unsurpassed. Our ideas and methods were cutting edge – we were pioneers without even knowing it.

Although on paper the Saudi experiment was a failure for us, it blazed a trail for other visionary projects. There is no doubt that CWC Africa and other organisations I work with will one day be at the forefront of future global rewilding networks.

However, as far as I was concerned, the one aspect that truly stood out was that the project involved large-scale repatriation of caged animals. All my previous projects involved wild animals, such as the Atherstone elephants or future plans to move the Tembe tuskers to other reserves to spread the gene pool.

The AlUla project opened my eyes to other options. Returning animals that had been caged around the world for generations to their ancient lands where they would run free and wild was simply magnificent beyond words. Yes, the AlUla project would have been a genuine Noah's Ark homecoming.

On a more sombre note, this also starkly shows that for many species there simply would be no gene pool left to repatriate without zoos and captivity breeding. Their work is essential.

I'm still hoping that the Saudis will rekindle the project and involve us. But in conservation nothing stands still and, while I was still pondering the 'what ifs' of AlUla, another man came on to the scene. He was not only closer to home, but also an African. And like the Saudis, he had money. Money to spend on wildlife projects. Or at least he said he did.

He also had the most unusual name. Henry Kissinger Siambone.

CHAPTER NINETEEN

Kissinger of Africa

L ike most of my generation, I'm an internet immigrant rather
than a native. I can navigate around cyberspace, but sometimes consider digital wizardry to be borderline voodoo, whereas
my daughters take it for granted.

So I suppose it should have come as no surprise when I
started randomly communicating on Facebook with someone
I thought was from a conservancy in the outbacks of Zambia,
only to discover I was actually e-speaking to a game ranger
enquiring about career opportunities.

Yet that chance meeting in the ether was potentially one of
the most fortuitous mistakes I have made.

It happened when my CWC Africa partner James Arnott,
who was consulting on a Zambian hydroelectric scheme, put me
in touch with a biodiversity project in the South Kafue region
of Zambia. This was something I was keen on doing with
Joe Pietersen's Nkombe Rhino charity, so I told James I
was interested.

I then got a Facebook message from someone called Fay
Munkombwe. I regularly get these random missives and seldom
take notice, but this time I replied as I thought Fay was part of

the Zambian project. He wasn't but, in a freak coincidence, it turned out he was a Kafue National Park game ranger and personally knew the tribal chief I was trying to get hold of. What were the chances of that?

However, in our electronic Zambian–English exchange, something got lost in translation and, instead of setting me up with the chief, Fay referred me to the owner of a lodge on the reserve. His name was Henry Kissinger Siambone. The name alone was enough to intrigue me, although I hoped there were no Watergate-style shenanigans involved. The only Henry Kissinger I'd previously heard of was disgraced American president Richard Nixon's national security advisor.

A few days later I got a text from Henry asking if I was interested in investing in a lodge in Zambia. I replied with an emphatic 'no', saying my sole interest was helping a tribal community in Kafue whose chief indicated he had land for biodiversity.

Then Henry phoned, and we hit it off right away. He's a gifted conversationalist and exceptionally easy to talk to. However, to disabuse him of any lingering notions he might have of me being an investor, I outlined the work I did, and what I planned to do in Zambia with Joe Pietersen. He suddenly interrupted me, 'You mean the rugby player?'

Wow – Joe must be really famous if they had heard of him in Zambia where rugby is about as popular as snowboarding. 'Do you know Joe?' I asked.

'Not personally. But I went to school in South Africa,' he said.

In fact, Henry had gone to Pretoria Boys High, the same school as SpaceX's billionaire engineer-entrepreneur Elon Musk. Topping that, his father had been a political prisoner jailed on Robben Island with Nelson Mandela.

There was certainly more to the African Henry Kissinger than met the eye, so I decided to hear him out. He said the reason for his call was that he was looking for a partner in a luxury fourteen-bedroom lodge in the Kafue National Park. The asking price was US$10 million. Could I help?

I'd had some expertise in this type of project while marketing Amakhala, so said I would be happy to advise on drawing up a prospectus. I also offered to set him up with the right people to find an investor, which he eagerly accepted.

'How many visitors does the lodge have a year?' I asked.

'None. It isn't open to the public.'

Instead, the Mumbuluma lodge was solely a wilderness playground for fabulously wealthy jetsetters. That certainly wasn't the market I was interested in, and Henry sensed my interest deflating.

'Hold on, I'll email over pictures,' he said.

A few minutes later I was looking at one of the most impressive lodges in wild Africa. It's the only private concession in the Kafue park and even has its own private frontage on a U-shaped bend of the Nanzhila River that flows into the Zambezi.

'Is there wildlife?' I asked. The sad reality is that in a significant number of Africa's remaining wildernesses, the most conspicuous missing ingredient is wild animals.

'Plenty. We have seven hundred elephants walking through the concession as I speak. There are lions basking on the river bank just in front of us. In fact, I have fourteen highly trained game rangers who have completely eradicated poaching in our specific area.'

Then he started telling me his incredible story. Apart from his father being a high-profile political prisoner, his grandfather originally came from Scotland, so he was a quarter Scottish and that side of the family owned property in Glasgow. He had worked at several jobs, including fashion modelling, and said he now ran a multimillion-dollar business called Abantu Holdings. It was registered in Andorra, a principality tucked high in the Pyrenees Mountains between France and Spain, where he lived for three months each year to maintain residency status. He also spent part of the year in Los Angeles, where his wife was a plastic surgeon. They had six children, including quadruplets, all of whom had all been educated at private schools in Switzerland or South Africa.

He's also extremely well-connected. He said his elder sister Matildah Siambone is employed by the United Nations and had sat near to American vice-president Kamala Harris at the inauguration of Joe Biden. She's also one of Henry's business partners. On top of all that, he said he planned to be the president of Zambia in ten years' time. He was deadly serious, but I'm not taking any bets on that just yet.

This all sounded extremely impressive and, on the face of it, it seemed I was dealing with a hugely influential person. But I couldn't help remembering the old proverb that if it seems too good to be true, it usually is. That's particularly pertinent in my line of work. I have dealt with what we call 'eco-scammers' before and so was wary. However, nothing Henry said or did indicated that he was not completely above board and, if he was a scammer, he certainly was the most charming one around.

He then said he wanted to meet me in person, suggesting Joe and I fly out to Zambia where he would show us his lodge and also introduce us to the Kafue tribal chief I had initially attempted to contact.

To get into Zambia required a COVID test, something that put Joe off immediately. He is as hard as iron on the rugby field, oblivious to pain, but any mention of sticking a swab up his nose has him running terrified for cover. He would sponsor my flight, but would not go himself.

I took the test – thankfully negative – packed my bags and was about to catch the plane when James Arnott phoned from Lusaka. He warned that I not only needed a COVID test to get into the country, but also to get out. The second test I would have to take in Zambia itself, and the red tape involved was horrific. Even worse, I would have to wait four days for the results. As I could only be away from home for a weekend, that made the trip impossible.

Henry was gutted, but the fact I had booked a ticket and paid for an expensive COVID test indicated I was serious. Consequently, he said he would instead fly to South Africa to meet me.

The idea was good, but the timing was terrible. I was already overloaded organising the uBhejane Xtreme mountain bike challenge, a major conservation fundraiser, as well as hosting potential backers from Kenya. Christmas was just around the corner, which I planned to spend with my family, and most importantly, my eldest daughter Jess was getting married at Amakhala in a few weeks' time.

'No problem,' said Henry. 'I won't take up your time. I just want to meet you, shake your hand and have a cup of coffee.'

I reluctantly agreed, stressing I was unable to host him. In fact, I had little reason to do so as there was no mention of him getting involved in my projects. Instead, I was helping him with his.

He flew first class, and when Joe and I met him at the airport, he looked as though he had stepped out of the pages of a glossy magazine. Tall, in his early forties, wearing designer chinos, silk polo shirt, top-of-the range dark glasses and clutching a leather briefcase, he gave new meaning to the word 'elegance'. Perhaps even more so when standing next to me and Joe in our creased bush khakis.

Once again, just as we had on the phone, Henry and I immediately hit it off. He has a wicked sense of humour and is great fun to be with. We chatted for about an hour, and as Joe and I got up to leave, I asked how long he was staying.

'Ten days. At the Hilton.'

'Ten days?' I thought he was just flying down for a quick meeting. 'You can't sit around for that long.'

'I'm fine. I'm worried about catching COVID so wouldn't be going out much anyway. The main reason for the trip was to meet you. Now that I've done that, I'm happy.'

I felt bad about him coming all this way to be cooped up in a hotel room, even if it was a presidential suite. It also seemed a bit rude to leave him alone in a strange city.

As it happened, I had been summoned to another conflict-resolution meeting the next day by the Stedham community whose land borders Loziba Wilderness. Coming with me were Zaynah Khanbhai from Kenya, her Argentinian husband Justo Casal, as well as my attorney, Peter Rutsch. I asked Henry if he wanted to tag along.

It was the start of a three-day road trip that I think none of us will forget. Zaynah and Justo own the conservation-tourism consultancy Merging Mundos, and Zaynah is also founder of South South Women, a global network of female role models. Henry, with his flair and international credentials, fitted in perfectly.

However, I had some nagging misgivings about taking such eminent people into a potentially volatile situation, particularly as our last meeting at Stedham almost erupted in violence. That time Richard Mabanga backed me up; this time I would have nobody as Richard was on a trip with Kingsley Holgate.

Just before we left, I received even more disconcerting news. The meeting would be in the form of a tribal court where I would be cross-examined by the community. I also learnt that the main complaint against me concerned the Mawana elephant herd.

I sighed. Not again. If the elephants weren't the perceived culprits, it was marauding lions, Kerneels van der Walt's hyenas or diseased wildebeest. I assumed the tribal court would follow the same procedure of forcing me to defend the Loziba project against increasingly exaggerated livestock loss claims geared to get maximum compensation. We knew with absolute conviction that most of the community supported the development, and that the inflated compensation demands were invariably made by the usual suspects – cattle rustlers. But even so, it was tiresome in the extreme.

What did seem strange, though, was that the elephants were the focus of supposed grievances on this occasion. The entire region was in the grip of a severe drought and the herd was many miles away at a section of the river still trickling. As far as I knew, the animals were disturbing nobody, so it would be difficult to manufacture 'incidents'. I would soon find out.

As I parked the car outside the community hall, I became increasingly nervous. Memories of the last meeting with angry men hurling belligerent accusations and machetes stacked in the corner of the hall came flooding back. What potential danger was I leading my eminent guests into? Was I right to risk their welfare?

I had no option as I didn't have time to drop them off at Mawana where we planned to spend the night. Consequently, I consoled myself knowing that Zaynah, Justo and Henry had specifically come all this way to watch me interacting with communities and, if nothing else, this was an excellent opportunity to do just that. I also had Peter with me in case I needed legal backup.

We arrived at the hall and I asked *Nkosi* (Chief) Mfanzele Buthelezi, who would be chairing the meeting, if we could speak privately beforehand. He had not been present at the previous unpleasant confrontation, so I told him I had international guests and wanted some assurance that we would be welcome.

'You are more than welcome,' he said.

I was not totally convinced as I was led to the podium, rather like an accused in a magistrate's court. I looked out at the sea of faces staring back at me. My guests, looking conspicuously foreign, were in the front row.

The only exit was at the back of the hall. It seemed a long way away.

CHAPTER TWENTY

Crocodiles Don't Cry

I was prepared for fireworks, which I either had to handle tact-
fully or give as good as I got.

But perhaps I was mistaken. As I stood facing the crowd,
Nkosi Buthelezi warmly introduced me and my guests, referring
to my Zulu praise name, *Nkunzi Ayihleli*, the bull who doesn't
back down. He certainly wasn't going to call me that if he knew
the community was hell-bent on making me do the contrary.
I briefly wondered if I was in the right place, let alone the
right meeting.

Then, even more surprising, he told me that the complaint
against the elephants was merely a minor encroachment that had
happened nearly a year ago, even before Beyers had been killed.
It had been formally logged and thus had to be acted upon, but
could only be aired now that COVID lockdowns had been
eased. As I had suspected, no one had seen an elephant in the
area for the past nine months thanks to the devastating drought,
so the complaint was redundant in any event.

The chief then said he would allow five questions to be
directed to me from the floor. The first question, now that the
elephant issue was settled, was about wildebeest *snotsiekte*

– which I pointed out had also been resolved when we removed the diseased animals seven months or so ago.

The next concerned crocodiles attacking livestock. I had never been called to give evidence on 'crocodile conflict' before, so this was a first for me.

According to the complainant, his goats were being slaughtered by crocodiles, which was bad enough. But what annoyed him even more was the reptiles weren't fighting fair. They lay on the riverbank as still as statues so the goats didn't notice them. Consequently, the animals thought it was safe to drink and were cruelly slain for their efforts. Not only that, the crocodiles were killing for fun, as they weren't eating the dead animals. Instead, they stored them in underwater lairs to rot, which, the complainant observed, was a waste of fresh meat.

This was hugely entertaining for the people in the packed hall, as the complainant obviously didn't know that crocodiles cannot chew on a carcass. They have to let it decompose. But how I was supposed to fix this problem, apart from offering to pay compensation for goats stupid enough to drink from a river full of crocodiles, I did not know.

One has to remember that such meetings can be the glue of the community. There are few TVs and no cinemas or shopping malls in rural villages, so tribal gatherings are meant to be entertaining as well as platforms to discuss neighbourhood issues. Those attending expect to be amused by maestro raconteurs and, believe me, Zulus know how to spin a good yarn. I usually love listening to the stories.

But not this time. Even the *Nkosi* had heard enough.

'*Hlala phansi* – sit down!' he instructed the crocodile man. '*Nkunzi Ayihleli* is here to help us. He is not responsible for your goats and some crocodiles that have nothing to do with Loziba.'

He then turned and faced the crowd. '*Nkunzi Ayihleli* is not the enemy. He is here to provide solutions. Stop harassing him.'

I saw most of the crowd nodding in agreement and decided this was too good an opportunity to miss. Before entering the hall, I had expected to be reeling on the back foot, fending off hostile accusations, and now suddenly I was the good guy. I had to grasp this unexpected windfall with both hands and asked the *Nkosi* if I could speak.

'My friends, look who I have brought to listen to you at this meeting today,' I said, pointing to my guests in the front row. 'You all know Peter the lawyer, and he has helped many of you in this community. He is an excellent lawyer with your interests at heart. The other people are from Zambia and Kenya and even across the sea from Argentina, where – as you know – they play good football. You are talking to people of the world here. They have come to hear your story. They have come to see what we are doing for this reserve, doing together, if everything goes right. They have come so see what we can do here with jobs and schools. Jobs for everyone who wants to work, and schools for our children.'

Again, I saw heads nodding in agreement as they scrutinised the four strangers in the front row. They were impressed.

Nkosi Buthelezi thanked us, and we left. I was still stunned as I walked out of the hall. The sudden change of mood was enough to give one whiplash. The success was not just thanks to a bright young chief who handled the meeting firmly and fairly, but rural people who believed no one listened suddenly found they had an international audience. The public relations boost from that alone was incalculable. I even dared to believe that we might have turned a critical corner with the Stedham community.

Next stop was Mawana where we would be staying the night in the Van der Walt farmhouse. Sitting around a fire for a *braai* – a barbecue – sparked much animated discussion about Loziba and the massive untapped potential of this continent. Henry in particular was enthralled, probably because he understood some Zulu and got the nuances of the meeting more than the others.

The next day we drove to the Makongo Hills Lodge at Ven-Africa, and all three foreigners were completely captivated by the beauty and folklore of the area. Henry then told me that he was part Tsonga, a Zulu sub-group in the far north of the country, so this area had a particular resonance. I looked at him in surprise as the Amatonga tribe live close to the Tembe Elephant Park, where we would be running the Tembe tusker relocation project.

'That's interesting,' I said. 'Because one day, at this exact spot, you will be looking at elephants from the same gene pool that your ancestors would recognise.'

His beaming grin said it all.

The reason for the Ven-Africa visit was, like Stedham, a conflict-resolution issue with a tribe that live in the Mkuze Valley. We wanted to incorporate some of their land into the Greater Mkuze Valley, alongside Ven-Africa and three other reserves, which eventually could link to the Ezemvelo-owned Ithala Game Reserve near Vryheid. Once again, it was a case of most of the community supporting the project, but we still needed to convince a group of diehards. This time, instead of a village hall, the meeting was held in a beautifully thatched *lapa* at the nearby Nkonjane Lodge, a traditional structure but with all the modern conveniences. We did this to show tribal leaders what sort of venture they potentially would be joining.

Kicking off the meeting, I told the headmen that the upliftment opportunities they wanted for their people and the land that we wanted for wildlife were mutually compatible. I had a fancy PowerPoint presentation available, but I never had to use it as our foreign guests spontaneously joined in. I had told Henry, Zaynah and Justo that they could speak if they wanted to, but otherwise they could just observe. It was up to them.

They decided to participate, and enthusiastically so. All were on top form. Zaynah said there were similar projects in her native Kenya, but the most successful ones all had a single common denominator: the communities took ownership themselves. They rolled up their sleeves and got involved. It was up to them to make it work, and they knew it.

This put a whole new slant on the project. Some leaders in the Mkuze Valley unfortunately tended to sit back and watch us do all the heavy lifting while they pocketed the royalty cheques. Zaynah said no, that was not the way to go. People like me would give them the ideas, tools and direction, but she said that ultimately their destiny was in their hands.

I watched closely to see the reaction to this, and it was extremely gratifying. The tribal leaders were blown away. I could see that they now realised how deadly serious we were when speaking about tangible upliftment for everyone.

Henry then spoke, agreeing with Zaynah. However, he said that as a Zambian, he was immensely impressed how far down the road communities in Zululand were in 'visionary projects'. They were trailblazers in their own right.

This was exactly what our audience wanted to hear. The meeting was a massive success – so much so that, a few weeks later, the deal was signed. Leased tribal land would be incorporated in the Greater Mkuze Valley, guaranteeing local jobs and investment.

At the end of the road trip, Henry took me aside. 'I can't believe how well you handled those meetings,' he said. 'You listened to everyone and treated them with respect. Even that guy who went on and on about crocodiles eating his goats.'

I hadn't thought about it that way, and hoped he was right. To me it was absolutely essential to use persuasion rather than coercion, especially in South Africa where trust is a precious commodity in short supply.

I thanked Henry for his kind words, and it was at that instant that our relationship did a complete flip. Up until now, as far as I was concerned, he was a guest from Zambia that I was helping. There was no talk of him being an investor in my projects. Now, suddenly, the roles reversed.

'How much will it cost to finish Loziba?' he asked.

'About 127 million,' I replied, wondering where this was going.

'Rand or dollars?'

'Rand.'

Henry smiled. 'That's nothing in dollars. I'll phone my sister to organise it.'

He could see the scepticism in my eyes, so explained further. He said he considered himself a humanitarian, but the trip to Loziba and Ven-Africa had radically changed his way of thinking. He now wanted to support the type of work that I was doing. However, if he did that in Zambia, any financial backing would be squandered by crooked or inefficient bureaucrats. In fact, he took it further, saying curbing rampant corruption was a key reason why he would be standing for president in a decade's time. But in the interim, he wanted to do good for people throughout Africa. Apart from that, his ties with South Africa were deep; from his Tsonga heritage to his father's legacy as a political prisoner against the unjust apartheid system.

He then asked about future projects. I told him I was sourcing investors to buy private game reserves along the Kei River in the Eastern Cape, primarily for black rhino range expansion. The wildly rugged Kei Valley, choked with thorn brush and inaccessible gullies and gorges, was ideal pachyderm country.

'I want to come with you.'

I hesitated. 'You mean you want to buy land in the Eastern Cape?'

He nodded. 'As long as it's for rewilding.'

I hesitated. This was going too fast. One minute I was helping a guy and his game lodge, the next he was talking about investing in projects I was working on. Henry was obviously well-connected, but how deep was his commitment, let alone his pockets? Would he really want to buy land in this country purely for rewilding? On the say-so of someone like me whom he barely knew?

So far his promises were purely verbal. We had nothing in writing. As such, I was putting my standing as an honest broker on the line more so than at any other time of my life. If it turned out that I had been conned by introducing an eco-scammer into the arcane world of buying and selling wildlife real estate, my reputation would not only be in tatters, I would be dead in the water. Stories of shady 'investors' manipulating the system to stay at five-star lodges with all expenses paid were – and still are – legion.

But . . . sometimes you have to go with your gut.

'OK, come along. But it's going to be a rollercoaster ride,' I warned.

For sheer feral beauty, the untamed lands rimming the Kei River are unrivalled. The bush is so thick in places that there is no way through even with a machete, while the crags and crevices are as wild as they were when this was South Africa's frontier two centuries ago. The history is equally fascinating as this area between the Kei and Great Fish rivers was where Boer and Xhosa first clashed, resulting in hit-and-run raids, vicious flare-ups and outright warfare lasting a hundred years. It was the longest running military action in African colonialism. Sadly, in a few isolated pockets, that war is still being fought and racism is real. I told Henry he would be the first black businessman some of the people we would be visiting had met.

Henry is no stranger to racial injustice, and still recalls how aggressively he was treated by some prison wardens when visiting his father on Robben Island. But he also remembers the opposite, the gruff Afrikaner guards who treated a frightened little boy with kindness, helping him on and off the island ferry.

This, understandably, introduced other issues. For example, estate agents bragging about how many Black people were employed on certain game ranches irritated Henry no end. Presumably the white person saying that meant it as Black empowerment, but Henry is far more interested in what someone genuinely thinks instead of trotting out spreadsheet audits. For example, on one of the farms we visited, the manager was an old-school Afrikaner who treated us courteously but we could see he was worried about his job. Henry assured him that he would only consider buying the property if he knew the manager would be staying on.

That was typical Henry. He has a gift for reading people, and his observations are uncannily spot-on. Oblique racial remarks, well-meaning or not, would torpedo any deal faster than an eye-blink.

A highlight of the trip was when I took him to Leeuwenbosch, our lodge at Amakhala, and put him in the same guest room that Prince Harry had used when he visited us during his African sojourn in 2015. Henry was delighted, and I'm certain we are the only lodge in Africa that has hosted both Prince Harry and 'Henry Kissinger'.

Two weeks later I dropped him off at the airport. As we shook hands, I wondered what would come of this strange encounter sparked off by a bizarre case of mistaken identity on social media.

I would know soon enough.

CHAPTER TWENTY-ONE

Burnout at Bongani

I sometimes think that the phrase 'Shakespearean tragedy' applies more to Africa than any other continent.

Like *Hamlet*, *Othello* or *King Lear*, an African tragedy is epic, apocalyptic and colossal – but yet something noble always seems to emerge like a diamond from the ashes. That, for what it's worth, has always been my experience.

But sometimes my optimism wavers. There are times when the flame of hope flickers as precariously as the proverbial candle in the wind. The saga of the Bongani Mountain Lodge was not just a wind – it was a hurricane.

The lodge is situated in the middle of an 8000-hectare, state-owned game reserve called Mthethomusha that borders the far south of the Kruger National Park. The area surrounding the park is the epicentre of a population explosion, ballooning like storm clouds in lands once prized as wilderness. The capital, Mbombela – formerly Nelspruit – is now one of the fastest growing metropolises in the country. It's also at the heart of the Maputo Corridor, a major trade route linking Pretoria to the Mozambican capital, which will eventually slice across the width of the southern part of the continent from the Atlantic to the Indian Ocean.

As a result, urban creep is spreading like lava from an erupting volcano, reminiscent of Brazil with crude shanty towns sprawling up rockfaces next to modern shopping malls, apartment blocks, sport stadiums and the ubiquitous speakeasy shebeens.

Nestling in granite cliffs 2500-feet above this seething mass is the Bongani Mountain Lodge, a true jewel of Africa. Not only is it situated on a Big Five reserve, it is crisscrossed with ancient paths once walked by the San hunter-gatherers. There are more than 250 rock art sites and the world's largest concentration of San paintings, which date back 1500 years.

From the lodge, the panoramic view on top of the Malelane Mountains stretches east across the Kruger National Park all the way to Mozambique, and north to the Blyde River Canyon. The Blyde is a 'green' canyon – unlike the arid Grand Canyon – and considered to be one of the world's most outstanding natural sights. Relaxing as the sun sets blood-red with a drink around a swimming pool hewn from granite rocks, it's hard to imagine the bustling mass of humanity below.

However, the outside world is encroaching rapidly, and the owners of the lodge know it. As Bongani caters for a substantial number of international tourists, it's the largest employer in the area and it is a responsibility the lodge takes extremely seriously. Consequently, much of the local heavy-lifting in ground-breaking community welfare work is spearheaded by Bongani's owners, and they are easily among the most committed charity and conservation-minded people I have met. For example, the lodge is heavily involved with an organisation called Shosholoza, started by Canadian Christine Menard that builds schools and soup kitchens, as well as the charity Imbumba, founded by the brilliant social entrepreneur Richard Mabaso. Imbumba, which is now better known as Caring4Girls, provides, among much else, free tampons. I cannot tell you how big a deal that is. Most teenage girls in the surrounding communities miss a staggering fifty school days a year because they do not have sanitary pads.

I first got involved with Bongani Mountain Lodge in 2016 through Trevor Barrett, a British photographer who was chronicling the work I do for Project Rhino. He introduced me to an amazingly energetic woman called Creina Schneier, one of the owners of the lodge, who liked what Richard Mabanga and I were doing with Rhino Art. As a result, she asked us to run roadshows in nearby schools. But she warned that the logistics of reaching out to the exponentially mushrooming communities were a 'challenge'.

I saw exactly what she meant when Richard and I first drove along the concrete logjam of buildings springing up on both sides of the Maputo Corridor motorway. I wondered aloud to Richard whether anything, or anyone, could control this abnormally rapid growth. That bleak remark was to some extent endorsed when we arrived at the front gate of the Mthethomusha Game Reserve to find it charred and smouldering from an arson attempt earlier that day. We had to drive for another hour and a half to get to an alternative entrance. It didn't take a genius to grasp that the much-vaunted Maputo Corridor was an interesting – if not volatile – crossroad of old and new South Africa, where hip-hop modernity increasingly clashed with ancient traditions.

Despite my negative first impressions, the project went exceptionally well. Over the next four years we visited all of the twenty schools in the Matsulu, Luphisi and Mphakema villages bordering the lodge, meeting thousands of schoolchildren and teachers. The shows included taking groups to Bongani Mountain Lodge, exposing them to the spectacular array of wildlife and San rock art, which was a huge success. The kids loved us, and I genuinely thought we were making excellent progress – so much so that we took a local group to the 2019 World Youth Wildlife Summit at the Kruger National Park. We also hosted the summit's Vietnamese delegation at Bongani for a night, which was one of the many highlights that year. The symbolism was crystal clear; Vietnam is the principal illegal end-user of poached rhino horn, and here we were, accommodating their children right next to the world's largest living concentration of rhino. They saw first-hand what this battle for the soul of the planet is all about. The importance of that for both the youth of Africa and Asia cannot be overstated.

Our man on the ground for the roadshows was a local artist called Fanikie Mlombo, who had contacts in all three surrounding villages. He arranged the meetings, set us up with head teachers and educators, and generally gave us good background information to work on. The fact that he was a well-known actor in a local radio soap opera certainly didn't do us any harm. Everywhere we went, the kids shouted 'Baba-Mnisi', which was his radio character's name. He also is an exceptional artist, and his 8-foot tall portrait of Nelson Mandela in the Bongani Mountain Lodge lounge had an appreciative international audience.

Another massive plus for our work was that we sometimes brought along Sibusiso Vilane, the first black African to climb Mount Everest as well as the Seven Summits, the highest peaks on every continent. He was born in Luphisi and his earliest contact with wildlife was at Bongani Lodge. Before becoming a world-famous mountaineer, he was a game ranger and we could not have picked anyone better for an ambassador as far as the local communities were concerned.

As we were making such strong headway with the youth, I decided to try and expand our work to include the tribal leaders. It was well-known that the headmen of Matsulu and Luphisi villages disliked each other intensely, so I tried to get them to a roundtable conference where they could talk face-to-face. It was tantamount to unravelling a centuries-old Appalachian feud, with both sides always finding an array of lame excuses not to attend. Also, the demands and pre-conditions just for a talk about talks were impossible to implement. A lot of NGOs and charities make the mistake of believing that rural communities are homogenous units, which is simply not the case. There are multiple conflicting political, social and economic undercurrents, and issues prioritised by one group may clash with others. Sadly, poaching gangs often form a vociferous group in these internal disputes, and while they may not be numerically strong, they are armed, ruthless and extremely dangerous. They can terrorise an entire community.

Anti-poaching education was a key issue in all Rhino Art projects, but perhaps it was even more pertinent with our Bongani area programme as the Mthethomusha Game Reserve is considered a 'pantry' for the gangs. This was further aggravated as not only did the reserve have rhinos, it also shared an eight-mile border with the Kruger National Park. However, we heard through the grapevine that the gangs operating in the Bongani lodge area stayed clear of Kruger as they were particularly frightened of a ranger called Don English. The pickings were far less hazardous on the Mthethomusha side of the fence where the Mpumalanga Parks and Tourism Agency (MPTA) rangers were not considered crackerjack, to put it politely.

The news did not surprise me. Don English is one of the most formidable anti-poaching warriors in Africa and deservedly won the prestigious 2020 Game Ranger of the Year Award. Tough, tenacious and totally fearless, he has taken the fight in the bush directly to the criminals themselves. In doing so, he has made a lot of enemies and has exposed corruption in high places. As a result, he has been smeared repeatedly and once suspended when accused of being a racist. Unsurprisingly, all accusations came from those being vigorously investigated by Don's predominantly Black anti-poaching team, and all were unsubstantiated.

On top of that, Don is tougher than a sjambok whip. An enraged buffalo once charged him and Don somehow managed to grab its horns, shielding himself, before being tossed into the sky like a rag doll. A buffalo bull weighs a ton and how Don survived defies logic, not to mention adding more spice to his already awesome legend – particularly among superstitious poachers.

Thanks to people such as Don, the two sides of the fence could not be more different. On the Kruger flank was a war being won; the other a Wild West corridor choked with lethal wire snares and illegal gunmen hunting almost at will. We asked SANParks (South African National Parks), which runs Kruger, to take down the fence and help the Mpumalanga rangers, but this was turned down. I suspect SANParks believed that removing the electrified barrier simply meant importing the MPTA's severe poaching problems, which was a valid concern. As a result, the Bongani Mountain Lodge was very vulnerable.

As we soon found out.

It happened on a Friday evening when lodge manager Johan Meintjies received a frantic radio call. It was from a patrol of MPTA rangers yelling into the speaker that they were under fire and needed urgent assistance. It seems they had shot a poacher in an earlier confrontation, and the gang was now attacking them.

Johan is a big guy and would have made a great rugby forward if he didn't love being out in the bush so much. He is hugely respected in the area, working extremely well with both people and animals. It was largely due to him that the lodge was well run and so popular with overseas tourists. He also was extremely committed to community projects, always making us feel more than welcome whenever we arrived for Rhino Art roadshows. His wife Surette is an equally committed wildlife enthusiast and, as they have no children, there are always orphaned wild animals in their home.

Johan fearlessly patrols the reserve on his motorbike, but does not have the resources to offer assistance in a firefight. Besides, he is employed by the lodge, not the reserve. However, he immediately alerted the police and MPTA, requesting urgent support.

Instead, to his astonishment, the MPTA refused any assistance. They categorically denied their staff was under attack or that a poacher had been killed. It was a surreal situation of men being shot at and calling for help only to be told by their bosses that they were imagining things.

Equally bad was the police response. Although constables arrived at Mthethomusha, they appeared to be reluctant to intervene and actually stop the firefight.

The battle in the bush raged throughout the night, with Johan getting increasingly panic-stricken calls that the security patrol was running out of ammunition. Unless help came soon, they would be overrun.

Once again, Johan begged the MPTA and police for help. Once again, his pleas fell on deaf ears. Eventually, at about 4 a.m., a guard radioed through, voice shaking with fear, saying they had no bullets left and were going to run for their lives while it was still dark.

Fortunately, all escaped.

But it wasn't over. On Sunday, twenty-four hours later, Johan's team at the lodge got calls from residents in nearby villages warning them that at least fifty heavily armed men were planning to storm the lodge. They were already marching up to the north gate.

Once again, Johan phoned the police. This time they set up a makeshift roadblock on the northern road leading up the mountain, which was circumvented by the armed mob with contemptuous ease. The gunmen then burnt down the reserve's locked gate and rushed towards the lodge.

It was now a race against time. Thankfully, there were no guests at Bongani due to the COVID-19 lockdown. So that was at least one problem Johan and Surette didn't have to worry about. They hastily gathered their staff and ran a convoy to the south gate on the far side of the reserve.

When the frenzied mob arrived, they found the lodge deserted. They torched the complex to the ground and ransacked the beautiful thatched guest huts, grabbing TV sets, computers, furniture, cutlery, bed linen – whatever they could lay hands on. Soon afterwards, untroubled by policemen standing placidly nearby, pickup trucks arrived to carry off the piles of stolen goods. Among the charred detritus was Fanikie's much-prized portrait of Mandela.

The rampage continued with large sections of the fence surrounding the reserve being torn down, virtually guaranteeing that fleeing animals would run straight into the snares and guns of poachers.

The lunacy of this is difficult to grasp. Mthethomusha had lions, buffalo and elephants in significant numbers. To let these dangerous animals loose around densely populated villages was beyond insanity. It would be a mere matter of time before elephants flattened a cyclist in their way or a lion killed someone stumbling home after an evening at the shebeen. Domestic cattle would wander on to the reserve's lush grazing, resulting in herd boys being attacked by buffalo. Once that happened, the MPTA would have little option but to shoot the animals.

Also in the crosshairs were rhino. Every horn poacher in the area would soon be making his way to Mthethomusha. It was a windfall beyond their wildest dreams – no anti-poaching patrols and no fences. For them, this was not merely a win. It was a complete and utter rout.

I heard about this tragedy through an email from Creina Schneier on the night it happened. I felt sick to my stomach. This was probably the worst community-conservation catastrophe in South Africa's recent history.

The immediate consequences were that the eighty or so Bongani Mountain Lodge employees had, in the blink of an eye, lost their jobs. It was unlikely they would get new jobs, as in a COVID-stricken economy with minimal tourists, work was in pitifully short supply. Not only that, the lodge's multiple contractors such as laundry operators, roof thatchers, stone workers, road builders, carpenters, even casual labourers clearing alien vegetation, had lost their prime meal ticket.

The long-term consequence was the crippling impact on outreach programmes. Some would take many years, if ever, to recover.

The tragedy was indeed Shakespearean – from the cataclysmic impact on people's livelihoods to the pending massacre of endangered animals and scandalous blundering of the authorities. Our work with local communities was severely hampered, if not doomed.

But was it?

A small light glimmered. For the people of the Bongani Mountain Lodge, one of the most pertinent questions arising from the bitter ashes was this: who came to their aid when they needed it most?

Not the timid police. Not the cowering provincial conservation authorities. Not the government.

It was instead the community. The silent majority, the people on the ground, who did not fail them.

There is no doubt that the true heroes are Johann, Surette and their staff who spirited everyone on the reserve to safety. But equally important is the courage of individual villagers. If they hadn't warned the lodge – at great personal risk as poachers invariably kill informers out of hand – I shudder to think how this sorry saga might have ended. When everything else collapsed, random groups of people living near the Bongani Mountain Lodge stood firm. They were indeed the line in the sand.

At times I feel like weeping with gratitude for the brave souls whom I meet wherever I go. In particular, I salute the people of Matsulu, Luphisi and Mphakema who did not waver; who did not cower before thugs and criminals; who had the guts to warn Johan and Surette what was about to happen and the danger they were in.

That courage, that loyalty, and that commitment to a better future are what makes many of us get up in the morning.

CHAPTER TWENTY-TWO

Another Fallen Comrade

The WhatsApp icon on my phone flashed. The name on the message was my lawyer, Peter Rutsch.

Except the message wasn't from Peter. It was from his daughter Janine.

'Sorry about this bad news. I'm on my dad's phone. He died peacefully in his bed last night.'

I grabbed the table in our lounge to steady myself. Even so, the room reeled. The shock was like a hard punch to the head, particularly as it came the day after I had translated a Xhosa eulogy to the staff of my late friend, also called Peter, at his farm in Darnall. Peter Goss had been a legend in the agricultural world and our families often shared Christmas holidays at his cottage, Black Sands, on the Wild Coast.

I forced myself to breathe slowly. I knew that Peter Rutsch had COVID-19, as he had told me four days previously. I also knew that he was diabetic. But even so, at seventy-nine years old, he was exceptionally fit, both mentally and physically. He still worked a full day, starting at around 5 a.m., and although a modest whisky drinker, he was a non-smoker and easily kept up with me during our hikes in the bush. Even though he was afflicted with COVID, his death took everyone close to him by total surprise.

I had spoken to him the week before, saying it was the start of the year and we had a lot of work to do. He sounded a little jaded as he had a sore chest and hacking cough that he assumed was from inhaling ammonia fumes while cleaning his barbecue grid.

The next day he visited his doctor, who immediately sent him for a COVID-19 test, purely as a precaution. The tests came back four days later; a time lapse in which he received no treatment. The results were positive.

Further tests revealed his partner Desire, or Des as we call her, and son Kiren were also positive. Janine flew up the next day from Cape Town, where she works as a chartered accountant, to care for the family. Miraculously, she never caught the virus.

There was nothing I could do, unable even to visit the bereaved family as they were all in isolation. Also, the mortuaries were overflowing due to the pandemic and Des had to wait two weeks before a cremation slot was available. The funeral for the immediate family was via Zoom, while a memorial service where Peter's ashes would be scattered in the bush would have to wait until the pandemic was over.

What a dreadfully sad ending to a remarkable man's life. In those awful times, hundreds of thousands of people took their last breath isolated in hospitals or nursing homes without any physical contact with their families. In Peter's case, the only consolation was that he died in his own bed surrounded by Des and two of his children. Des had been with Peter for the past thirty years and was the love of his life. She was an explosives expert, owning her own blasting company, which was a highly unusual and tough job for a woman at the time. As Peter was a cerebral legal eagle, it was a carbon-copy case of opposites attracting one another.

Des then sent me a transcript of an interview Peter had done in 2008 with the Legal Resources Centre (LRC). I read it enthralled as revelations of an extraordinary and courageous life unravelled before my eyes. I knew that Peter had been a frontline lawyer combating the apartheid regime last century and had fought the system tooth and nail. But I had little idea of what that actually entailed.

Peter had worked for many years for the LRC, mainly providing free legal assistance to victims of apartheid. The majority of clients came from the most marginalised elements of society, many unable to comprehend, let alone combat, the complexities of the system that callously ruined their lives. Peter had initially been particularly active in representing political detainees when the security police locked up activists in solitary confinement without bothering to inform their families. Peter would get calls in the middle of the night from distraught parents saying they had no idea where their son or daughter was. He and the LRC teams would tirelessly track them down, demanding those detained be charged or released, and giving them the best legal advice possible. All free of charge.

He also was prominent in representing people evicted from their homes under the Group Areas Act, where Black South Africans were forcibly removed from so-called white areas. He tells of one instance where a family that grew commercial flowers on a plot of land they had owned for generations received a piece of paper instructing them to immediately up sticks and move to an Indian area. Their 'compensation' was a sliver of township land the size of a pocket handkerchief, unfit for weeds let alone market flowers. In one swoop, a family were stripped of their home and livelihood. Peter, enraged beyond words, took the authorities to court, demanding that if the family be booted out by junk law, they at least receive reparations marginally commensurate with the incalculable loss of a home that had been theirs for the best part of a century.

As the apartheid judicial system was rigged against them, the LRC probably lost more cases than they won. But the fact that such iniquities were at least contested by lawyers such as Peter gave countless numbers of anguished people hope in bleak times.

Peter's approach was not to instruct people what they could or couldn't do. Instead, he outlined the various legal options available, then let his clients have the final say. Many communities did not want to take Western options, and Peter would advise them on what was creatively possible within the framework of dubious laws.

This type of legal work, grindingly hard, often tedious, hated by officialdom in particular and white South Africa in general, was incredibly gruelling and Peter paid a high price. His first marriage failed and he was shunned by many fair-weather friends and colleagues who considered him too 'liberal'. But Peter never wavered.

In the 1990s, when South Africa became fully democratic, he finally left the LRC to become involved in assisting rural communities evicted from tribal lands. After decades of fighting evictees under apartheid's colour-coded Group Areas Act, this was at least a fight on a more level playing field. He was particularly active in Maputaland, and suddenly his work was being recognised and his practice was in demand. He seamlessly switched from activism to conservation, being elected to the boards of both Ezemvelo KZN Wildlife and the Wildlands

Trust. Indeed, it is largely thanks to people like him that modern conservation in this country is so grassroots orientated. No community in South Africa today is kicked off their ancestral lands, although not all claims have been settled.

Looking back, now that apartheid has been irrevocably relegated to the rubbish bin of history, most white South Africans realise that Peter and his colleagues were the good guys. But as I say, I knew little of this until after his death. To us he was just Peter, a humorous, fun-loving, hugely likeable man and skilled lawyer who by the grace of God was on our side.

I first met him in 2017 when I phoned for advice after butting up against official obstacles to the Loziba Wilderness project. To my surprise, he knew all about Kerneels van der Walt and Mawana's somewhat chequered past. In fact, he is significantly responsible for the fact that Mawana still exists today as wilderness. In the 1990s a large bank wanted to buy the land and transform it into low-cost rural housing, and Peter was at the forefront of the legal team opposing it. The thought of such magnificent bush being converted into drab sub-economic housing is too ghastly to contemplate, and thankfully Peter and his colleagues had the application overturned. As a result, he not only personally knew what a conflicted situation we were facing but also most of the tribal chiefs, making our task in establishing dialogue and trust immeasurably easier. When working with communities, I never referred to him as 'my' lawyer. Instead he was 'our' lawyer.

Seeing how useful he could be to us, I took him to meet Beyers. Despite different backgrounds – the tough Afrikaner and English-speaking liberal – they became close friends with Peter doing work for the Coetzee family as well as Elephants, Rhinos & People, who were also involved in the project.

The Loziba connection with Peter expanded into untangling other conflict situations such as the Jozini elephants, relocating Tembe tuskers and rewilding the Mkuze Valley. Not only was he a Herculean pillar in particularly grim times, his input was essential. We could not have done without him.

On top of that, he never sent us a single bill. This was a godsend beyond our wildest dreams as we were almost always severely strapped for cash. That's just the way it is in conservation, as most donations are for project implementation, not 'incidentals' such as salaries, stipends or services rendered. Eventually, I decided I could not ignore it any longer. I took him aside and said, 'You know, Peter, we must owe you at least a million rand.'

He laughed. 'I suppose if you add up all the timesheets, it would come to that. But it's not about money. Anyway, what would I do with all that cash?'

Whenever I brought it up again, he replied, 'This is important work.'

Indeed, Peter never complained about the amount of work we asked him to do, often at inhospitable hours, or even the fact that he was off-the-clock. The only time I saw him irritated was when some of our partners conjured up pipedream ideas and presented them as 'visionary'. Peter was very much into the here and now, and any plan had to be both rooted in common sense and financially viable. He ruthlessly cut through fantasy and concentrated on reality.

Eventually he agreed to cap his fees at R250,000 (about US$18,000) and, if we felt like it, we could give him a plot of land at Loziba Wilderness when the project was completed. That's a commitment I will keep, come hell or high water, although sadly Peter will not be able to enjoy it. However, future generations of Rutschs will, and that will be part of his fine legacy.

I didn't know it at the time, but when he came on that memorable road trip with Henry, Zaynah and Justo in December 2020 to northern Zululand, it would be our last. I treasure it more and more with each passing moment.

A month after his death I was on the cusp of negotiating possibly the most lucrative conservation deal of my life. It also involved the animal that has loomed larger in my life than any other. Rhino.

Without Peter at my side, I did not know if I could pull it off.

CHAPTER TWENTY-THREE

Riding the Rhino Range

Whenever I visit wild areas, I subconsciously run a cursory checklist in my head evaluating how good the land would be for my favourite animal – rhinos.

This is even when I'm working on projects for other species, such as elephants. Or in other countries, such as Angola and the DRC. After food and water, what I look for most is space – and a vast expanse of it. Because of all creatures on this planet, the black rhino is not only one of the most endangered, it's also the most claustrophobic. It needs more individual room to roam than any other. In its search for solitude, it will often refuse to breed if it feels confined. Simple as that.

Consequently, it was no surprise when I discovered that the most successful black rhino breeding programme in Africa today is predominantly about wide-open spaces. Instead of penning males and females together to ensure maximum physical contact, it does the exact opposite – moving the animals to larger and less inhabited reserves. In short, the less contact the better.

The seemingly crazy logic behind this is that, as extremely reclusive black rhinos only interact during the breeding season, they are far more inclined to mate if they are not bunched together during the off season. A true case of absence making the heart grow fonder. So in order to get them to procreate faster, the solution is to keep them apart for most of the time.

It has worked beautifully. With excess black rhino moved off the more congested reserves wherever possible, the happy result has been a remarkable upswing in newborn calves. Equally gratifying to me is that the two most thriving regions where this is happening are KwaZulu-Natal, where I live, and my native province, the Eastern Cape.

This does not mean that rhino numbers are anywhere near healthy – in fact, the polar opposite. Even so, the success of these space-orientated breeding programmes has resulted in the urgent need for more remote bushveld to keep the breeding momentum going. A huge amount more.

So it was inevitable that with my rewilding work I would cross paths with the man who pioneered the concept of more room equals more baby rhinos. His name is Jacques Flamand, founder of the Black Rhino Range Expansion Project.

BRREP is supported financially by the World Wildlife Fund (WWF) but owned by Ezemvelo KZN Wildlife, and what Jacques does is exactly what it says on the tin: he moves black rhino on to new ranges. But although the theory of increasing range resulting in more rhinos is simplicity itself, the actual implementation can be a nightmare. For obvious reasons, moving rhinos has to be stringently controlled, with security tighter than a gold vault. There are only 5455 black rhinos left in the world, so vigilance is absolutely vital. Also, BRREP will not look at land that does not have a carrying capacity of at least 1000 hectares per animal. That works out at almost 4 square miles of habitat for each individual rhino, and BRREP will only move a viable breeding population of at least twenty rhinos, with more males than females. This is because the animals do not pair and thus more males ensure that all fertile females will fall pregnant.

Such relocations are further complicated as the new land has to be relatively free of other rhinos. BRREP has learnt from hard experience that placing black rhinos in already established populations can be disastrous. Settled alpha males will challenge all newcomers, and as rhino fights are often to the death, this was a serious problem.

Finally, there has to be community involvement. If a reserve does not support clinics, bursaries, schools and beneficiary ownership of the rhino offspring, BRREP is not interested.

So four inviolate factors have to be met: security, size, community and suitable habitat. Without those criteria, a relocation project is dead in the water, which makes finding a perfect range-expansion area exacting, if not extremely difficult. We may have land that is ideal habitat, but there is not enough community involvement. Or vice versa. We may even find that all criteria are in place, but then the owner gets cold feet over the exorbitant costs of maintaining twenty-four-hour surveillance.

Despite this, BRREP is more than significantly responsible for the overall black rhino population increasing by a staggering 49 per cent, albeit from a critically low base. To give an idea of the extent of the project, since Jacques started it in 2003 there are now thirteen BRREP-created populations on a total of more than 300,000 hectares. Crucially, five are on tribal-owned lands in some form or another, thereby making local communities genuine stakeholders in rhino conservation. Indeed, in 2019 BRREP hit a milestone in relocating its two-hundredth rhino. That triumph is truly phenomenal.

As a result, BRREP today is a victim of its own success. Much of the project's land is now nearing full carrying capacity, and new habitat has to be found. Under BRREP's constitution, Jacques has to deliver a new project a year, and with 2020 having been a write-off thanks to COVID-19, he now needed to urgently deliver.

I first met Jacques about ten years ago at Project Rhino meetings, but basically just to say 'hello' as he thought I was primarily involved with Rhino Art. However, when he realised I was also deeply committed to rewilding land, we struck up a professional relationship before becoming good friends.

He already knew about Loziba Wilderness and the Greater Mkuze Valley as both projects were earmarked for rhino expansion. In fact, when I first took Jacques to Loziba he remarked that it was among the most perfect rhino habitats he had seen in KwaZulu-Natal.

He now wanted more of the same. And that was the thrust of his first question when we met up again – did I have anything in mind?

I hesitated for a moment. As luck would have it, I had been approached by an investor in the Eastern Cape but the intricacies of the proposed deal were so complicated that I was sworn to secrecy. The short version was that the investor was pledging more money for wilderness expansion than I had ever before imagined. Although the potential deal did not specifically mention any species, I knew that if it went through the investor would want rhinos. Hopefully as many as he could get.

On top of that, I was expecting an answer from Henry Kissinger Siambone within a month. Henry had promised me money for both the KwaZulu-Natal and Eastern Cape projects, but I was also playing that close to my chest. The biggest mistake in conservation is to count unhatched chickens.

'Funny you should ask,' I said, replying to Jacques's question. 'I've got some interesting stuff going on in the Eastern Cape. Possibly also access to investors.'

His eyes lit up. He had already relocated rhinos from the Great Fish River area during a previous BRREP operation and, in his opinion, the Eastern Cape could soon become the beating heart of black rhino breeding. This was looking more and more likely as poaching continued to soar in many areas of the Kruger National Park, while the Eastern Cape not only had near-zero rhino killings, it was on the cusp of relocating more black rhinos than anywhere else.

But there were other reasons why Jacques was keen to see what I was doing in the southern tip of the continent. Much of the remaining bush in that part of the world is impassable thicket, ideal for black rhinos who browse the sweet thorn brush, and local anti-poaching units were proving to be highly successful in protecting the animals. This was due to several factors, not least being that the province has no giant harbour like Durban with Far East trade routes, and no porous borders with Mozambique like Kruger. In short, the area has a lot going for it.

But most of all, it has genuinely wild land that is largely untouched, rugged and beautiful, if you know where to look. And I believed I did.

'OK, what areas are you talking about?' asked Jacques.

'Pack your bags and I'll show you.'

A week later we drove south, resulting in the most intensive rhino safari I've ever been on. It was to be our sole focus – to find new ranges for these glorious beasts.

Personally, I have more experience dealing with white rhino rather than black. In fact, one of my initial projects had been trying to save the last remaining northern white rhinos in the

DRC, a venture started by one of my heroes, the late Lawrence Anthony. Lawrence courageously visited the hideout of the Lord's Resistance Army, a vicious terrorist outfit led by the CIA's then most wanted man, Joseph Kony, to try and get the last of the northern white rhinos out of harm's way. Sadly, we both failed and the animal is now officially extinct in the wild.

The main difference between black and white rhinos is not their colour. In fact, both are greyish, although the black rhino is usually darker, sometimes even brown. The most marked disparity is that black rhinos have a hooked upper lip for browsing trees and shrubs, while white rhinos, which are savannah grazers, have a wide square mouth. One theory, albeit discredited in some circles, is that 'white' is actually a bastardisation of the Afrikaans word '*wyd*' which means 'wide'. The white is also larger and heavier, but – relatively speaking – more placid. Indeed, if a black rhino sees you, it will charge without hesitation and the only escape is up the nearest tree. Unfortunately, many trees in rhino territory have sharp thorns that will shred your hands. But believe me, that's the least of your problems when two tons and a horn comes at you.

This was something rhino-expert Jacques knew all too well, having clambered up his fair share of spikey acacias with a slashing horn just yards behind. He is a true hero of conservation, largely unsung as much of his crucial work has not been in the limelight. As a child growing up during the 1950s in South Africa, he loved venturing into the wilds, stirred by true-life adventure books such as Percy FitzPatrick's *Jock of the Bushveld*. This inspired him to pursue a life of action, either as an explorer or game ranger, and his father gave the most useful piece of advice imaginable for a restless and headstrong youngster: 'Get a profession that lets you do what you like.'

Jacques hit on becoming a wildlife vet, which meant he could explore the world, live in the bush, and get paid for it. He obtained his veterinary degree at Cambridge University and returned to South Africa to complete a postgraduate degree in wildlife management. In 1975 he was appointed the sole field vet at Kruger National Park, but left a few years later to join the Natal Parks Board (now Ezemvelo KZN Wildlife), which was at the forefront of rhino management. It was there that his love for these persecuted creatures became a passion.

He then worked for six years in Saudi Arabia with the rare Arabian oryx, followed by a four-year posting at the Chitwan National Park in Nepal. While in Asia, Jacques witnessed the virtual extinction in the wild of the Sumatran rhinoceros. It was, he says, one of the saddest moments of his life. He vowed that the African rhino would not share the same fate.

Interestingly, despite having immobilised several thousand black and white rhinos in a career spanning half a century, Jacques's most serious injury in the bush came from an elephant, which broke his arm. It happened while releasing a herd into the Hluhluwe-iMfolozi Park and Jacques was snipping off identification tags around the animals' ankles.

'One then put his back foot down on my arm,' he said. 'I couldn't move it. I realised then that with their protruding eyes elephants can see what's going on at their feet – that's why they walk so quietly. He was looking at me; he knew exactly what he was doing. Eventually he stopped and I could withdraw my now broken arm.'

He also has been bitten in the foot by a wild dog, but fortuitously its razor-sharp fangs sunk in the gap between his toes, while his most unusual patient was a highly venomous Gaboon viper, whose spine had been damaged when struck with a spade.

The first area I took Jacques to was the Great Fish River, where BRREP already has a seed foundation herd, but I also wanted to show him other range expansion areas. From there, we went to the remote Mpofu Nature Reserve, an 11,000-hectare reserve which is in the old Ciskei homeland; and then to the Kei Valley, where I knew of several large properties for sale. It was the same area I had visited with Henry Kissinger Siambone, and if he came up with the money as promised, we would be able to buy the land and start BRREP relocations right away.

Much of the Kei Valley is little more than thick virgin jungle, too wild for sheep and cattle, but a black rhino heaven with ideal shelter among the thorn-strangled dongas. Jacques, a bush veteran for most of his life, was blown away by the sheer beauty and diversity of the land. He didn't know such unspoilt wildernesses still existed in pockets surrounded by population explosion.

In fact, the bushveld in both the Kei Valley and the Kat Valley – where we were going to next – is unique to the region. Protected plants such as the giant cycad and red and white milkwood trees grow gloriously wild while, in a tributary of the Blaauwkrantz River, small schools of a tilapia-related fish found nowhere else in the world still swim. Jacques remarked that by reintroducing black rhino, these valleys could become among the most valuable conservation strongholds in Africa.

The final area we looked at in the Kowie Valley was Buffalo Kloof, the 20,000-hectare game reserve owned by my cousin Warne Rippon and his wife Wendy. Warne already has several rhinos thanks to a previous relocation scheme organised by BRREP and WWF in 2019, but he was happy to take more on the eastern section of his land. However, we needed to get permission to use an area of commonage to round off the deal with BRREP.

And that is where things suddenly went wrong.

CHAPTER TWENTY-FOUR

Forgiveness or Permission

Warne has stepped up to the plate for me on several occasions.

He had taken in a herd of elephants from Atherstone, which he initially didn't really want. Now, having fallen head over heels in love with the matriarch, one of the biggest females in South Africa, he couldn't imagine Buffalo Kloof without her.

This time he was offering to help out again with a crucial BRREP relocation. But with Warne, you are never sure how things are going to pan out as he does not believe in doing things strictly by the book. However, I always take comfort in the fact that he is extremely successful at almost everything he turns his hand to, even if his methods are unorthodox.

Warne's key characteristic is that he is not scared of taking risks. In fact, he thrives on it. A self-made millionaire and genial hellraiser, when Warne is around you know things are going to get interesting. In the 1980s he was part of the Transvaal (now Highveld Lions) cricket team dubbed 'The Mean Machine', which to this day is considered by many to be the best-ever domestic side in the world. Warne was a big-hitting top-order batsman who did not know the meaning of the word 'defend', often to the exasperation of his captain, the legendary Clive Rice. In one notable match he was facing Stephen Jack, a lightning-fast bowler, who was peppering him with 90-mile-an-hour bouncers. As Warne stands fractionally under 6-foot-7 in his socks, to get the ball ricocheting higher than his head was no mean feat.

Warne had glared at Jack. 'If you bounce another, I'll smack you out of the ground.' We were not sure if he was talking about hitting the ball or Stephen.

The next ball bounced skull-high. Warne steadied himself and swung like a baseball player. The ball skyrocketed out of the stadium and into the road. Then, in a thousand-to-one chance, landed in the back of a garbage truck.

'Now bugger off and fetch your ball,' he bellowed to Jack as the truck headed off in the direction of Soweto. To this day, that story is repeated with loud guffaws.

He loves living on the edge and owns racehorses, undeniably one of the riskier ways of making money. In 2008, his favourite horse, Sun Classique, which he co-owned with renowned trainer Lionel Cohen, won the richest race in the world, the Dubai Sheema Classic. In true Warne tradition, his horse defied all bookmakers' odds by winning in a nail-biting finish after being jammed tight against the rails. After that epic race, Sun Classique was tipped to win the even more prestigious Prix de l'Arc de Triomphe in Paris and the Kentucky Derby, but tragically broke her ankle and was put out to breed.

So, Warne is not your average Joe. His philosophy is that it's far better to ask for forgiveness than permission – something he's very good at. He once built a 'small' dam on his property without council planning permission that ended up so large it could be seen by satellite. He was forgiven.

Consequently, when he heard that BRREP needed to move surplus black rhinos, he put up his hand to say that Buffalo Kloof would take some. He also started putting up a game-proof fence for the animals' new home, despite the fact that he had no permission to use the commonage it would cross. His reasoning was that the land was far too wild for agriculture, and as the community would be paid considerably more than what the lease was worth, it was too good a deal to waste time worrying about irksome red tape. He would ask for forgiveness once the fence was in place.

Unfortunately for Warne, the community didn't see it that way. The result was a major outcry with both the council and tribal leaders angrily saying they had not been consulted. Not only that, they claimed the boundaries between Warne's land and the commonage had not been clearly defined, so summoned Warne to a meeting to explain himself.

Warne asked me to accompany him as, although his Xhosa is workable, it's not fluent. He needed me to be his interpreter as even the slightest mistaken nuance could kill the project stone dead. That I knew. But I had no inkling that I would be walking into a maelstrom that would make some of the hairier community gatherings I had attended look like a left-arm throw.

The meeting was in Bathurst, one of the original 1820 settlements where English immigrants were shipped out to form a human frontier against Xhosa tribes coming from the north-west. The town is rich in folklore and we parked outside the historic community hall, a stone's throw from the Pig and Whistle, South Africa's oldest pub dating back to 1832. I joked that we might have to beat a hasty retreat there to down a few stiffeners if the meeting got too hectic, little knowing that I was not speaking entirely in jest.

COVID-19 restrictions were still in force, so face masks were mandatory, muffling voices as well as possibly preventing pathogens, and the chairman ensured we all sat 6 feet apart. The downside was that initially no one could hear what was going on, but this was soon rectified as tensions rapidly ratcheted up and eventually became so heated that the meeting could be heard in the next town, let alone the next seat.

As expected, Warne was the focus of the ruckus, with whoever took the floor demanding to know who had given him permission to start putting up the rhino fence.

Warne tried to reason with them, with me interpreting. 'This is a win for the community,' he said. 'I'm going to give you water for your cattle, fix your roads and fences and you will be paid ten times what the land is worth. All I want is 200 hectares to join the land where rhinos will be. I am giving you far more than I'm taking.'

He argued that the land he wanted to lease was only suitable for leopards, rock-climbing baboons and, most importantly for us, rhino. There was little the community could do with it, whereas the rental money they would get could buy more feed for their cattle, grow more crops and do more important infrastructural work.

It was to no avail. Speaker after speaker angrily pointed out that the community had fought the previous apartheid government for that same land that Warne wanted, which was partially true, and that it belonged solely to them, which was definitely not true. It was commonage, not tribal land.

Then, to my amazement, one man got up and started ranting about people in helicopters shooting at him and other villagers. I was about to shake my head in disbelief when Warne leaned over and grabbed my arm.

'Don't say anything,' he mumbled into his face mask. 'I was flying that chopper for the Anti-Stock Theft Unit. That guy is probably a cattle thief.'

He quickly whispered that several weeks ago the police had asked if they could use his helicopter to chase cattle rustlers, who were operating almost at will in some areas. It appeared no one in the hall linked the helicopter to Warne but, even so, it was best if we sat out that part of the discussion.

This was without doubt the most hostile community meeting I had attended. Even worse than the bitter clash at the Stedham Community Hall where I had been accused of introducing *snotsiekte* from Loziba and allowing elephants to trample fences. Whenever Warne and I tried to explain that the deal was good for the everyone as well as conservation, the catcalls got shriller.

'I don't think this is going our way,' I whispered to Warne, and he shrugged with a half-smile. That was the understatement of the year but I could see by the glint in his eye that he was not giving up. That rhino fence would be built, no matter who we had to persuade. However, at that moment, I couldn't have cared less – the more pressing matter was whether we would get out of this meeting in one piece.

Then suddenly the entire mood altered. I could sense a shift of gravity in the room, and we were no longer the focus of the acrimony. Instead, the community started turning on itself, accusing one another of giving Warne 'illegal' permission while each competing faction claimed ownership of the commonage. The increasingly strident denunciations were now becoming politicised, with councillors and chiefs harping on about what seemed to be longstanding feuds.

Relieved not to be in the direct firing line any longer, Warne and I sat back to watch. The meeting eventually ended without us having to beat an ignominious retreat to the Pig and Whistle, but it had been a close call.

However, as I feared, nothing was resolved. Warne was not given permission to put up the fence, and the council and tribal leaders were still at loggerheads over land claims and various other internal issues. Although somewhat shaken by the antagonism shown towards us, I was not disheartened. Africa moves at its own pace, and anyone expecting to hit a home run in a single meeting and get exactly what they want is seriously deluded. We would be back, hammering home our belief that the community was getting a fair deal until there was a resolution, one way or another.

Even so, there was no denying that this was our first major setback in the 2021 BRREP plans, and I was more concerned than I cared to admit. Not only had the Buffalo Kloof relocation been put on hold indefinitely, but Henry Kissinger was no longer returning my calls. I knew there had been cataclysmic weather in Zambia with floods and storms, so perhaps he was stranded at his lodge in the South Kafue reserve. But most worrying was that it was now almost two months since I had last seen him, and I still had nothing in writing. Everything was based on handshakes, which was far from ideal.

Then I got the message I half dreaded, half expected.

CHAPTER TWENTY-FIVE

Karoo Capers

The bad news came via an email from Matildah Siambone, Henry Kissinger's sister.

She was apologetic, but said events were not turning out as expected. Apparently she was due US$5-million in COVID-19 assistance from the United States federal relief bill, which had been delayed. This meant she could not invest that money to get further loans and pay us the 20 million euros promised by 'Kissinger', as she called her brother.

While Henry was adamant the money would still be forthcoming, it unfortunately would not be in the timeframe that I envisaged. That was a major problem in the current situation as we had to move fast.

The reason for the urgency was that the week I received the Siambone bad-news email, the government announced that almost all COVID-19 lockdowns were about to be lifted. While this was great news, particularly for the wildlife tourist industry, it meant conservationists had to be on full alert. There were worrying indications that the pre-COVID rhino poaching crisis was about to spike again with a vengeance.

We all suspected that the dramatic decline of horn poaching

during lockdown was merely the quiet before the storm. With lockdown being lifted, airports and harbours would soon be open for travel again. Borders with Mozambique and Zimbabwe would swarm with hungry people who hadn't earned money or had a full stomach for more than a year and were now desperate for work. International horn syndicates previously unable to enter the country now had even larger orders and backlogs to fill, and we were getting increasing reports of 'persons of interest' with known cartel links being seen at reserves that have rhinos.

We had made some progress at the start of the pandemic with the shooting of poaching kingpin Baas Leon Stoltz, and the dehorning of multiple animals in the North West. Before that, we had rescued eighty animals at risk with Chris Holcroft. We needed to keep that momentum going with lockdown restrictions easing, and if Henry couldn't deliver in time, I had to find alternative options.

In any event, another door seemed to be creaking open. It came from an old friend, Declan Hofmeyr, a veteran wildlife ranger, whom I had met several years previously at the Madikwe Game Reserve on the Botswana border.

Declan had been Madikwe's operations manager, and as it is one of the largest Big Five game reserves in the country with significant numbers of rhino, it was an action-packed job. He was also in charge of a thirty-nine-man security team that relentlessly chased poachers. As a result, Declan has been involved in every aspect of rhino protection from intelligence gathering and forensic analyses to firefights in the bush. Few others have been as consistently involved in the struggle against horn cartels as he has and, as a result, rhinos are a particular passion of his. As I suffer from the same affliction, we had hit it off immediately.

Unfortunately, as sometimes happens in state game parks, politics interfered and Declan was moved to a less high-profile job as reserve manager of the Molopo Game Reserve in the Kalahari Desert. Much of his work involved personnel and programme management – a far cry from the poaching wars in which he had previously been so successful.

Declan missed the intensity and 'vibe' of Madikwe, so in 2020 he and his wife Carmen, also a qualified game ranger, moved to manage another Big Five reserve in the Karoo, the 16,700-hectare Magic Hills Private Collection.

Declan is a great guy, bull-shouldered with a bushy black beard, and he knew I was always on the lookout for rewilding projects. Once he had settled into his new job, he contacted me suggesting I look at the Karoo, which is one of the most desolate areas of South Africa. This is largely because it's semi-desert and relatively unpopulated, but Declan said the thorny thicket covering the arid scrubland was black rhino utopia. Conversely, the lack of savannah made it virtually uninhabitable for white rhino, even though he had some on Magic Hills.

Much of the low-rainfall Karoo is used either for hardy goat and sheep herding or antelope hunting, particularly trophy kudu. One of the true ironies of conservation is that strictly controlled hunting concessions finance more wild land than almost any other industry, and that is something more and more African conservationists are beginning to accept, if not embrace. Hunting is also deeply entrenched in the Karoo's psyche as the area spans the ancient tracking trails carved out by South Africa's first nation, the Khoikhoi, who pursued migrating herds of springbok, blue buck and the now extinct quagga. Legend has it that in those days Karoo 'thunder' was not the sound of a storm but a stampede of a million springbok migrating east. It would take an entire day for the herd to pass. The fact we know this is thanks to beautiful, eons-old rock art still surviving on cliff ridges and cave walls.

The Karoo has its own unique beauty with mountains shimmering like mirages on the cobalt-blue horizon, dramatic sunsets that bounce shades of gold off the steep rockfaces, stony valleys slashed with green strips of spate river foliage and aloes sprouting red blossoms like cathedral spires. The language is almost solely Afrikaans and there was no need for my Xhosa or Zulu linguistic skills. Fortunately, I am fluent in that language as well.

Declan told me that COVID-19 had crippled the professional hunting industry with no big-money overseas trophy seekers coming to the country, while farmers were reeling from the worst drought in living memory. As a result, at least thirty-five farms and hunting concessions in the Jansenville area – including Magic Hills – were up for sale or in need of diversification. The options were either to find investors to snap up bargains, or to get owners to agree to drop fences and allow free migration of wild animals.

I was interested. 'How much land are we looking at?'

'Difficult to say. Maybe bigger than Madikwe.'

I whistled. Madikwe, where Declan had previously been based, was 65,000-hectares. That was a huge chunk of wildlife real estate. It certainly was a grand vision.

I arrived in the Karoo a few days later and immediately started looking around. It was everything that Declan had promised, and the blow of Henry's possible withdrawal eased considerably. The black rhinos Declan showed me were fat with glistening hides as the thorn bush was ideal for the browsers to thrive. But only if we could protect them, and we were already doing that successfully in other areas of the Eastern Cape.

Of the thirty-five landowners approached, only two were against rewilding or black rhino relocation projects and both were wealthy enough not to be affected by the crippling economic climate. They would survive no matter what happened. No tempting offer would change that.

But then a seemingly insurmountable obstacle suddenly cropped up from the last place I expected. Just as everything was going exactly to plan, I mentioned to a landowner that one of the potential partners was the owner of Magic Hills, Erik Kovacs. In other words, Declan's boss.

The shocked look on his face said it all. He wanted nothing to do with Mr Kovacs and immediately withdrew his support. The news spread like a forest fire to other landowners and, one by one, they backed out. At the mere mention of Mr Kovacs's name, the project fell flat.

Indeed, it seemed there was no one in the area he had not offended. If the reaction of his neighbours was anything to go by, he was as disliked in the Karoo as much as the late Kerneels van der Walt had been in the communities surrounding Loziba.

I had never met Mr Kovacs, so could not give an opinion. But what astonished me most about the intensity of his unpopularity was that he didn't even live on the game reserve, only coming out for a few weeks each year. His home was in Bratislava, Slovakia, where he ran a highly successful pharmacy business. He had first come to South Africa in the 1990s on a hunting safari and fell in love with the Karoo, so much so that he bought a game reserve and hunting concession called iBamba, which he renamed Magic Hills Private Collection.

This resulted in the most lavish upgrade of a reserve ever undertaken in the area. The most notable feature was the construction of a gigantic luxury chalet on one of the highest peaks in the Oudeberg Mountains, which Mr Kovacs and his wife Alexandra, an international fashion model, called Sky Lodge. It's an engineering marvel as it towers into the heavens, but most locals think it would look more at home in the Swiss Alps with yodelling and après-ski as a backdrop rather than rugged African bushveld. Be that as it may, the views are panoramic and on a clear day it is possible to see all the way to the outer boundary of the famous Addo Elephant Park 20 miles away.

Some of the disputes between Mr Kovacs and his neighbours regarded business dealings, but the one that seemed to rankle the most related to the death of a twenty-nine-year-old game ranger and professional hunter, André de Villiers.

Magic Hills had recently acquired a new buffalo bull and André, an employee of the reserve, was eager to see how it was settling in with the rest of the herd. Nobody knows exactly what happened, but it appeared that André got out of his vehicle and walked down the bank to a riverbed to find the animals.

When he didn't return, his parents and wife went looking for him in the veld. André's father Jéanne eventually came across his son's lifeless body in the bush, trampled and gored. It's not certain whether the new bull had killed him, but further controversy erupted when it emerged that the animal may have been potentially rogue and had apparently been destined to be put down before being sold to Magic Hills. The rest of the herd was considered placid, although buffalo are always extremely dangerous.

But the most distressing aspect for the De Villiers family was that they say there were no condolences from Mr Kovacs or his management team at the time, which was long before the arrival of Declan. I heard that story repeated on numerous occasions when speaking to neighbouring landowners.

Jansenville, the nearest town to Magic Hills, is about two hours' drive from Amakhala, and I knew the area well as it was in the heart of goat-farming country. As a boy, I had reared Boer goats and regularly attended auctions and agricultural shows in the Karoo, so bumping into some of the landowners was more like renewing old acquaintances. This time around I wasn't competing with them for the best goat on show; I was on the other side of the fence, wanting their land for conservation. Not only that, many years ago my father had worked as an agricultural estate agent and sold some of the properties to the present owners. This gave me a foot in the door, but even that was to no avail when I mentioned Mr Kovacs.

Fortuitously, Mr Kovacs also wanted to sell his land and, if that happened, he would leave the area and our problems would be solved. But the asking price was too high, close on US$35 million. I would need an angel investor with bottomless pockets to put that deal together. Coupled with what appeared to be mutual antagonism between him and his neighbours, I was starting to think that Mr Kovacs was too big a problem for me to solve. It seemed unlikely the Karoo option would see the light of day.

Then everything took a tangential turn one morning when Declan, who knew I was looking for an angel investor, gave me a phone number.

'This guy could be interesting,' he said. 'He says he has money and wants to spend it on wildlife.'

Declan stressed he didn't personally know that man, whose name was Hans, so couldn't vouch for him. However, Hans had expressed interest in buying Magic Hills, so maybe it was a lead worth pursuing.

Hans's phone number had a prefix code that looked suspicious – one of those that charge exorbitant rates – so I hesitated in calling at first. Then I decided that nothing ventured meant nothing gained and dialled the number.

It was legitimate. Not only that, Hans said he had been waiting for my call as he had heard that I was 'the right guy to talk to' about his vision.

'What is your vision?' I asked.

He said he had made a lot of money diamond mining at Port Nolloth on the west coast. The town is one of the roughest-and-readiest places in the country where fortune seekers, adventurers and 'cowboys with boats' once flocked to mine alluvial diamonds along the 252-mile stretch of coastline leading to the Namibian border. Today, few diamonds are left for the freelance adventurers, but it still attracts some of the wilder fringes of society. It's dangerous, gruelling work, sucking precious stones from the ocean floor with high-pressure hoses on small boats in some of the most turbulent seas in Africa.

Hans said he had made a fortune during the diamond boom, not only as a rig operator, but also from buying gear and bridging finance for equipment before being bought out by a large offshore mining company. Since then, he had concluded a multimillion-rand deal, which he said had 'government connections', and was just waiting for the money to be released. Consequently, he was looking for other outlets, and as he loved the bush – or so he said – he wanted to invest in game reserves.

I had heard such stories before in various guises. In fact, so much so that I almost yawned. Some come from serial liars, some not. Some have money, others don't. I normally only talk to those who have at least some form of tangible asset. For example, Henry Kissinger was credible as he part-owned a luxury bush lodge in South Kafue, but I must admit that Hans was the first precious-stone miner I had met. He was worth listening to, but was this once more the too-good-to-be-true scenario? He could be either an eco-scammer – someone who steals money from well-meaning urban greenies – or an eco-dreamer – someone who gets a kick out of pretending to be a conservation-philanthropist. Or he was legitimate.

Hans then said he wanted to meet me face-to-face. I replied that I was currently in the Eastern Cape. No problem – so was he. In Port Elizabeth, he said.

That intrigued me. I know all the big money names in what is basically my native backyard, but had never heard of Hans. Was that an alarm ringing in my head?

At first glance, Hans looked exactly what he had said he was: a tough diamond miner. There were no airs or graces, no elegant mannerisms, designer clothes or dark glasses, which were the trademark of the immensely likeable Henry Kissinger. In fact, Hans and Henry were at the opposite ends of the sophistication spectrum; flamboyant elegance contrasting with apparent hardscrabble no-nonsense. I hoped Hans's bank balance reflected that as well.

We got straight to the point. He told me his cash was tied up for a month in a restraint of trade deal, but soon his considerable funds would be released. And they would be in American dollars, not increasingly depreciating South African rands. He was now at a stage where he could do what he liked with his money, and he liked conservation. He liked the bush – particularly in the Eastern Cape as he had been to school in a town about 30 miles inland of Port Elizabeth. But most of all, he liked Magic Hills in the Karoo. He wanted to buy that. Then we could talk about the other land for wildlife.

This put me in a bit of a quandary, as there was no doubt that even with the alpine-chic Sky Lodge, Magic Hills was hugely overpriced at close on US$35 million. With that amount of money, Hans could buy a reserve double the size. Also, buying at a grossly inflated price would upset other landowners as it would skew the market. As the reaction to Mr Kovacs had shown, we desperately needed the support of all our potential neighbours.

But, on the other hand, if Hans bought the Big Five reserve at whatever price, it would remove the most obvious obstacle in our way – Mr Kovacs himself. Once the Slovakian pharmacist was out of the equation, all the other landowners would possibly fall into line, potentially giving me access to about 70,000 hectares of prime Karoo bushveld. This was far bigger than what I had been trying to achieve in the Great Fish, Kei and Kat River valleys. The Karoo could overtake all other areas to become the core breeding hub for black rhinos. It was more than worth my while to encourage Hans to buy the place.

Despite that, I decided instead to be an honest broker and tell Hans the truth that the deal was not a good one. The price was too high.

'I don't care,' he replied. 'I want it for the view, not because it's a good or bad business deal.'

He then asked if I had any other projects on the go. I mentioned Loziba, and he immediately cut me short. He said he had heard of the Bongani Mountain Lodge being burnt to the ground and believed Loziba, which was also heavily reliant on community consent, could go the same way.

'I don't want any partners,' Hans said. 'That is non-negotiable.'

I soon gathered that by partners he meant community involvement. Dealing with various tribes and their different agendas, cattle rustlers, marauding lions and elephants – as we had in Loziba – was the last thing he wanted. Ironically, Hans was the third potential investor in a row to tell me exactly that. The harm done by torching Bongani was immeasurable.

However, not wanting partners could pose a problem, as many donors like to feel good about their investments, and helping even the most intractable communities is considered worthy and noble. Many NGOs have that cemented in their constitution, and it's a sentiment with which I usually agree.

But this was irrelevant in the Karoo for the simple reason there were no indigenous rural communities with whom to negotiate. There were no sacred tribal grounds, ancestral burial sites, historic grazing rights or land claims that would take decades to hammer out in courtrooms. Any deal would be a straightforward transaction between buyer and seller.

Another of Hans's stipulations was that I would be the frontman in any negotiations. He wanted nothing to do with any haggling. He said meeting landowners, persuading families to sell properties they had owned for generations and rushing around getting signatures were alien to him. It was, in his view, the equivalent of politicians kissing babies. He would sign cheques if I persuaded him something was a good deal, but I would have to do the legwork.

'I can fix anything with these,' he said, showing me his work-hardened hands the size of shovels. 'But I don't like talking, and then more talking. You must do that.'

I nodded. 'But I can't do anything without a written guarantee from you,' I said.

'Give me the name of your lawyer. I will give you sole mandate.'

We shook hands and, with that, I got the job. It had taken a single meeting, and I had been told I would soon have access to a multimillion-dollar budget. If it was all above board, that is. At this stage it was still verbal. I desperately needed Hans to be legitimate.

I would soon find out.

CHAPTER TWENTY-SIX

Eco-dreaming

I was busy putting together the deals to buy various properties in the Karoo on behalf of my supposed angel investor when Hans inexplicably went quiet.

We'd had six weeks of hectic phone calls and talks after our initial meeting in Port Elizabeth, when suddenly my calls weren't answered. Nor were emails, although Hans had warned that he wasn't good with 'electronic media' and other 'new-fangled' stuff. Instead, I had to resort to sending messages via WhatsApp, which were not answered.

I began to have serious misgivings. It's one thing to go 'quiet' – it's another to be a non-starter. And Hans was certainly starting to fall into the latter category.

I then had to ask myself some hard questions. Who actually was this guy? Was he in fact the 'rough diamond' multimillionaire he claimed to be? Was his rustic 'trust me I'm a son of the soil' mantra too folksy and rehearsed to be true? Was he expecting me to proceed on the basis of a single meeting and a handshake, without any proof of bank accounts or investments?

In other words, did he really want to buy up a chunk of the Karoo for wildlife conservation, or was he just someone who got a kick out of leading a fantasy double life? In his case, a Walter Mitty version of a fabulously wealthy, no-frills environmental do-gooder?

These were all valid concerns, especially as I had been burnt before by an alleged animal activist who contacted me several years ago saying he ran an elephant rescue fundraising organisation. He wanted me to join his board of advisors, and promised to raise funds to move the Atherstone elephants.

Then I discovered that the 'do-gooder', without my knowledge, was also inappropriately using the reputation of Amakhala to raise funds for something that seemed very dubious to me. Appalled, I demanded that my name immediately be removed from his website. Thankfully I have not heard from him since.

So was Hans merely a clone of this person in a different guise?

I had no idea, but certainly had growing reservations about which direction the Karoo deal was going. Even worse, I couldn't fall back on the wise counsel of my attorney Peter Rutsch, who had died the previous month from COVID-19. I needed that guidance more than anything else at that moment.

Eventually, I decided to visit my former attorney in Grahamstown, who has a 'bulldust' detector second to none. He had represented me when I ran a dairy farm in the Eastern Cape thirty years ago and stared bankruptcy in the face after a consortium of wealthy Johannesburg investors pulled the rug from under my feet. Ultimately, I lost the farm but, even so, my tenacious attorney made those 'suits' think twice about tangling with the locals in future. He is also an expert in conveyancing law and has handled more buying and selling of farms in the Eastern Cape and Karoo than anyone else I know. Sniffing out the creditworthiness of people like Hans is what he does in his sleep.

I told him my concerns, and he smiled. 'Grant, in the property game, there is no shortage of fantasists. I know all the stories. I have heard them all. This one appears to be a classic.' He told me he had eight acid-test guidelines that he used to weed out clients suffering from severe delusions of grandeur. 'And my gut instinct is hardly ever wrong.'

Firstly, they never sign a document. This is a major warning sign, and everything Hans had promised me was either verbal or based on a handshake.

Secondly, they say everything is good-to-go once foreign exchange delays have been sorted out. This is one of the most common ruses, but easily exposed as foreign exchange transfers take at most forty-eight hours to go through internet banking accounts. Again, this was more or less true with Hans. He had claimed to have concluded a 'top deal' that he couldn't divulge due to a 'restraint of trade' clause.

Next, suspect buyers always claim they are prepared to pay the asking price or go even higher. I nodded my head at that as Hans had repeatedly stated he would buy Magic Hills for way more than I thought it was worth. But whenever I said that, he replied he 'didn't care' as he had more than enough money. The reality in the property game is that hardcore investors fight for every cent and go for the best deal they can. Hans claimed to be such a businessman, yet was not interested in whether the deal was good or bad.

Dubious buyers also never disclose who their lawyer is. This, too, was true with Hans. He regularly told me to get my lawyer to draw up papers, but never once mentioned his.

They never haggle over details, either big or small. That makes sense, as they have no intention of signing the document in any event. Again, in Hans's case, whenever I mentioned any of the finer points, he would shake his head saying he didn't sweat the small stuff. Now I thought I knew why.

They hesitate to pay for any service. Hans also fell into this category by never once offering to pay for any expenses I incurred.

They have little or no internet profile. Search engines such as Google or any other analytics either come up blank or with minimal, insignificant information. For example, there was no reference anywhere on Google to Hans being a hugely successful west coast diamond miner. As he regularly referred to his digger days, some mention of that should have been on the web. If there was, neither I nor my attorney found it.

Finally, they talk big but have low delivery. In Hans's case, it was not 'low' – it was 'no' delivery.

As my lawyer's credentials were rooted as much in solid, down-to-earth wisdom as in hard experience, I tended to agree with his gut instincts. Unfortunately, Hans appeared to have fallen short on every one of the eight tests. That, at the very least, indicated that something was a little out of kilter with the story of the rough-and-ready businessman with bottomless pockets.

Not that this in itself was proof of any wrongdoing. On the contrary, my attorney was at pains to point out that it seemed unlikely Hans was a fraudster. He appeared instead to be living in la-la eco-land and getting a kick out of his supposed philanthropic credentials. So having dealt with the suspected eco-scammer it seemed I was now dealing with an eco-dreamer. The problem is that even though it's not a crime to invent big, unattainable schemes, it wastes a huge amount of other people's time.

Of course, we could both have been completely wrong and I would potentially be throwing away possibly the biggest conservation deal of my life.

But maybe not. As I was mulling all this over, an email from a friend who manages a big cat game reserve further north in the Karoo popped into my inbox. I knew he'd also had dealings with Hans, so wanted his opinion on which route I should take.

He said he first met Hans when a Bloemfontein-based property agent called on behalf of a client wanting to buy the reserve and arranged a meeting in Port Elizabeth. The client was Hans, and at the meeting he said he had just sold his diamond and coal mines to a Chinese investor, but the deal was not completed. The holdup was – you guessed it – foreign exchange regulations. Once that was ironed out, he would buy the reserve.

Hans also claimed to have put together more than 100,000-hectares of additional land in both the Free State and Northern Cape provinces, which would make this one of the largest big cat sanctuaries in the world. My friend took him at his word, but since then not only had no money been forthcoming for the project, Hans had not even visited the property.

This story was frighteningly similar to my own. Hans and I also first met in Port Elizabeth, but on that occasion he said he was 'fortuitously' visiting as he was usually in the bush. In fact, it appears that is seldom the case.

Then, just as he said that 'forex transfers' with Chinese investors were holding up the big cat project, in my case it had been a 'restraint of trade', possibly concerning top political figures.

Also, just as Hans had not visited the Karoo big cat reserve, he had not visited Magic Hills, even though he professed it to be his 'dream home'.

This was all a little too close for comfort, as far as I was concerned. It seemed at the very least that Hans was great on generating high expectations, but a little short on providing funds, or proof of any.

I think the reason people took him at his word was because he seemed to be the complete antithesis of a slickly eloquent confidence trickster. Craggy-faced, roughly dressed and a little unkempt, when he said he used to be a hardscrabble diamond miner, people believed him. When he said he rarely used 'new-fangled electronics' and preferred handshakes to lawyers, it fitted the character he was portraying. The fact that he was the polar opposite of a smooth talker gave him a veneer of hillbilly credibility far more authentic than a pinstriped suit. If my suspicions were correct, he was actually a very shrewd operator indeed.

But apart from the wild goose chase, no harm was done. In fact, I was lucky. I only spent six weeks running around trying to pin Hans down. My friend had spent two years.

The bottom line was that this was the second would-be angel investor in a row to disappoint. With Henry Kissinger Siambone, the problem was the time-sensitiveness of the project more than anything else, and we are still on good terms. I half expect one day to get a call out of the blue telling me to 'hold the line for the president-elect of Zambia'. With Hans, I have a feeling I was wrong all along.

But, as always, another project cropped up. This time there was no talk of diamond mines or luxury lodges. No claims of foreign-exchange holdups.

It was true grassroots conservation in its purest form.

CHAPTER TWENTY-SEVEN

Mozambique Miracle

Kingsley Holgate is not known as Africa's greatest living adventurer for nothing. Every time he finishes an expedition which everyone says will be his last, he sets off on another.

He is now seventy-five years old, but the thought of a pipe and slippers by the fireside doesn't remotely enter his grizzled head. And sure enough, the moment COVID-19 restrictions were fractionally eased in September 2020, he was off again into the wild.

All his missions have a humanitarian focus, and this was no exception – to alleviate hunger in remote areas. However, what was different was that the Mzansi Edge Expedition was his first to take place solely in South Africa, following the country's 6250-mile border as close to the edge as possible. In some cases, the wheels of the expedition vehicles would be turning exactly on the dividing line between Mozambique, Swaziland, Zimbabwe, Botswana, Namibia and Lesotho. Nothing Kingsley does is without adrenaline, and there would be no shortage of that in this trip – not least being the scores of crocodile-infested rivers his team would be wading through. The word *mzansi* means 'south' in Zulu, and as we are the southernmost country on the world's most misunderstood continent, Kingsley wanted this to be as much of a voyage of the mind as a physical journey.

Belonging to the working class, I couldn't take time off to do the entire expedition but was at the Kosi Bay starting point on the shoreline of the Indian Ocean. The next day I was driving along the Mozambique border when I spotted a wild elephant bull in the distance, a solitary figure in an eternity of savannah. Incredibly, it was a tusker, and a unique snapshot of wild beauty and unfettered freedom was caught in a single blink of an eyelid. It was absolutely breathtaking. With me was Jeffrey van Staden, CEO of the Babanango Game Reserve, and we agreed that if there was a wilderness dream ticket project, we would choose Mozambique. It has vast empty space and an incredible biodiversity of pristine habitats ranging from coastal plains and hardwood forests to sub-tropical jungles. It has mangrove swamps and grasslands that seemingly stretch to infinity. In fact, it has everything one could wish for on an eco-paradise bucket list, but somehow we never seemed to be able to do the right thing with it.

The idea itself of a conservation 'dream ticket' was nothing new, as trans-frontier parks incorporating reserves along the South African, Swaziland and Mozambican boundaries have been on the drawing boards for decades. We just needed someone with the political will and energy to run with it.

I spent several days with Kingsley's expedition, driving along the perimeter of the Tembe Futi Corridor linking the elephant reserves, and on my return decided to pursue my dream-ticket conversation with Jeffrey further. Instead of just talking about what a wildlife utopia Mozambique could be, why not do something about it?

The Tembe Futi Corridor is a 68,800-hectare historical elephant migration route from Mozambique to South Africa along the Futi River, but I had no idea who was actually in charge of it on the Mozambican side. Were they conservationists or bureaucrats? Or both?

First step was to find out and, while I was researching this, an international organisation called Biofund caught my eye. It's a private financial institution based in Maputo with the aim of bankrolling Mozambican biodiversity conservation, and it was active in the proposed trans-frontier parks.

I then discovered Biofund had money available for victims of the COVID-19 recession in the Maputaland district, and as we were doing similar work feeding wildlife communities on the South African side, I contacted its finance director Sean Nazerali to suggest we worked together. The bottom line was that if we had more funds we could deploy skilled project managers such as Richard Mabanga and Abe Nzuza to go in and feed Mozambicans in the corridor.

At first Sean, a Canadian who has lived in Mozambique for more than twenty years, was suspicious. In fact, it went further – he accused me of implying in my email that Biofund had already allocated us money, which was not my intention at all.

Well, that was the end of that. Or so I thought. Then a couple of weeks later, I met Nathan Sage, a USAID environment officer based in Mozambique, at former game ranger Paul Dutton's house in KwaZulu-Natal. Paul had been chief warden at Mozambique's Gorongosa and Bazaruto reserves during the dying days of colonialism, and was once imprisoned by the notorious secret police, PIDE. He was falsely accused by the Portuguese of being a spy, but as a result his 'post-colonial' credentials are impeccable. He still has many good contacts in the country.

I mentioned to Nathan that I had approached Biofund with an idea but had been turned down, and also invited him to visit Amakhala as he was travelling to the Eastern Cape. He took me up on that, and during a brief visit I showed him the rewilding, rhino protection and community work we were doing.

At the time, I didn't realise the far-reaching implications of that visit. Nathan liked what was happening at Amakhala and immediately phoned Peter Bechtel, an American-Mozambican conservationist who was also connected with Biofund, suggesting he and Sean 'revisit' the email I had previously sent.

Peter Bechtel was the missing Mozambican link I needed. He has spent his entire adult life working to improve rural communities and conserve nature in remote areas of Africa. A biologist originally from Philadelphia, he arrived in Africa in 1982 as a volunteer with the US Peace Corps and never left. He bought a farm in Swaziland, where he met his wife Ruth, then moved to Mozambique, eventually acquiring citizenship. His conservation achievements are phenomenal, and among much else he is a founder member of three major reserves: the Quirimbas National Park, a UNESCO biosphere; Lake Niassa Reserve on the Tanzanian border; and a marine sanctuary on the dazzling Primeiras e Segundas archipelago in the Mozambique Channel.

He is also a sought-after consultant to various prestigious clients including the World Bank Group, and advises the Mozambican government on anti-poaching and wildlife law enforcement.

Thanks to Nathan's intervention, a whole new world of Mozambican conservation opened up. Peter said he would get together a team to discuss 'mutually beneficial projects', and suggested I do the same on the South African side.

I knew exactly who I wanted on my team: stalwarts Chris Small and Joe Pietersen who are always ready to help out in any situation. Both were also deeply involved in the lifesaving Feeding the Wildlife Community programme during COVID, which we hoped to roll out in Mozambique as well.

Another reason for including Chris was that, apart from being a committed conservationist, he is a dynamic businessman and his international telecommunication company Savuka has an office in Tete, north-western Mozambique. This was incredibly beneficial, as it meant that we would have local audits and bank accounts already in place, eliminating a mountain of red tape specifically designed for foreigners. Chris immediately set the wheels in motion to register a 'conservation arm' of Savuka, which would give us an internal base from which to operate.

Joe was equally keen to go into Mozambique. As fate would have it, he was on the Mozambican border when I phoned as his charity Nkombe Rhino was busy dehorning rhinos in a private section of the greater Kruger National Park.

'It's going crazy here,' he said. 'Poaching is starting up again big time. Everyone is saying that if we could just close the Mozambique corridor we would only have one side of the border to fight.'

I knew exactly what he meant. Mozambique is the Achilles heel in the poaching wars as that's where most cross-border raids are launched, and unless we brought some semblance of control to the wildlife corridors along the Lubombo range, it would be an endless game of playing whack-a-mole.

I then contacted Peter Bechtel, introduced Chris and Joe, and said: 'Let's talk.'

Although I told Peter that Joe and Chris were my partners, I was using the phrase loosely as we have no formal agreement.

Instead, we are good friends who not only have the same interests but the same vision. Both men love adventure almost as much as they do wildlife, and having a loose alliance rather than a rigid structure ensures they do not drown in bureaucracy. That's their biggest nightmare – they want to be a highly effective reaction force protecting animals at risk, but at the same time they want to enjoy doing it. This was almost exactly what Chris Holcroft wanted to do with Wild911, which sadly had stalled with his death.

I have a foot in both worlds. Like Joe and Chris, my heart is in the bush, but I also have to deal with paperwork as that's what donors expect. Thankfully, my partners at Communal Wild Conservancies Africa do the bulk of the number-crunching, freeing me up to spend most of my time outdoors.

Chris and Joe were happy to be excluded from any pen-pushing, and that's why Mozambique was so appealing to them. It had everything going for it: an adventurous off-the-grid project in some of the most primordial wildernesses on the continent. This is not to say Mozambique is an unblemished paradise – on the contrary. It has suffered two brutal wars: the decade-long colonial liberation struggle against Portugal, followed by a fifteen-year civil war between the FRELIMO government and RENAMO guerrillas. The amount of blood spilt was colossal, not only from civilians slaughtered in the crossfire, but wildlife in most national parks was all but wiped out to feed marauding armies. When the smoke cleared, the only creatures left standing were those in the remote north of the country and some of the privately run *coutadas*, or hunting concessions, that were more vigorously defended against plunder.

Today, wildlife populations throughout the country have recovered spectacularly, particularly in the Gorongosa National

Park where American humanitarian Greg Carr and his team have worked miracles. Before the COVID-19 catastrophe struck, the world-renowned park was in the throes of attracting hundreds of thousands of international tourists, and that alone is enough to give the country a glimmer of hope.

In short, Mozambique is a land in search of revitalisation with unlimited potential, vast natural resources and enough wild space to become a global environmental beacon. That's why it is so important to make it work.

Peter then introduced us to his three partners: Simon Norfolk, founder of the Mozambican environmental consultancy firm Terra Firma with international clients such as UN-Habitat; Roberto Zolho, a graduate of Edinburgh and Queensland universities with more than thirty-five years' experience managing protected areas; and Tiago Félix Lidimba, also a university graduate specialising in wildlife and environmental administration.

I must say, my own academic CV looked somewhat sparse compared to our illustrious Mozambican counterparts, but I hoped my hands-on experience from a lifetime in land management and conservation would counter that. But what struck me most about our Mozambican friends was their notable list of government contacts, including Mr Mateus Mutemba, head of the National Administration of Conservation Areas (ANAC). They would do all the heavy lifting with the Mozambican authorities, ensuring we would be welcome anywhere in the country with top-level approval.

Our initial hook-up was done on a Zoom conference call. Peter kicked off the meeting, outlining six potential wildlife and community regeneration projects his team already had on the table that they would like us to consider.

251

First was the Lubombo trans-frontier area, which included the Masintonto Corridor, a joint venture with the South African-based sugar giant Tongaat Hulett, which owned the land. I could see Joe's eyes light up, as this would involve tackling poachers on the Kruger border.

Next was Coutada 4, north of Save River. This was a hunting and conservation concession, although we obviously were more interested in the latter. The licence for Coutada 4 would only cost about US$10,000 as no one else wanted it, mainly because it was in a historic conflict zone. In fact, the Save River had been a crucial dividing line; FRELIMO armies in the south and RENAMO in the north. Even so, it was an interesting tract of land as it bordered the 1500-square-mile Zinave National Park. Wildlife had been relentlessly butchered in the Zinave during the civil war, but like Gorongosa, the reserve was staging a remarkable comeback. I envisaged linking Coutada 4 to the greater Zinave area, which is unique in that it includes a dramatic transition section between wet and dry tropical zones.

A little further south was the Coutada 5 Extension, which was also linked to the world famous Bazaruto archipelago, home to the critically endangered dugongs. However, the Bazaruto marine reserve – extremely popular among South Africans as it has some of the best black marlin fishing in the world – is run by Africa Parks, so this would have to involve a partnership.

Next on the list were the Mahimba and Marromeu reserves in Sofala province. These span the banks of the Zambezi delta, where one of Africa's greatest rivers meets the Indian Ocean in myriad estuaries that spread for more than 70 miles.

Of particular interest to us were a vast 160,000 hectares of open land between the two reserves. As this was largely uninhabited, Peter said we could practically and legally set up a corridor of protected wilderness almost all the way inland to Gorongosa.

The Zambezi delta is also home to the largest herds of Cape buffalo in Africa, which survived the war as the animals were difficult for soldiers to shoot in the swamps and muddy floodplains. As a result, the area is beautiful beyond description, yet also frighteningly feral. When the Zambezi floods, the water can come down in tsunami-like torrents and it's not unheard of for whole groups of buffalo to be swept away, either out to sea or as crocodile fodder.

Next was Massingir Safaris. This was owned by three South Africans, and from what we could gather was an extremely well run 8000-hectare reserve, home to a variety of game species. The key attraction was a buffalo herd of 250 disease-free animals – extremely rare anywhere in Africa as Cape buffalo are prolific carriers of Corridor and foot-and-mouth diseases.

This particular project immediately caught my attention as the reserve is just east of the massive Great Limpopo Transfrontier Park, where Rhino Art had taken root. It happened during Kingsley Holgate's expedition to communities living around the largely unexplored Lubombo Mountain range in 2013, and one of their stopover points was Massingir. The town was the 'capital' of the poaching crisis as most of the criminals crossing into Kruger to kill rhinos lived there, and, while visiting the local school, Kingsley had a brainwave. He handed out paper and crayons to the kids in the packed classrooms and asked them to draw their perceptions of wildlife. The results were staggering. The common thread in all sketches was animals being slaughtered, helicopters chasing men with AK-47s and gangster-style gunmen wearing bizarre bling jewellery living in big Portuguese-era colonial houses. Kingsley decided from then on to target rural children living in wildlife areas as that directly tapped into the future of the continent. Rhino Art has now reached almost a million schoolchildren around Africa.

Finally, there was the 1374-square mile Magoe National Park on the south bank of the giant Cahora Bassa Dam. It is also extremely striking country, supporting a variety of wildlife that escaped the worst ravages of the civil war due to its remoteness.

We could focus on one project. Or we could take all six, depending on what we could bring to the table. And that was the fundamental question from Peter and his team: what would be our contribution?

I started off by saying that we would be interested in a service-level agreement, providing expertise in community outreach, environmental education, and marketing and tourism skills.

We would also run anti-poaching training, aerial surveillance, ranger support, relocation of game from South Africa as well as tagging and monitoring animals. This included assistance in creating wildlife corridors between the various reserves and *coutadas*, something we were already doing on a significant scale in South Africa.

On the community side, we would spearhead projects such as Feeding the Wildlife Community. Again, we had a proven track record having provided more than 1.2 million nutritious meals under exceptionally demanding conditions during the COVID pandemic. We would also mediate in community–wildlife conflict situations, something I personally had been involved in at all levels for the past decade.

The Mozambicans nodded. All were extremely experienced in both community and wildlife management, but the logistics of operating in such a vast, underdeveloped country were challenging beyond belief. However, a lot of what they were experiencing were situations we had already been through.

Nothing happens fast in Africa, and Mozambique is no exception. But we were given a tentative green light. Chris, Joe and I agreed that this could be one of the most exciting projects we had undertaken.

However, there was another problem. Something that none of us dared mention at the meeting.

It could be summed up in one acronym.

ISIS.

CHAPTER TWENTY-EIGHT

Terror in Paradise

When speaking of fundamentalist terrorism in Africa, most people think of Boko Haram abducting schoolgirls in Nigeria, or al-Shabaab's bombing campaigns in Kenya and Somalia.

Predominantly Christian Mozambique would be far off the list. Or so you would think.

But today, in the remote north-eastern corner of the country, ISIS and al-Qaeda-linked terror is surging with a vengeance. At first, it seemed to flare up from nowhere with a raid on Mozambican security forces in the Cabo Delgado province that took everyone by surprise. Even more surprising was that the perpetrators claiming culpability were an obscure ragtag group that referred to themselves as the 'Islamic State of Central Africa Province'.

Then it went quiet, with a few sporadic attacks here and there, but nothing dramatic. Suddenly, in 2019 it exploded again, and there is now an attack reported on average every week. Even worse, they are increasing in ferocity and today more than 1500 people have been killed and quarter-of-a-million displaced.

Mozambique is a big country with poor infrastructure, so an insurrection happening even a few hundred miles away is often not as critical as it may sound. To drive that distance in a vehicle can take up to fifteen hours on roads that are so potholed it's sometimes easier driving in the bush. But even so, Boko Haram, which started in the same seemingly insignificant manner, has now destabilised northern Nigeria, and ISIS virtually brought the Middle East to a standstill when it occupied much of Syria and Iraq. Although the uprisings are localised in Cabo Delgado on the Tanzanian border, it would still be prudent to compute risk factors into any strategies.

Most of the projects we were looking at were in the southern or central areas of the country, so the only two marginally in danger of being caught up in a terrorist brawl were Cahora Bassa and the Zambezi delta.

The main faction of Mozambique's ISIS-linked groups is called Ansar al-Sunna (Supporters of the Tradition), and they are as fanatical as they come. Even so, few people in the West would have initially heard of them if it were not for an attack on the Quirimbas Islands, where a handful of the more adventurous A-list celebrities holiday. Among them are James Bond actor Daniel Craig, Irish pop singer Bono and footballer Cristiano Ronaldo. Consequently, when Ansar al-Sunna struck, it was the trigger for a tabloid feeding frenzy that catapulted the jihadists on to the global terror map.

Quirimbas is an archipelago in the Indian Ocean off north-eastern Mozambique, close to Pemba, the provincial capital of Cabo Delgado. It consists of about thirty-two islands spreading up to the Tanzanian border and is as close to a tropical paradise as one can get. Palm trees fringe the startlingly white beaches, and the turquoise ocean is so clear you can see the bottom glistening 60 feet below. Coral reefs rim the lagoons, and shoals of multicoloured fish flicker in the sun like strobe lights. Nelson

Mandela loved visiting with his Mozambican wife Graça, the widow of FRELIMO leader and liberation hero Samora Machel. One regal visitor was Prince Albert of Monaco.

However, terror came to paradise in April 2020. Eyewitnesses said the jihadists arrived in small boats from the mainland, taking sixty people hostage, burning one alive and shooting another. Three other people drowned as they fled panic-stricken into the sea. The insurgents then torched the local primary school, a health centre, the residence of the head of the Quirimbas administration and homes of the local population. Hotels on the island were also set alight although, with COVID rampant, there were no international tourists.

The militants returned to the mainland and stormed the port town of Mocímboa da Praia, overwhelming the government forces, some of whom had to be evacuated by boat after running out of ammunition. The jihad flag was hoisted and Ansar al-Sunna proclaimed the town to be their capital administered under Sharia law. Fortunately, the town was later retaken by the security forces.

Thanks to the media, this was the most high-profile attack to date. Most of the other attacks have been hit-and-run raids, where insurgents behead a local headman and a couple of prominent villagers and steal food before melting into the bush. Civilians are overwhelmingly the main targets, and are sometimes used as human shields in firefights with the security forces. Another target is young boys, presumably abducted to be used as child soldiers, one of the worst scourges of the continent.

Ansar al-Sunna also hit headlines when jihadists killed a group of Russian mercenaries who had been working with the Mozambican security forces. The Russians were employed by the Wagner Group, which is either a private military company or an extension of the Russian military, take your pick. The Russian PMCs (private military contractors – the polite word for mercenaries) were first bloodied in Ukraine and then in Syria, supporting the army of President Bashar Assad, before getting involved in Mozambique. The company won the government contract in 2019 after undercutting other bidders, some of whom had far greater experience in fighting African wars.

With the arrival of 160 Russian mercenaries, the Mozambicans pushed Ansar al-Sunna deep into the bush. But not for long. The militants regrouped and ambushed the security forces, killing seven Russians and twenty Mozambican soldiers. This was a serious setback, and analysts said the Russians were too inexperienced in African conditions to be effective.

The question facing Chris, Joe and me was how seriously we should take the ISIS/Ansar al-Sunna threat. Or was it too far away from where we would be operating to be concerned?

Equally important was to find out who these guys were. Sure, they had burnt down James Bond's favoured hotel on the Quirimbas and killed some Russian guns-for-hire. But who actually were they?

The truth is no one is quite sure. Ansar al-Sunna is possibly the most shadowy of all ISIS-linked movements, and information on the size of the jihad army, or even who the real leaders are, is still sketchy.

What is known is that the guerrillas speak Portuguese or Kimwani, the local dialect, indicating that most are native Mozambicans. However, survivors of terror attacks say that Tanzanians and Somalis are also involved and speak Swahili, the East African lingua franca.

That makes sense as the original Ansar al-Sunna group was formed by radical Kenyan cleric Aboud Rogo, whom Interpol believe assisted in the 1998 bombings of the US embassies in Nairobi and Dar es Salaam. Rogo was assassinated in Mombasa in 2012, but just before his death he had been charged with possession of multiple weapons and police said he was leader of a terror cell plotting to bomb Kenyan targets. Samantha Lewthwaite, the British widow of Germaine Lindsay, one of the London Underground suicide bombers in 2005, was also said to be part of Rogo's cell. Dubbed the 'white widow' by the tabloids, she is still on the run.

After Rogo's death, some members of his Ansar al-Sunna movement fled to Kibiti, Tanzania, and then – it is believed – into Mozambique, where they started recruiting local youths. The isolated bush and woodlands of Cabo Delgado provided unlimited hideouts, and it is believed the recruits were trained by hardened al-Shabaab terrorists, mainly from Somalia.

Like Boko Haram, Ansar al-Sunna is against all Western concepts and wishes to prevent people from attending hospitals or schools, which it considers anti-Islamic. The punishment for disobedience is death, and several mosques have been targeted for not being 'Islamic enough'.

From what the police gather, the jihadists do not have widespread support but have succeeded in terrorising the local population, both Christian and Muslim. If the army was better equipped, the uprising would possibly be quelled fairly quickly. But as that is not going to happen overnight, it was something we had to insert in our forward planning.

Possibly just as alarming is that Ansar al-Sunna funds itself through criminal activity, and as a result is in cahoots with local gangsters. And we're not talking about holding up the local *spaza* store. This is big league with the main sources of terror cash coming from heroin, contraband and – most worryingly – blood ivory. If that is the case, the elephant herds that had escaped much of the civil strife in the remote north would be targeted with a vengeance. Conservationists would be increasingly drawn into the fray.

As I was involved with several other projects in South Africa, I would be less hands-on in Mozambique than I would have liked. For example, I would not be out with anti-poaching patrols or driving through landmine-infested bush. Instead, I would be organising animal relocations, community feeding schemes, building materials, fuel drops and finances from the South African side to hold up our end of the bargain. I would be part of a greater vision in another country and use my marketing and fundraising skills, rather than doing field work. But still, I had to know what was happening on the ground.

With that in mind, and with COVID travel restrictions finally dropped, Chris Small and I decided to spend a few days flying over the two northernmost projects we would hopefully soon be partnering in.

First was the Magoe National Park on the banks of Cahora Bassa. This is the fourth largest human-made lake in Africa, and for sheer magnitude and beauty, it is unsurpassed. It reminded me of what Lake Kariba must have been like in its glory days, the same wild bush, rocky valleys, and thousands of tranquil bays and claw-shaped inlets where the lake snuggles into nooks and crevices that were steep ravines before the gorge flooded. From above, we could see forests of partially submerged mopane trees that provide superb habitat for fish life. These trees are referred to as 'ironwood', as instead of rotting in the water, they solidify

261

to become as hard as iron, with the added advantage of not rusting. Their tops poking out of the water also provide nests for fish eagles, and there were scores of these majestic birds, whose ululating cry is the haunting echo of wild Africa, gliding across the watery expanse.

Flying low over the southern shore we spotted plenty of elephant and roan antelope in the lush grasslands as well as countless crocodiles and hippos basking on the banks. There are also leopards and lions, and together with high-adrenaline tiger fishing on the lake itself, this reserve is custom-made for the adventure tourist.

One aspect that also gave me hope of tourism expanding was that Cahora Bassa is isolated from Cabo Delgado by the southern edge of Malawi, which juts into Mozambique. Any insurgents wanting to infiltrate west would need to cross an international border.

Next we headed for Beira airport, refuelled, and then towards the Zambezi delta about half an hour's flight away. I knew this was dramatic country, but it was even more so from a bird's-eye view. The swamp grasses are so high that herds of buffalo are at times invisible in the jade green foliage fanning in the wind, while the delta's 70-mile-long estuary of lagoons and beaches rivals anything in the Caribbean. From the sky, the multiple creeks flowing into the Indian Ocean look like blue fingers stretching from the 'wrist' of the Zambezi.

I could feel my gut tighten with excitement. This was going to be one of the most ambitious projects yet. And we had six of them!

But Cahora Bassa and the Zambezi delta would have to wait. Chris, Joe and I decided our first project would be near the town of Massingir, the former poaching 'capital' bordering the Great

Limpopo Transfrontier Park that incorporates Kruger in South Africa and Gonarezhou in Zimbabwe.

This was the most pressing and, for us, the easiest to handle logistically.

CHAPTER TWENTY-NINE

The Bottom of the World

One of the most fascinating aspects of conservation is the number of unusual people one encounters. I suppose that's because it's a career path not many choose.

Take, for example, ex-Royal Marine Barry 'Baz' Gray, whom I don't think I would have met under normal circumstances. He is an English mountaineer, survival expert, extreme adventurer and polar explorer, specialising in the remotest, coldest regions of the world. While we both have a love of wild places, mine tend to slant more towards the warmer climes and I doubt our paths would typically have crossed.

The chance meeting happened due to another fortuitous encounter. I met Baz's boss, William Bowen-Davies, while giving a talk at a rhino fundraiser in Piccadilly, London. An old school friend, Pete Henderson, introduced us and mentioned that William had recently founded a conservation charity called the Reuleaux Foundation with the aim of supporting philanthropic eco-projects. William lives in England but was born in South Africa, so I instinctively understood his interest in wildlife. In fact, that night we held a charity auction to raise money for rhino conservation and

William bought my traditional Zulu *umbhulaselo* bead and patchwork jeans for £200.

I thought nothing more of it until a year or so later when Pete asked me to contact William, who was in South Africa doing background work for the Reuleaux Foundation. As the foundation had interests in African conservation, he said perhaps we could find some common ground.

However, at the time William was stranded as some of his team had tested positive for COVID-19. Even though they had completed their quarantines, they could not return to the United Kingdom, which was still in hard lockdown.

At that stage, the foundation had not expressed any interest in the projects I was doing with CWC Africa or with Chris and Joe in Mozambique. Even so, conservation is a broad church and I wanted to give as much help as I could. Consequently, I phoned William asking if he would like to do a walking safari in the iMfolozi wilderness with Nunu Jobe. William jumped at the opportunity, but said he had a large team with him, including his partner Heather, his two sons and his operations manager, Baz Gray.

Baz, who has spent time with Sir Ranulph Fiennes and survival expert Bear Grylls, had specifically come to South Africa for hands-on training in conservation and community work. I had never heard of him before, but decided a walk in the woods with Nunu would do more for his grasp of grassroots environmentalism and the primal atmosphere of Africa than anything else I could imagine.

Nunu was happy to take along a large party at short notice, and afterwards all agreed it had been a life-changing experience. With Nunu as a guide, trekkers not only see large animals up close, but are also introduced to lesser known wonders of the wild, such as trapdoor spiders that spin hinged nests to snare their prey. Baz, in particular, was enthralled.

That night we camped under the stars and Baz and I drank 'lockdown' rum around the fire until the small hours of the morning, discussing life, nature, adventure and stuff we thankfully now don't remember. William went to bed earlier, regretfully saying he had peaked before midnight, but he still woke with a throbbing head. He learnt a popular Xhosa metaphor that morning – 'Tsho Tsho' – which literally means that if you put your hand in the fire, you get burnt.

Baz wanted to see more of the country, so a few days later I took him on a Feeding the Wildlife Community road trip to deliver food parcels in the KwaZulu-Natal Midlands. It was a joint operation with the Do More Foundation, a children's charity, and the distribution point was on the Tugela River at the historic Spion Kop hill near the town of Ladysmith.

I told Baz that Spion Kop is one of the most famous Boer War battlefields, a no-holds-barred brawl fought at close quarters in January 1900 when the British Army attempted to relieve Ladysmith, which was under siege by the Boers. Baz had been a regimental sergeant major in the crack British Royal Marines before becoming an explorer, and the story of the battle fascinated him.

The name Spion Kop means 'Spy's Hill' as it provides excellent strategic high ground, and was held by the Boers who were outnumbered almost three-to-one by the British. There was much heroism on both sides with brutal hand-to-hand fighting involving bayonets and hunting knives, but the Boers retained the crucial vantage point, mainly thanks to the mindboggling incompetence of the British high command. A stand at Liverpool Football Club's famous Anfield ground was nicknamed the Spion Kop just a few years later, and the name Kop has stuck ever since.

One of the most fascinating aspects of the battle was that the Boers were led by General Louis Botha, later to become South Africa's first prime minister. On the British side, Winston Churchill was an officer and a unit of volunteer stretcher bearers was led by Mahatma Gandhi, who was decorated for bravery. So in a single battle lasting less than twenty-four hours, the fathers of modern India, modern South Africa and modern Britain converged on the same killing field. I think that was a key moment for Baz in realising what an interesting continent Africa is.

Returning home afterwards, I mentioned to him that one of my conservation colleagues was Sibusiso Vilane, the first black African to summit Mount Everest. Sibusiso had also been part of Sir Ranulph Fiennes's 2005 Everest expedition, so Baz was keen to speak to him. I phoned Sibusiso and told him to speak in English as a big fan of Sir Ran's, who had also been to the South Pole, was on the line. The two adventurers from vastly different backgrounds hit it off right away, showing that kindred spirits know no boundaries.

After the trip Baz kept in regular contact, asking me to take him wherever I could as he was learning more about community conservation than he would from any textbook. By his own admission, he couldn't tell the difference between an impala and a nyala, but his unpretentious eagerness to learn was inspirational. I have since taken him to our projects in Loziba, the Kei Valley and the Greater Mkuze Valley, and hopefully we will do something together there in the future.

Baz has been a soldier for most of his life, enlisting soon after his sixteenth birthday and was one of the Royal Marines' youngest-ever recruits. When he passed his selection test – one of the toughest and lengthiest in any army – he was too young to go to war, but not for long. He was deployed to hotspots around the world, including Northern Ireland, Kosovo, Iraq and Afghanistan.

However, it soon became apparent that his true calling, mentally and physically, was in extreme cold climate survival. So much so that in 2008 he was appointed chief instructor of the Mountain Leader Branch, an impressive post that is responsible for all mountain and cold weather training in the British Army.

It was thus no surprise that when Baz left the elite unit after twenty-six years' service he became a specialist adventurer. He was part of the team that re-enacted Sir Ernest Shackleton's epic rescue mission from Elephant Island to South Georgia in an open 22-foot boat. It's a feat regraded as the most incredible small-vessel voyage in maritime history as Shackleton and his crew had to sail 800 miles across the Roaring Forties, where 60-foot combers are not considered unusual. One wave was so high that in the darkness Shackleton thought the foaming crest was the early morning sky as it crashed down on them. A howling gale then drove them on to the west shore of South Georgia and to reach the island's whaling station they had to climb an ice-covered mountain range that had not yet been mapped.

Not only did Baz and his colleagues faithfully retrace Shackleton's steps, they did so in similar flimsy clothes, eating similar unpalatable survival food and using similar rudimentary equipment. No other re-enactment has been able to achieve that.

In 2019, Baz set the third fastest time for a solo, unsupported journey to the South Pole, completing the 745-mile trek dragging a 187-pound sled in thirty-nine days in some of the worst weather imaginable.

This was a training mission for his next expedition, so was not a world record attempt. However, he did set a record as being the South Pole's first 'postman'.

It happened like this. Baz was skiing on the thick polar icecap when a plane flew overhead and dropped a parcel. As he was on an unsupported mission, a maildrop would have been strictly illegal and thus it was obviously a case of mistaken identity. Baz knew there were supported expeditions in the area, and as some are millionaire vanity shows, supply planes are used for special deliveries. These are often for luxury items, and can be something as insignificant as a box of chocolate bars.

However, this presented Baz with a problem. If he left the parcel on the pristine icecap of the world's least-polluted continent, it could remain there frozen for eternity. But if he so much as laid a finger on it, his unsupported expedition would be disqualified.

What he did next gives me hope for conservation. Rather than leave litter behind, he radioed back to the expedition base – the exorbitant satphone rates eating into his tight budget – asking what to do. He was given special clearance to take the parcel to its rightful owners who were more-or-less on the same axis to the pole as he was.

Doing this was actually the last thing Baz needed. An extra 16 pounds on his sled could have cost him a world record time to the pole. But he didn't hesitate in doing the right thing.

Baz's next expedition is the most ambitious imaginable: a world record solo dash across the entire 1700-mile width of Antarctica in less than a hundred days. It was originally scheduled for December 2020 but had to be postponed until the COVID-19 pandemic had subsided. If he succeeds, it will be the first ever solo, unsupported and unassisted coast-to-coast crossing of Antarctica via the South Pole. Unlike other expeditions, he will not be using kites to wind-ski.

Equally daunting is that if he is delayed on the ice for any reason, he could starve to death. His food stock is calculated in calorie fractions to last a maximum of a hundred days – anything above that would be surplus weight which would slow him down. That's how fine the margin is, and even the smallest mistake could be life-threatening.

The solo unsupported crossing of Antarctica is said to be the final frontier for polar adventurers. It's the last 'big' expedition still remaining. But for Baz, the motivation to do it is more than just a notch in the belt.

'We would all still be sitting in caves if people did not want to explore and try to achieve new things,' he said. 'Apart from that, there is something very special about being somewhere extremely remote, where very few people have been before. No maps, guide books or previous notes is what makes the adventure so real, generates excitement and can be a constant thrill as well as extremely daunting.'

I sat riveted, listening to his exploits, often told around a campfire in the bush. They seemed surreal, doubly so as we were in the middle of a South African heatwave and fair-skinned Baz was literally slathered in sunscreen lotion. But even so, it suddenly struck me that if we treated the rest of the planet as we do Antarctica, where people such as Baz are prepared to go out of their way to make sure a single parcel does not blot the landscape, the world would be a better place. Perhaps that could be one of the messages from Baz's expedition?

I never said that to Baz. Instead, he said it himself, and came up with an idea so brilliant that I was momentarily stunned.

It happened during an unforgettable evening with Kingsley

Holgate, an equally intrepid explorer. As expected, the two adventurers instantly connected, swapping entrancing yarns about their escapades on roads less travelled by ordinary mortals. During the high-octane conversation, Baz noted that both Kingsley and I use a Zulu 'talking-stick', an *induku zophefumula*, when we sit around a campfire telling bush stories. Whenever it's someone's turn to speak, they are handed the bead-decorated stick. This stems from a deeply rooted Zulu tradition that whoever has the designated stick during an *indaba* (gathering) holds the floor. It's a great idea as it stops others from interrupting. I have taken my *induku zophefumula* to six of the seven continents and Baz suggested he takes it to the South Pole and will use it when he delivers a global conservation message. On his return, he'll return the stick to continue its 'energy of storytelling' – and it would also mean that my *induku zophefumula* has 'talked' on all seven continents. It was a brilliant, uniquely African idea, thought up by a madcap English explorer.

However, both Kingsley and I pointed out that this would be extra weight on a polar sled on which even toothpaste is considered a luxury. Would the stick not be a burden similar to the parcel he had to deliver during his dash to the South Pole?

No, said Baz, as all unsupported expeditions are allowed a single bag of promotional merchandise such as national flags and sponsorships banners. This is dropped for photographs at key points, including the Pole itself, and my *induku zophefumula* would be packed in that bag.

As a result, Baz would be the first polar explorer to deliver a message from the bottom of the world using a Zulu talking stick.

It would truly be a voice in the wilderness.

CHAPTER THIRTY

Chimanuka

I'm always slightly apprehensive whenever an email from John Kahekwa pops up in my mailbox. It's either a brilliant, heart-warming story about another victory against all odds. Or the complete opposite.

Unfortunately, this time it was the latter. Devastatingly so. I had to read it twice. The alpha silverback of the Kahuzi Biega National Park, a prime specimen called Chimanuka, was missing, presumed dead.

'Dear family,' John wrote, in his delightful blend of French-English-Swahili grammar, 'It goes softly straight into my heart. You know they haven't found Chimanuka since December last year [2020] yet. A gold illegal digging site was established by gunmen in the territory of Chimanuka's. Many gunmen against the few rangers in such area . . . although the search and patrols are continuing, on my side I am worried, expecting Chimanuka to have already been eaten for bush meat.'

John was inconsolable. The email was sent to his legion of followers around the world, and I knew the shock would be massive. What made the tragedy doubly heart-breaking was not just the probable blood-and-gore murder of Chimanuka, but what he stood for. Without doubt, he was the most iconic eastern lowland or Grauer's gorilla in the world.

When Hutu militia fled into the DRC after the Rwandan genocide in 1994, triggering the DRC's civil war, many of the mass murderers hid in the 2600-square-mile KBNP. To feed themselves they exterminated much of the wildlife and it was thought that all the park's gorillas had been slaughtered.

Then, one morning in 2002, a ranger saw a muscle-ripped silverback emerging from the mist. At first, he couldn't believe his eyes. It was like a phantom, a ghost coming down Mount Kahuzi to haunt humans for the industrial-scale slaughter of fellow primates.

It was no apparition. It was Chimanuka.

The excited ranger radioed the park's headquarters at Tshivanga. He was almost garbling over the mic: 'There is a gorilla. I have seen him. On the mountain.'

Wildlife staff immediately contacted John saying that at least one silverback had survived. John rushed out to confirm the sighting, the first since the end of Africa's most vicious war which saw 6 million people killed or displaced. He had started patrolling the park again as at one stage even he, the undisputed doyen of the KBNP, had to flee at gunpoint.

When John saw Chimanuka, he broke down in tears. He recalls it as being one of the happiest days of his life. The elation among rangers, many of whose colleagues had given their lives defending these persecuted creatures, was equally ecstatic. The celebrations were epic. Chimanuka, whose name means 'good fortune when you need it', became a shining symbol of hope for gorillas in general and the KBNP in particular. His survival was a beacon of light, tantamount to a resurrection.

Game rangers then intensified their search. They found more gorillas, and eventually concluded that of the original twenty-five families in the highland sector of Kahuzi Biega, more than half had been massacred during the conflict. Awful as that was, in the DRC you take what wins you can. The half-full cup was the fact that about a hundred animals in the vast park were still alive. They had survived against every expectation.

Chimanuka was a solitary male at the time, but he soon rectified that, gathering wives and a family after a series of fights. One of the fights was against Mugaruka, the one-handed silverback our trekking group encountered during a trip to the DRC the previous year.

Despite his ferocious reputation as a brawler, Chimanuka was a gentle giant with his family and even reared an orphan called Marhale, which is unheard of for a male gorilla. Marhale's mother Makali (meaning 'fiery-tempered') was killed during the clash between Chimanuka and Mugaruka, and Chimanuka personally took charge of the traumatised baby.

I have never seen Chimanuka but Angela and I met his eldest son Bonané on both of our previous gorilla treks. It was a privilege I will always cherish.

Now Chimanuka was missing. At first, when rangers sighted his family without him, they thought little of it. The jungle is so dense that it is almost impossible to see all of a gorilla group at the same time. Chimanuka's clan of twenty members is one of the three families in the park habituated to humans, and after several sighting without the silverback, alarm bells started ringing. A silverback never deserts his family unless he has been ousted by a competitor, and that was unlikely to have happened to the extremely powerful Chimanuka.

KBNP management issued a red alert. The guard force was

doubled thanks to funding from my friend Peter Eastwood and the Tanglewood Foundation, while John also threw all of the Pole Pole Foundation's grassroots resources into the desperate search.

They found nothing. After a few months, it seemed almost certain that the colossus of the KBNP had been killed, most probably by humans. Illegal miners in game parks live off the land and the fact that no corpse was recovered sadly indicated that Chimanuka had been eaten. The outnumbered and outgunned park rangers could do nothing about it. The miners were a law unto themselves.

We didn't know for sure how Chimanuka died, but one thing was for certain. He would not have gone quietly into the night. If illegal miners had attacked his family, he would have fought to the death, no matter how many guns shot at him.

The tragedy is even more distressing as Chimanuka's father Maheshe was also killed by poachers in 1993. Like Chimanuka, Maheshe was in his day the world's most famous gorilla as his muscled image appeared on the Congolese 5000-franc banknote. Everyone in the country, which was called Zaire at the time, referred to the note as a 'Maheshe'. So much so that much trading was done in the silverback's name and shopkeepers priced items in 'Maheshes', doing far more for gorilla awareness than any public relations campaign. Indeed, Maheshe was as well-known and infinitely more loved than the kleptocratic president of the country, Mobutu Sese Seko. The sad irony that the gorilla made famous on a banknote was himself killed for cash was more than heart-breaking. It was a bad omen. An omen that came true with his son.

I scratched my head, wondering yet again how the gods of fortune could allow such bad karma continuously to plague such a spectacularly beautiful country. The resource-rich land was seemingly cursed beyond redemption. I knew that wasn't true, but at times it was difficult not to feel that way.

Artisanal, or subsistence, mining has been problematic for many years in the DRC and is particular prevalent in the eastern districts near Bakavu. The KBNP may be one of the world's most beautiful parks, but it is also slap-bang in a fabulously rich mineral area with prolific deposits of gold, tin, tungsten and coltan – a key rare earth metal used in cellphones. The distressing consequences of this are far-reaching and today there are believed to be more than nine hundred illegal mining sites in the protected area, about half of which are run by ruthless militias. So with uncontrolled poverty and greed running rampant, what chance does a handful of rangers with aged rifles have in halting it?

On a national scale, the picture is even bleaker. An estimated 10 million Congolese make a living from subsistence mining, either by scratching the soil and panning rivers or by smuggling, charging 'taxes' and providing muscle against rival militias.

The environmental damage is staggering. Since gold mines are almost always near rivers, acids and chemicals such as mercury are washed directly into waterways. Mercury kills fish, as well as people who eat those fish and animals that drink the poisoned water. On top of that, crucial streams and creeks that feed jungle rivers are redirected or dammed up by mass strip-surface excavations, while large sections of forest are slashed and burnt to get at the minerals. The illicit industry is so vast that the only way to stop it would be to evict all militias from all national parks. However, that could only be done as a full-scale military campaign, and some conservationists are already suggesting something similar to a United Nations peacekeeping task force should be formed. This is unlikely to happen. In many desperately poor regions of the DRC, subsistence mining is not just a job, it is the only job.

As always, it is the wild animals that suffer in the race for the land. Chimanuka's murder was merely the latest instance of horror and barbarity in the long list of crimes against the planet.

On the news of his death, I expected an uproar. The scandal that a national icon had been chopped up and put in a pot on a fire somewhere deep in the bush should be shouted from the rooftops. Voices of outrage and furious indignation should thunder across the world.

Yet there was silence.

The main reason for this was the timidity of the Congolese conservation authorities. The KBNP is a World Heritage Site, and if it was discovered that rogue gold miners had eaten one of the world's most famous gorillas, UNESCO could withdraw its prestigious status. If that happened, what little international aid the KBNP received could shrivel on the vine.

To some extent, I understood that. Perhaps silence was a necessary strategy to try and protect the rest of Chimanuka's severely threatened fellow forest dwellers.

But on the other hand, if illegal miners got away with murdering and eating an animal as famous as Chimanuka in a World Heritage Site, what chance do other creatures have?

There was no clear answer. But for me, one thing was crystal clear. Chimanuka's most distinctive identification – in fact, his trademark – was a teardrop-shaped protrusion below his right eye. From an angle, it looked like he was weeping. That melancholic feature was beyond prophetic. It will forever haunt us. Of that I have no doubt.

I sat staring at John's email for several minutes, wondering what, if anything, we could do. In South Africa, we have much experience in protecting threatened wild animals. With Project Rhino, CWC Africa and BRREP, we are fighting rear-guard battles to save a species that is almost as critically endangered as gorillas. With Chris Holcroft's legacy, and people such as Chris Small and Joe Pietersen, we are using rapid-reaction tactics to defend vulnerable individuals and herds, such as the elephants of Mawana. We use many strategies, ranging from electronic tracking collars to aerial surveillance. We have the best elephant relocation experts in the world with people such as Kester Vickery. We train and equip skilled anti-poaching units. We educate children in rural areas on the long-term commercial and spiritual value of wildlife. In times of drought and pandemics, we show that the wildlife community cares by feeding hungry villagers.

But all of these projects are backed by advanced technology as well as using modern concepts of marketing and fundraising. So how could we replicate that in the DRC, which is so vast, so wild, so poor, and so remote?

For example, John's son Eddy Kahekwa once asked me if we could donate tracking collars to put on the Kahuzi Biega gorillas. We would then know where they were at all times, and if they were attacked by poachers. It was a good idea, but a more pertinent question would be this: what could the park staff do if the animals were attacked? The reality on the ground was that poachers not only outnumber game rangers, but they are also far better equipped. More often than not, KBNP staff don't even have enough fuel for their patrol vehicles. With the best will in the world, the phrase 'rapid reaction' in the vast jungles of the DRC's national parks is often an oxymoron.

Relocating the gorillas is also impractical. The forests of Central Africa are not replicated anywhere else on the continent. We could not, for example, move gorillas to safe havens in South Africa, as the habitat is alien.

We could, of course, move some to zoos. In fact, many zoos already have gorillas, and they are among the most popular attractions among visitors. That at least preserves the gene pools, but for conservationists such as me who believe in big-sky wilderness, it would be heart-breaking. To remove gorillas from Kahuzi Biega would rip the soul from Africa's equatorial jungles. Even so, I may have to accept that, with the explosion of subsistence mining and bushmeat poaching, this may be one of the few options available.

We could also attempt to raise money for heavily armed international eco-armies to turn the last jungle outposts of the DRC's gorillas into impenetrable fortresses. But the massive amount of money and political resolve necessary to do that are not anywhere on the horizon at the moment.

So what could we do?

Then it dawned. We did have an answer. In fact, it was already in place. It had been introduced by John Kahekwa and his charity Pole Pole and then rolled out in some of the villages surrounding the park. And, despite everything, it was by and large working.

Strange as it might sound, all one needs to do sometimes is step back, take a deep breath and look at the bigger picture. The seemingly insurmountable problems I have outlined have been in existence for decades. Poaching, slash-and-burn agriculture, strip mining and other forms of eco-devastation are nothing new. But yet the animals are still there. In fact, in some small pockets – such as Bonané's growing family – they are thriving.

The bottom line of this seemingly endless litany of tears is that the KBNP and John's Pole Pole team have somehow kept thirteen families of gorillas alive in the face of every obstacle imaginable.

It defies logic. It is a true miracle. Yet they have done it. While others have wrung their hands, John's team has been chipping away at the granite rock of despair by providing alternative choices for destitute people who would otherwise swell the growing ranks of strip-miners and poachers. It has been slow, as the name Pole Pole implies, but they have established spirulina, mushroom and fruit farms that now flourish on land surrounding the KBNP. They have built nursery projects, planting more than 4 million saplings to prevent villagers from logging indigenous forests. Rural women are taught skills such as basket weaving or fish farming. Ex-poachers become game guards. While all of this might pale against the explosion of illegal mining, it is still keeping the wheels of conservation moving in the right direction. And they have done this on a shoestring budget that can't even afford the shoestring.

The answer is not relocating gorillas or hiring heavily armed eco-mercenaries. It is instead providing the vital resources for Pole Pole and the heroically resilient staff at KBNP to keep going. To keep on doing what they do. They cannot do it alone forever. They need help from the rest of the world – help on a vast scale. They need a modern-day international Noah's Ark programme of aid and education, and massive investment driven by a dogged refusal to surrender. John Kahekwa has shown us the way. We have to follow it.

The death of Chimanuka has to be the turning point. Or else he will have died in vain.

CHAPTER THIRTY-ONE

Back to the Future

I'm told the shortest period of making a movie is the most crucial part – the actual filming. It can take as little as four months to roll the cameras, compared to four years of pre-planning, raising finance, script changes, dealing with agents and writing out hefty cheques to actors delivering the lines.

That's a little like many of my conservation projects, apart from the hefty cheques, of course. What many would consider to be the most important aspect, the actual relocation of vulnerable animals, is almost always the shortest and simplest. Obtaining suitable habitat, putting up fences, security and permits can take years. In the case of transnational parks such as those on our KwaZulu-Natal borders, it can take forever. That's why so much of my time is spent sourcing wildernesses. Without the land, we can do nothing.

At the time of writing, I have several projects on the go, some of which I initially despaired would ever see the light of day. Thankfully, despite COVID being the perfect storm for the worst of all possible times, the majority of my projects are at least still standing, if not completed.

The one I had been working on the longest, Loziba Wilderness, was also the most time consuming. However, the tide is at last turning in our favour with the most vociferous community, Stedham, slowly coming around. Also, Beyers's memorial ceremony and Andries Botha's poignant speech had to some extent compelled the Van der Walt family to work more closely together. The sensible siblings are realising that they are in danger of losing everything if their land in Mawana is not incorporated into Loziba. It's as basic as that. The lawyers will simply put the game reserve up for auction, and in today's market still struggling with the aftermath of the pandemic, not to mention possible community land claims, Mawana may go for a song. It's terrible that it takes a tragedy to move things forward, but sometimes that's just the way it is.

Also, it is now clear to everyone that the Loziba deal will go ahead, and those who don't jump on board could miss the boat completely. Apart from substantial money from the Chris Holcroft legacy, we also received a million rand from a donor, which we will use to bid for more surrounding land. We now have a viable project as a crucial financial hurdle has been cleared. The venture can stand on its own, even if the original dream of a 35,000-hectare reserve is scaled back somewhat. But one thing is now certain: rhino will again roam this lush northern Zululand thornveld that is their ancestral home.

Also topping the success of the project is that the Mawana elephants are safe. We had successfully stemmed, if not completely reversed, calls for the destruction of the two askaris that killed Beyers. We had also moved diseased wildebeest away from community cattle herds, but I was not sure how long that would last as rustlers still drive pilfered animals across private land, and any contact with wildebeest can reignite a *snotsiekte* crisis.

In effect, Loziba is now operational as a makeshift conservation area, if not a fully fledged game reserve. We have completed all the necessary due diligence work and most interested parties, with the notable exception of livestock bandits, are on board.

Unfortunately, my vision to rewild the former war zones of Angola and bring back elephants whose ancestors were slaughtered by marauding armies is still up in the air.

But even in that there is cause for some optimism. We came to within a hair's breadth of pulling off a deal with the Namibian government when that country's wildlife authorities put out a tender for the capture and relocation of several elephant herds. We submitted a bid for ninety animals through Joe Pietersen's charity Nkombe Rhino, stressing that we wanted to move them to Angola.

Unfortunately, our bid failed, but mainly on a technicality. The Namibian government said they would only consider a cross-border programme if it was done at government level, which was understandable. However, as the Namibian government does not physically handle capture and relocation procedures itself, it indicated that any future Angolan elephant deal could be assigned to us. Obviously we would have to provide the funding, but the 'war elephants' project is not dead in the water by any means. The fact that the Namibian and Angolan governments have exceptionally close ties dating back to their respective liberation wars augurs well for us. We also have the Angolan hotel and tourism minister Pedro Mutindi and former FAPLA General Fernando Mateus on our side, as well as Johan Booysen of 61 Mech's Veterans Association, which was doing humanitarian work in Cuito Cuanavale. Suffice it to say I am cautiously hopeful.

The Greater Mkuze Valley project is firmly on track with Ven-Africa, Amakhosi Safari Lodge and Chamanzi Wilderness joining forces. We have already relocated our first elephant and a blueprint is being drawn up to construct a corridor that will eventually stretch from the Tembe Elephant Park in the east to Ithala – which also has rhino – in the west. At the time of writing, five other private game reserves and a 5400-hectare stretch of community land called Mpondwane have expressed interest in joining the umbrella conservancy.

The Maldonado family have also formed the Conservation Initiative of Ven-Africa (CIVA), which includes myself, Sam and Veronica Maldonado, Venezuelan biological scientist Rafael Antelo, Alwyn Wentzel of Amakhosi Safari Lodge, and Tim and Susan Machpesh. We have begun an intensive rewilding process and land is now suitable for the ultimate goal of reintroducing the Tembe tuskers.

I want BRREP to include black rhinos in the Greater Mkuze Valley conservancy as well, and CIVA is in the process of establishing a world-class anti-poaching unit with the construction of ranger housing and a dedicated base for operations.

We are now also taking local school children to Ven-Africa for educational trips, and Susan Machpesh is on the verge of opening a small school and library as part of a community outreach programme.

On a personal note, the Maldonados have invited me to visit Hato El Frío, their Orinoco delta reserve in Venezuela, once sanity returns to the oil-rich country. I hope that happens.

At Lake Jozini, the problems with Mr Steenkamp's determination to shoot elephants eating his sugar cane still persist. He is a multimillionaire with a lot of financial clout, but our war chest has been considerably boosted with a hefty donation from the international Elephant Crisis Fund (ECF). This will mainly be used for emergency measures such as scattering concentrated chilli powder on fences and establishing beehives to deter elephants, as well as financing emergency helicopter callouts, installing solar-powered monitors and legal costs.

But despite our clashes with Mr Steenkamp, the southern Lubombo corridor through the Mkuze gorge will go ahead. This is a long-term project and will take at least five years, but the fact we are committed to doing it will save the lives of several elephants earmarked for culling on Lake Jozini's eastern bank. One of our main successes in this regard is that no one any longer disputes that elephants are absolutely vital for eco-tourism in the entire Lake Jozini area. Or to be more precise, no one except, perhaps, those planning to plant sugar.

The biggest failure, as far as I was concerned, has been the Saudi Arabia AlUla conservancy. In this regard, I am referring purely to our involvement as the project itself appears still to be on the cards. Judging by the amount of international TV advertising, Saudi Arabia has not deviated from its expressed goal of becoming a world-class tourist destination by 2030. Even though we are not currently involved, it was an interesting exercise for me as one thing it did prove was how advanced South African environmentalists are in global conservation. The concept of rewilding a park and bringing back indigenous species is nothing new to us. In fact, I think we are world leaders and our ideas are cutting edge.

The biggest conservation setback for us within South Africa during the awful COVID pandemic was the burning down of the Bongani Mountain Lodge. The unfortunate ripple effects of this on grassroots conservation are devastating, with at least three deep-pocketed donors telling me that they were no longer interested in projects involving what they call 'volatile' communities. The sentiment, usually implied rather than spoken, is that any future ventures involving unresolved land claims, divided communities and cattle rustlers are more trouble than they are worth. This is unfortunate, as these problems are manageable. We faced such issues on an almost daily basis while putting the Loziba Wilderness project together, and the fact we have to some extent succeeded should go a long way to allaying donors' fears. Only time will tell.

The torching of the Bongani lodge was followed by setbacks in the Eastern Cape and Karoo, although I am sure Henry Kissinger Siambone will feature again in our eco-projects. His fact-finding trip to South Africa at the start of the COVID lockdown left an indelible mark on him. On the other hand, my angel investor Hans once again proved the old adage that if something appears too good to be true, leave it well alone.

In summary, only the Saudi Arabian and eco-dreamer Hans's projects were outright failures for us. And this has to be viewed in the context of COVID, the bleakest, most depressing and frightening period many people have faced in their lives. Ironically, they were also the projects where the most money had been promised.

But looking at it from a glass half-full angle, we have done remarkably well. Two ventures are on the threshold of success (Loziba and Ven-Africa), a third is being fiercely fought for (Lake Jozini), while the Angolan elephant project could go either way.

Even better, we had also done the groundwork for an equally visionary project in Mozambique. In fact, six of them.

Then disaster struck.

CHAPTER THIRTY-TWO

Blood on the Beach

For many people in more affluent parts of the world, Mozambique's main claim to fame is that Bob Dylan wrote a song about it.

Even that was clouded in controversy, as the song came out in 1975, just as Portugal abandoned its colonies and FRELIMO took over Mozambique. FRELIMO was a hardline Marxist liberation movement in those days, but Dylan's lyrics didn't reflect that. It was more of a whimsical song about beautiful women frolicking on Mozambique's sublime beaches. Even so, the right wing considered it to be a paean to communism, and the left wing regarded it as frivolous bourgeois nonsense.

Despite Dylan's 'Mozambique' reaching number 54 on the *Billboard* Hot 100, the country is little known internationally. It has always played second fiddle to Portugal's richer African colony, Angola, with little investment coming its way. When it gained independence, it took a double whammy with crippling cross-border raids from South Africa for harbouring ANC insurgents, and Rhodesia, which repeatedly bombed Robert Mugabe's ZANU camps below the Chimanimani Mountains. Also, when the Portuguese administration fled in disarray, the country had perhaps a couple of dozen Black university graduates out of a barely literate population of about 20 million. Then it plunged into a civil war lasting fifteen years. As a result, this beautiful, resource-rich country with some of the most outstanding wildernesses in the world did not exactly have a running start.

Now, just as it is beginning to get its act together with a firm commitment to progress and prosperity, the threat from ISIS-linked Ansar al-Sunna in the far north erupted.

We had to take the jihadist situation into account regardless of what we planned to do in the country. Even though most of the projects we were looking at were some distance from the heart of the insurgency, it could easily flare up elsewhere.

Then, suddenly, this conflict came close to home. Frighteningly so.

It happened in April 2021 when a heavily armed Ansar al-Sunna group raided a town called Palma in Cabo Delgado, specifically targeting European expats as well as local villagers. Their actions were barbaric beyond description, with more than a hundred people being disembowelled, beheaded and slaughtered in the sort of random cruelty not seen on the continent for ages.

Also killed was a South African. His name was Adrian Nel, and any doubts that this was getting personal were dispelled when I discovered he lived in Zinkwazi, a town just up the road from where I live on the KwaZulu-Natal coast.

A professional deep-sea diver, Adrian had previously worked in the DRC (another of my stamping grounds) but lost his job due to the pandemic. He then joined his stepfather Greg Knox and brother Wesley to work on the French energy company Total's multibillion-dollar gas project in Palma, Mozambique. It was scheduled to be the largest liquefied natural gas venture on the continent, and many, including the Mozambican government, claimed that the poverty-stricken province of Cabo Delgado would soon be transformed into Africa's 'Dubai'.

Describing the events leading to his brother Adrian's death, Wesley Nel told TV reporters that they were in the Amarula Hotel a few miles outside Palma on the Tanzanian border when Ansar al-Sunna fighters surrounded the building. Along with other expat workers staying at the hotel, Wesley said they hunkered down in the bar making repeated calls on their cellphones for help. When these went unanswered, Adrian risked his life to retrieve an AK-47 stashed in an abandoned military vehicle. He would use it if the insurgents stormed the hotel, but otherwise it was of little use against the jihadists' RPGs and mortars.

In fact, the besieged workers' only protection was from a few makeshift helicopter gunships circling overhead, flown by a private South African security company, Dyck Advisory Group (DAG). However, DAG had no ground force and the small choppers had little or no passenger-carrying capacity. Even though they were doing heroic work in holding off the insurgents from overrunning the hotel, they could not launch an actual rescue mission. They also were not equipped to fly at night, and as Total has a policy not to supply fuel to private military contractors, DAG would soon be out of operation.

After three days of fruitlessly pleading with the Mozambican army for rescue, it was clear to those holed up in the Amarula that they had no choice but to make a run for it. The few DAG pilots could not keep the jihadists at bay for much longer, and Adrian and his besieged colleagues had no illusions of what would happen to them if captured. It was well-known that Ansar al-Sunna favoured decapitating any Christian or 'Crusader nation' prisoners.

The men drew up a rudimentary plan to rush out of the building and commandeer whatever vehicles they could in the hotel parking lot, smash through the insurgents' roadblocks, and just keep going as fast as possible until they reached the beach. They had heard that local fishermen, at huge personal risk, were using dilapidated dhows and anything that could float to get people out of the killing zone.

Adrian, Wesley and Greg were among the desperate group's leaders and gave the command to run for the vehicles. Making sure that women and children were secure in the sole armoured vehicle outside the hotel, the men scrambled for the cars. Adrian, Wesley and Greg jumped into one of the front vehicles and Adrian grabbed the steering wheel. As he keyed the ignition, Wesley said, 'It's going to be the drive of your life, bro.'

The seventeen-vehicle convoy raced along a dusty bush-lined road and within minutes came under intense fire. Somehow they managed to plough through the roadblock, but shortly afterwards they ran into a second ambush. Adrian was shot in his shoulder and leg but, despite bleeding copiously, kept driving for several miles.

Eventually he passed out, and Wesley grabbed the wheel while Greg frantically tried to staunch his stepson's gaping wounds. It appeared that an artery had been hit.

Finally, they reached a quarry that the convoy drivers had designated as a rallying point. Wesley felt for his brother's pulse. There was none.

The forty-year-old father of three would have celebrated his birthday in three days' time. It had indeed been the drive of his life and, although he had saved others, it cost him his own.

Stepfather and brother then pulled Adrian out of the car and fled into the bush. They were damned if they were going to let the gunmen find Adrian's body. They hid in the dense undergrowth for two days while jihadists sped up and down the roads searching for survivors to behead.

When help eventually arrived, seven of the hotel group were dead and several others wounded. Of the original seventeen vehicles, only seven made it to the beach.

Most of those who survived the jihadist attacks at both the Amarula Hotel and the town of Palma owe their lives to DAG pilots. However, the company, led by African bush war veteran Colonel Lionel Dyck, only had three helicopters, two micro-light gunships and two fixed-wing planes in Mozambique. But that shoestring air force was the sole lifeline for fleeing expat workers and Palma residents. About three hundred people were directly saved by DAG, while countless others were able to run for their lives as the mercenary pilots held back the advancing insurgents.

Colonel Dyck, who fought for both the Rhodesian and Zimbabwean armies, made his name in Mozambique fighting poachers and landmine clearing before landing the contract to assist the local police against the ISIS-linked jihadists. Interestingly, at least from my point of view, another South African company helping the Mozambican authorities is Paramount Group, whose chief negotiator is Ahmed Kassam, my neighbour who introduced me to the Saudi Arabian rewilding project. However, unlike DAG, Paramount doesn't supply mercenaries, instead providing training and military equipment such as armoured vehicles and aircraft. Ahmed could later prove invaluable in providing on-the-ground assessments for our future projects.

His help would be needed as Colonel Dyck believes that unless the Mozambican military roots out Ansar al-Sunna, the northern province of Cabo Delgado will be 'lost'. The jihadists, he said, were now integrated with established, well-organised criminal networks trafficking in ivory, drugs, rubies and emeralds: 'However, the big billion-dollar business is heroin, which is transported through the area and distributed to the north and south. This has now taken on an Islamic face and is a highly effective combination with strong external support.'

This was not what I wanted to hear. Suddenly, Mozambique took on a new dimension. Everything now seemed to loom much larger. As the story of Adrian Nel graphically showed, we would be targets if the insurrection spread. There was no skirting the fact that this is the price one pays for doing business in some of the world's rougher neighbourhoods.

Chris, Joe and I chatted about this at length, then decided to be philosophical about it. In Africa, there is always risk. We knew that, and we had to accept it. To fret too much is tantamount to not getting out of bed in the morning.

For us, there was no turning back.

A month after the ISIS-linked attack, Chris and I drove into Mozambique to meet our new partners. We had also earmarked the Mozambican project we were most interested in kicking off the new venture.

This was Massingir Safaris.

CHAPTER THIRTY-THREE

All the President's Rhinos

Even though we arrived at the Kosi Bay border post at the 8 a.m. opening time, the queue was already horrific, stretching back hundreds of yards.

I was also concerned about our COVID credentials as although Chris Small and I had tested negative, we still had not received the paperwork confirming this. Which meant we might have to wing our way through.

As it happened, COVID was the least of our worries and, to my surprise, the efficient South Africans whisked us through the gates in a relatively short time.

It was a different story with the Mozambicans. We had to pay several seemingly random taxes, including third party insurance and a road tax for our vehicle, and whenever we handed over money, the customs official said he had no change. He didn't bother to conceal the wads of banknotes in his desk drawer as he spoke.

He then came out to inspect our truck, packed with Adidas-sponsored footwear and footballs that I planned to donate to local communities. Shaking his head as if exasperated by the extra paperwork, he said these would require extensive import taxes.

'But we aren't selling them. They are donations,' I replied.

He continued shaking his head clucking sadly, when I suddenly had a brainwave. 'These shoes and footballs are for Mozambican communities. Would you like some for your children?'

He stopped, as though in deep thought. Then he started smiling. 'Do you have a packet?'

That was the game changer. He had accepted the bribe, and the negotiations were now on, although he didn't want his colleagues to know this. We needed to put the shoes and footballs in a bag.

We were through. But not for long. We had barely travelled 200 yards when two plain clothes officials ran out of the bush and waved us down. They wanted to see our receipts as proof that we had paid the correct taxes.

For some reason, we couldn't find the road tax receipt. True to Murphy's law, it was also the most vital piece of paperwork we needed. Without it, we could not drive in Mozambique, so we had to return to the border post. Fortunately, I was able to get hold of our previous official, now with new shoes, who joined the search for the missing receipt. We eventually found it at the bottom of all the Adidas gear in the back of the overladen truck – no doubt left there while the customs official searched for the right pair of trainers.

Finally, we set off to Maputo minus three footballs and two pairs of track shoes on a brand-new road built by the Chinese as part of its Belt and Road Initiative in Africa. The impressive 1.9-mile Katembe toll bridge spanning Maputo Bay is the longest suspension bridge on the continent. However, it seems the Chinese are extracting their pound of investment flesh for this through other ventures, most notably fishing. Maputo Bay is choked with Chinese trawlers.

I would like to say it was a pleasure to travel on this new, sleek-surfaced road, but it was the absolute opposite. By the time we had driven 100 miles, we had been through four roadblocks and fined at every one. These ranged from supposed speeding to allegedly taking a wrong turn, and even giving the wrong reason for being in the country. At one roadblock I explained that, among other things, we were donating wild animals to game reserves, thinking that would impress the police.

Sadly, not. 'So you are on business?' he thundered. 'But you have a tourist visa. That will be an extra 2000 meticais [about US$36].'

Eventually I refused to give out shoes or footballs. We would have none left by the time we reached Massingir.

Considerably lighter in pocket, we finally met up with our potential Mozambican partners, Peter Bechtel, Sean Nazerali and Roberto Zolho, at a promenade coffee shop. I still had to pay for a COVID test to exit the country and was worried I would run out of cash. But even with Mozambicans in the car, we were hauled over at roadblocks or flagged down by cars with flashing blue lights. We weren't alone; it seems every vehicle with a foreign number plate was considered a cash cow. Peter, Sean and Roberto were acutely embarrassed by the rampant police corruption and said the only way to counter it was to waste the crooked cops' time at every given opportunity. This included demanding to see their badges, asking to take cellphone photos of them – anything to stonewall the shakedown. The logic behind this is that by being as uncooperative as possible, police would miss out on other opportunities to fleece motorists. It actually works. On one occasion I could see them mentally scanning foreign number plates as cars went by, calculating how much money they were losing while bickering with us.

Having said that, this was the only major blight on our time in one of Africa's most beautiful and friendliest countries – epitomised by our new friends, Peter, Sean and Roberto. As we still had a six-hour journey to Massingir Safaris, it would give us plenty of time to get to know them better. It was time well spent as Chris and I realised right away that we were dealing with creative and dynamic people. Peter Bechtel is a big guy in very sense of the word, but I must say his dress sense is 'interesting'. He was wearing garish African-print cotton trousers that made my brightly coloured Zulu *umbhulaselo* bead and patchwork jeans look like a Savile Row suit. An American by birth, Peter has adopted thirteen African children and has adapted to the unique warp and weft of the continent better than many native white Africans that I know. Roberto Zolho, whose German wife works for the World Wildlife Fund, was a respected former head warden of Gorongosa, mentored by my old friend Paul Dutton. Roberto is an incredibly unassuming man, despite his impressive conservation credentials, and was raring to get going on our proposed new projects. He said he was busy 'planting trees' at the moment and hankered to be working with large animals and big-sky conservation again. Sean Nazerali seemed to be the most academic of the trio, but his conservation record is also right up there. An avid birdwatcher and photographer, his connections to Biofund resources could be invaluable to doing work in Mozambique – as could his knowledge of Mozambican law. When we were stopped at roadblocks, he would rattle off various legal clauses in immaculate Portuguese to stonewall bemused police expecting an easy payday.

Our Mozambican friends also gave us some background on the proposed Massingir Safaris project. It is a well-run, 8,000-hectare game reserve about 13 miles east of the town of

Massingir, and established in 2008 as a *duat*. This is a type of long lease with the Mozambican government that allows the leaseholders to do as they see fit. Private land ownership is restricted in Mozambique, so many consider a *duat* to be the most effective and secure form of tenure. The main shareholder is Scot Lawrence, whom we would soon meet, but at the moment he had two South African partners who were keen to sell their shares. If all things worked out as planned, we could be the new partners.

In effect, Massingir Safaris is the first post-civil war privately run game farm in the country, and our Mozambican colleagues seemed extremely excited to be showing it to us. Their enthusiasm was infectious, and now that the number of police roadblocks appeared to be diminishing, I started enjoying the trip. I could see Chris was as well.

After about a three hours' drive from Maputo we reached the town of Chokwe, which was a crossroads between the famously beautiful beaches of Xai-Xai and Bilene and the game reserves in the Gaza province. We now were off the Chinese-built roads and started hitting potholes with a vengeance. These were in some cases even worse than the ruined roads of the DRC, but still passable in a two-wheel drive vehicle. However, most of the traffic were multi-wheel logging rigs ferrying massive 200-year-old mahogany trunks, or heavily laden charcoal trucks, both a major concern for the environment. Dilapidated shacks lined the road, while sun-scorched maize crops and flooded rice paddies indicated the extent of hunger and poverty. I learned that the average daily wage in these areas was about R40 (US$2.8) compared to about R200 (US$14) in South Africa.

We eventually reached what used to be dense mopane forests, but even these were being systematically axed for charcoal. Every mile or so, piles of charcoal bags destined for the market were stacked high at the side of the road. There was obviously not a lot of community work being done in the area, and I made a mental note that this was where our expertise would be extremely useful in any future partnerships. I could picture the flamboyant Richard Mabanga standing on top of our 2-ton Rhino Art truck with loudspeakers blaring *maskandi* music as he urged local people to refrain from poaching and destroying the forests. Obviously we would have to replace that with other forms of income but, again, this was something in which we had a proven track record.

Arriving at Massingir Safaris was another world from the shanties and chopped trees we had just passed. We drove through a beautiful entrance towards a solar-powered bungalow camp and finally met Scot Lawrence and his wife Judy.

If I was taken aback by the rustic beauty of the reserve, I was even more surprised when I met our hosts.

'We know your family,' said Scot. 'Judy was best friends with your sister Ros.'

This was the first I had heard of that. Ros, who was born a year after me, and her husband Dale Paul had lived for many years in Duiwelskloof, a small agricultural town close to the Mozambique border where the Lawrences had owned a farm. In fact, Scot and Judy's children had grown up with Ros's son Tyler Paul, a professional rugby player now under contract to the top Japanese club NTT Docomo Red Hurricanes.

I shook my head, stunned at the coincidence. Ros had never mentioned the Lawrences before, but why would she? I wouldn't have known who she was talking about in any event.

But the coincidence went further. Scot was born in Rhodesia, but his family moved to South Africa in the 1970s as the bush war in the country soon to become Zimbabwe intensified.

He went to Grey High School in Port Elizabeth, not far from where I grew up, and it turned out that not only were his wife and Ros best friends, I also knew most of the people who had been in Scot's class.

The Lawrences were on the verge of getting Mozambique citizenship as they had lived in the country for almost ten years, originally buying a house at Xai-Xai, and ending up owning a hotel on the beach. Many politicians and government officials holidayed at Scot's hotel, and he is extremely well-connected. He is also an astute, no-nonsense businessman, and as he has always loved the outdoors, he ended up buying the major share in the Massingir Safaris business.

So here we were, talking about friends, family and acquaintances we never knew we shared in a distant chunk of wild bush in a foreign country. It certainly broke any ice between us, and the business discussions after that went a lot smoother than they would have done under normal circumstances. But, above all, when we spoke about conservation, I instantly saw that Scot bought into my vision.

He showed Chris and I around the property and, I had to admit, it was easily one of the best-managed game reserves I had come across. Although they 'officially' only had two of the Big Five – buffalo and leopard – elephants occasionally broke into the reserve, and there were a few lions on the premises that had somehow also got in. But it was no real problem as whenever elephants smashed through, the electric fences were repaired within hours – not days like much of the rest of remotest Africa. The administration in every aspect, from solar power in the immaculately kept bungalows and tented camp to road and infrastructure maintenance, was top notch. But most inspiring of all was their security. The reserve had four tracker dogs personally trained by Scot and his sons Courtney and Chad that were better than any I had seen before.

Before becoming Massingir Safaris, the area was primarily used for cattle grazing and the mass logging of trees for charcoal. Poaching was also a constant headache due to the proximity of the Limpopo Transfrontier Park – a problem which Scot's dog team had brought under control. Today it is beautifully rewilded and the main focus of the reserve is breeding game species for the Mozambique market. However, to pay the bills, some top-end hunting for buffalo and trophy antelope is also permitted. This is done on a highly selective basis with minimal impact on the environment and no more than two or three hunters on the reserve at any given time. Scot says he eventually wants to shut down the hunting side of the business, concentrating on game breeding and eco-tourism, which was one of the reasons why he was talking to us.

Not only that, he and Judy were about to acquire an additional 3,770 hectares bordering the western section of the reserve, which would give them close on 12,000 hectares of pristine bushveld.

Apart from being superbly managed, Massingir Safaris also has a lot going for it due to its location. It's only 50 miles from the Giriyondo border post with South Africa and directly on the main road to Xai-Xai and Inhambane. It's an ideal stopover for South African tourists wishing to incorporate five-star game viewing along with a tropical beach holiday.

However, our Mozambican counterparts believe most tourism will instead come from the rapidly growing Maputo metropolis only 160 miles away, which now has a burgeoning and wealthy expat population. The Massingir Lake on the Olifants River just up the road from Scot is already a sought-after destination as it rivals Cahora Bassa for wild beauty and tiger fishing, but is a fraction of the distance away.

What also appealed to us was that Massingir Safaris is increasingly promoting eco-tourism. Unlike South Africa, which has thousands of eco-tourist projects, Mozambique has very few. Most of the *coutadas* are hunting-orientated, so Massingir Safaris will not be competing in a crowded market.

Apart from everything else, the reserve is a stone's throw across the border of arguably the most famous game reserve in Africa, the 7523-squaremile Kruger National Park.

Chris and I looked at each other and nodded. All of a sudden the Mozambican conservation projects were looking to be likelier success stories than almost anything else we were looking at. In South Africa, some of the provincial wildlife authorities were on the verge of collapse, while 'volatile' communities were scaring off both donors and investors – as the torching of the Bongani Mountain Lodge tragically showed. In the DRC, many of the reserves didn't even have a main gate, let alone fences. Yet here in dirt-poor Mozambique we were seeing visionary projects that rival many developments in wealthier parts of the world. For me, this was a sea change of stereotypical perceptions.

On the negative side, of course, was the ISIS-linked insurgency up north. Cabo Delgado was well over a thousand miles away but, even so, there was a stark reminder that it was closer to home than we imagined when I noticed a bullet-riddled light aircraft on a nearby grass runway. Scot told us the plane had flown out the body of Philip Mawer, a British contract worker murdered by jihadists. Mr Mawer had been in the convoy that tried to break out of the Amarula Hotel in Pemba, when Adrian Nel and five others were also killed. Private military contractors had to use angle grinders to cut his body out of a mangled, shot-up vehicle and hurriedly loaded it on to a plane to fly it out of the warzone.

But we had already made the decision to be philosophical about that. There was no turning back.

Once we decided that there was no shortage of potential, Chris and I got down to the nitty gritty of hammering out an agreement with our Mozambican colleagues. Apart from upfront financial investment, the Mozambicans wanted our experience and expertise in the conservation industry as well as community projects. We were streets ahead of them in that regard as South Africans had been involved in eco-tourism for decades, while Mozambique had been sucked into a crippling civil war. Unsurprisingly, we were in a different league, as they would have been if the roles were reversed. Now, we could pool resources as they had the contacts, the land and the projects, and we had the knowhow. More importantly, we shared the same vision.

The security display Scot had put on for us was simply stunning, and as soon as I had seen how efficient the anti-poaching measures were, I started thinking about introducing rhino. These critically endangered animals need more protection than any other creature, and Scot's patrols and tracker dogs had demonstrated that Massingir Safaris was up to the task.

But Scot was one step ahead of the rest of us. Not only did he want to reintroduce white rhino, he wanted them to belong to the president of Mozambique, Filipe Nyusi, whom he knew personally. In fact, he had already told the delighted president of his plans.

All he needed was the rhinos: a small, core breeding unit that would be bequeathed to the Mozambican people through their democratically elected head of state.

The problem was that there are very few white rhinos left in Mozambique. Many believe they are extinct. So I told Scot we would find the animals for him in South Africa. Off the top of my head, I could think of ten reserves where I could get rhinos that weren't exactly surplus, but whose owners would consider buying into the long-term vision of providing animals for this magnificent project.

Mozambique, despite being the sixth poorest country in the world and being riven to the core by decades of conflict, has huge potential. It yearns for peace. And here we were talking about doing exactly that – bringing back 'presidential' white rhinos whose forebears had been annihilated in the country. The symbolism was beyond poignant. Not only would they return, but they would belong to the people of the country in the purest form – through the highest office in the land.

Maybe I was being idealistic, but it would be Africa's first peace herd.

We would be bringing the rhinos.

CHAPTER THIRTY-FOUR

Cruel Planet

The impact of COVID-19, and what it did to global consciousness, will be with us for some time. Maybe forever.

Even more significantly, it has finally removed the arrogant belief that we can control events. Or that nature can be bent to suit human needs.

The key question will be exactly how profoundly this pandemic will linger on in our lives, and how we adapt to future viral threats. In short, what – if anything – will be the new normal?

COVID affected virtually everyone on this planet. In the big metropolises, many people were stunned to see congested streets and packed sidewalks suddenly empty. Or the skies above the concrete and steel high-rises devoid of airplanes and the vast crisscross of vapour trails. There were reports of migrating birds being sighted in urban gardens where they had never been seen before. City dwellers said they heard the sounds and smelled the scents of spring for the first time in their lives. They were breathing cleaner air, living a quieter life – albeit enforced by regulations – and overall the entire planet seemed to spin at a more tranquil pace.

By law, people had to spend more time at home. They were encouraged to take strolls in parks and walks in the countryside, as those were the only places they were allowed outdoors. Their lives were not dictated by noisy offices, catching crowded trains and buses to work, or bosses barking orders in boardrooms.

Not all of this was good. Domestic abuse rates soared, so did alcoholism, drug taking, boredom and lethargy. Suicides reached record levels in many developed countries. Neighbours looked at each other suspiciously, obeying the quaintly phrased 'social distancing' laws and wearing face masks that made meek clerks look like highway robbers.

Good or bad, what cannot be denied is that COVID-19 showed what happens when events as uncontrollable as a charging buffalo take hold. And that Mother Nature answers to no human laws. We can hack down her forests, slash-and-burn her jungles, pollute her waterways, scale her mountains, sail her oceans and slaughter her creatures – but we cannot subjugate her. And the more we defy her, the greater the payback will be. A pandemic such as COVID is a mere reminder. Or a warning.

What will life be like after COVID? Will we heed the good lessons – greener energy in the skies and streets? Will we be more in tune with nature? Will first-hand knowledge and daily newspaper headlines that we tamper with natural forces at our peril finally sink into our collective psyche?

Or will we return to the bad old ways? The brutal rhino-horn cartels, bacteria-riddled wet markets, barbaric wildlife trafficking and casual extinction of species that have roamed forests and savannahs for millennia? Will we continue our abusive relationship with the planet?

Leading scientists are more or less unanimous in believing that the outbreak was a 'clear warning shot' that COVID-19 is a forerunner of other, far deadlier wildlife-based pathogen outbreaks. In fact, many believe that this time we dodged a bullet as COVID was, by pandemic standards, relatively mild. Far more people died during the Spanish flu outbreak in 1918, which killed up to 50 million. The next plague could be much more lethal.

This was articulated at the highest level when Inger Andersen, executive director of the United Nations Environment Programme (UNEP), said today's civilisation is playing with fire if it continues to ignore nature's message.

I could not agree more. If COVID-19 was not nature sending us a message, then what was it? No matter where the pandemic originated, wet markets and wildlife trafficking remain among the most plausible causes. The trafficking and treatment of animals are not only a disgusting scar on the conscience on humanity, it's a threat for the entire human race. That's about as clear a warning as one can get.

The main lesson learned should be that we cannot revert to business as usual. We cannot go back to the pre-COVID world. We cannot continue to keep forcing wild animals into smaller and increasingly degraded habitats without paying a massive price. Those who don't believe that should consider this – it's highly likely that a humble bat, a tiny mammal most people have never seen, pretty much brought the world to a complete standstill for almost two years. Not even the two world wars of last century managed that.

However, from a conservation point of view, wild animals were not only by and large unaffected by the actual pandemic, they actually thrived. Obviously there was an increase of hungry people subsistence-poaching for the pot, although we did try to counter that with Feeding the Wildlife Community and other projects. But generally speaking, the bigger picture was positive. Wildlife smugglers, horn and ivory poachers and wet-market butchers were halted, albeit temporarily, while animals in game reserves around the world flourished from lack of interaction and stress from millions of tourists. Eco-tourism is undoubtedly a crucial industry but, even so, it does show that without human interference, nature takes care of things in her own way.

The bottom line is that many believe that COVID-19 could be a point of no return. Some are talking about a great 'reset' – both economic and political. I don't know about that as I'm a conservationist, not a political economist. But I do know that the pandemic provided us with a potentially defining moment. It still is too early to tell whether we have grasped that.

However, from an intensely personal point of view, the early signs are that we sadly have not. There has been no change. In fact, it seems to be business as usual. Just more of the same.

First, there was the killing of Chimanuka. Next was a magnificent rhino, which was a favourite of barefoot safari guide Nunu Jobe, at Rhino Ridge Safari Lodge in Hluhluwe. He was the dominant bull in the area and knew Nunu well – in fact, so well that he would allow us to come up close as long as he could hear Nunu's voice. It was beautiful watching how he calmed down when Nunu spoke, soft and soothing, so the animal understood perfectly that we were no threat. It appears that he was killed by poachers on a hunter's moon, and the bull had no idea whether the humans that appeared from nowhere were good, like Nunu, or bad. Tragically, it was the latter.

Nunu phoned me with the news while vets were doing a post mortem. He was distraught, pleading with me to do something. I promised to try and get more armed rangers to go on patrol, but the reality was that we didn't have the funds to hire them.

Then, barely a fortnight after lockdown was lifted, I got a call from my old friend Sibonelo Zulu, the game ranger who had shot the poaching kingpin Baas Leon Stoltz.

Sibonelo told me that two nights previously he had heard gunshots in the eastern section of the Hluhluwe-iMfolozi Park. Rallying his men, he did a sweep across several thousand hectares of the reserve and found nothing. Sibonelo summoned a helicopter, and finally from the air he spotted two rhino carcasses with bloody, machete-hacked faces bloating in the sub-tropical sun. As another rhino had been poached the week before, the tally was now three since lockdown eased – one a week in the Hluhluwe-iMfolozi Park alone – and they were hearing gunshots on a daily basis.

Sibonelo and his rangers then inspected the fence and found no holes, which alarmingly indicated that the gunmen could brazenly still be in the reserve. Or else they had calmly exited through one of the main gates with blood-soaked horns in the boot of their vehicle. Even worse, the poachers now seemed tactically more prepared than ever with splinter groups scattering into other areas of the reserve, firing decoy shots to divert the rangers from the actual killing.

'My heart is bleeding,' Sibonelo said. There was little more that I could add to that.

As I write this, Sibonelo never leaves his house without wearing a Kevlar bullet-proof vest. It is as natural to him as putting on a shirt. He is a marked man. The poachers are after him with the same deadly intensity that they murder rhinos.

But Sibonelo will never back down. He does not know how to. That is the price one pays to keep animals safe from humans on this cruel planet. Sibonelo would never give up fighting for his beloved rhinos.

We are lucky to have such men still with us. But for him nothing has changed. There is no post-pandemic line in the sand. There is no defining 'COVID moment', if indeed there was one. There has been no great reset. No brave new world.

For Sibonelo, and for me, the war for the soul of our planet is the same as it ever was.

I hope we are wrong.

From the sky, he was beautiful. Although he was still a teenager, his tusks were already showing promise, larger than many of the elephants that renowned wildlife veterinarian Dave Cooper had come across during his long and adventurous life in the bush.

About 50 yards away was another juvenile. Perhaps a year younger. If anything, his tusks were even bigger.

Dave pointed at the animals. Next to him the helicopter pilot Jason Fischer nodded. Operation East Cape Tusker was now in full swing. The choice had been made. These two Tembe elephants were going to be transported to Warne Rippon's Buffalo Kloof reserve near Grahamstown to spread one of the continent's most precious gene pools. But even though the decision had been made, Jason did one more cautious circle around the two animals, waiting for Dave's final thumbs-up signal. There could be no mistake this time.

The translocation to the Eastern Cape of the first Tembe tusker, the previous year, had ended in tragedy. The animal died soon after being moved into the world-renowned Addo Elephant Park and, to this day, none of us is sure why. There were no obvious wounds indicating he had been in a fight. He wasn't crushed at the bottom of a steep ravine, so he hadn't fallen or been shoved off a cliff by a rival bull. No poachers had been in the area and, in any event, the Tembe bull's hugely impressive 5-foot long tusks were intact.

It was a mystery. However, the most credible reason was that some form of confrontation with other elephants had taken place, even though there was no evidence of battle. The Tembe elephant was an adult and introduced into an area where other mature resident bulls had already established their turf. Addo specifically wanted an elephant with both tusks weighing more than 100 pounds, which meant that we had to translocate a fully gown animal from the Tembe park. The upside was that Addo knew they were getting a genuine tusker, but the downside was that the animal would have to fight for mating and territorial rights from the word go. As elephant fights are seldom fatal, this was a risk worth taking.

Sadly, it didn't work out that way, so this time we wanted to try and do something different. Instead, we would move two teenagers who would be subordinate to the aggressive, home-grown alpha males and not pose a threat by stealing their harems. At least, not an immediate one. They would not be involved in any fights or hostilities with established bulls for about five or six years, which would give them time to familiarise themselves with their new home and size-up the other males that they would be up against. They would not pick fights they had no hope of winning. In the previous Eastern Cape relocation, it's possible that the Tembe tusker did not have that choice. As a developed bull he had no option but to stand his ground. But as he did not know the terrain like his opponents, he had no home advantage.

The main risk with choosing teenage animals is the obvious one: the young male may not grow into an adult with tusks larger and far heavier than an adolescent human. Just because Tembe bulls come from a big-ivory gene pool, it doesn't mean that they will all be tuskers, just as big human parents might not necessarily have tall children. All we could do was choose juveniles that already had large ivory for their age and hope for the best.

That is what Dave Cooper and Jason Fischer were doing, scrutinising potential young tuskers from the helicopter circling above the game reserve's trademark sand forests. Dave was the darter as well as spotter as his gut instinct in the bush is second to none. The two teenage bulls below seemed as good as anything else he and Jason would find.

The chopper banked, swooping down to hover two dozen or so feet above the elephants as Dave steadied his aim. The dart-gun fired, and the first animal ran off, a syringe full of tranquiliser quivering in its rump.

Dave loaded another dart, and a few minutes later both elephants were down.

Kester Vickery was in charge of the ground crew, and as soon as Jason radioed that the animals were darted, we sped to the scene with two transport trucks. I was there as an observer rather than part of the capture team, and with me was my niece Hannah Rippon, Warne's daughter. Although still in her early twenties, Hannah is going to be a force to be reckoned with in conservation circles, and I'm not saying that because she's family. The facts speak for themselves: a Stellenbosch University graduate, a qualified Field Guides Association of Southern Africa (FGASA) game ranger, and a licensed helicopter pilot. At Buffalo Kloof she is much more than the boss's daughter and already has major responsibilities running both rhino and elephant monitoring programmes as well as the reserve's extensive social media network. She is also a talented wildlife photographer, mentored by the maestro Chris Holcroft himself.

Working rapidly, Kester got a sling on the first young bull. The crane driver expertly manoeuvred the animal on to the truck that looked like a North Sea oil rig with hydraulic jacks at each end. If we didn't have those, the 4-ton animal could topple the truck as it stood. Kester jabbed the antidote into the elephant's inch-thick hide and we bolted the doors.

Once the second animal had been loaded and given an antidote, the painfully slow twenty-eight-hour journey south to Buffalo Kloof began.

The next day the potential tuskers, one weighing 4.4 tons and the other 3.7 tons, stepped off the trailer, making history as the first of a hopefully successful Tembe bloodline breeding programme in the Eastern Cape.

From a personal perspective, they were also making history for my extended family as they were taking their first steps in their new home on land belonging to our bloodline. Warne is not just a first cousin, but 'doubly' so as his mother is my father's sister, and his father is my mother's brother. It's first blood on both sides.

My father is also Warne's godfather, while Warne's dad Kyle Rippon was my godfather. Warne and Tick Bird share the same irreverent zest for life, while I was also close to Kyle, although, unlike me, he was never in a hurry. A deep-thinking man, we called him Father Time and the family joke was that although the Swiss invented the clock, it was Kyle who owned the hours and minutes. Sadly, Kyle died from diabetes complications several years ago.

When I say these Tembe beauties were the first wannabe tuskers on Rippon–Fowlds land, it's not strictly true as we already had a tusker at Amakhala – or he would be if he still had his tusks.

We call him Norman, named after Norman Hardie, a close family friend who gave him to us. For many years Norman ruled supreme with his giant set of ivories and was the undisputed Amakhala champion. Then one day the unthinkable happened and he was challenged by another large bull called Macaulay.

In the ensuing fight, Macaulay somehow headbutted Norman down into a steep valley. As Norman slipped, his tusks got entangled in the dense growth on the side of the gorge and the enormous gravitational wrench – more than 7 tons – yanked his massive ivories out of their sockets.

The first we knew of Norman's plight was when we saw him a few days later trumpeting in agony and spraying sand into the suppurating cavities where his hundred-pound tusks had been. We initially wondered what had happened as we hadn't seen the fight. Equally puzzled veterinarians diagnosed the ivory loss as some form of calcium deficiency. Whatever the reason, the end result was that he was now an outcast. Without tusks, he could not defend himself or guard his turf and was constantly harassed by other males – even those half his size.

About a year later, the mystery of his missing tusks was solved when we found them wedged deep in the gorge scrub where he had been pushed. We had two choices; either put him out of his misery with a mercy bullet, or move him to the northern section of the reserve where there were no other elephants. This would at least give him time to heal. We chose the latter, and today Norman minus his tusks is happily lording it over his stretch of turf.

Norman Hardie, who now lives in Canada, has generously promised to pay towards the costs of relocating a tusker to Amakhala from Tembe, and I plan to hold him to that pledge. I have always wanted a tusker to replace Norman, who is now in the winter of his years. But the problem is we already have thirty elephants at Amakhala, which we co-own with five other partners. Elephant herds double every ten years, and if we hadn't rewilded more farmland, Amakhala would today be facing the same problem of 'surplus' elephants as Atherstone and Lake Jozini.

Thankfully, with Warne stepping up to the plate, that is no longer an issue. We now have tuskers on family bloodline land. At least we hope so, as only time will tell whether Buffalo Kloof's Tembe elephants will actually turn out to be massive-ivory animals.

Maybe I'm an incurable optimist, but I believe that is exactly what is going to happen. At Buffalo Kloof, a new gene pool of an African icon will take root and, in some small way, our clan will have personally assisted in the process. The old tuskers were shot to virtual extinction for the 'crime' of having abnormally large ivory. Instead of lauding their magnificence, humans came within a hair's breadth of exterminating them. These fabled creatures had the cruel misfortune of living in a time of rampant greed and cruelty. At least on one patch of land in the far southern tip of Africa, those unlamented days are now gone forever. A new bloodline will spawn, and perhaps one day gradually spread throughout the continent.

On a recent trip to the Eastern Cape, I took time off to visit Warne, Wendy and Hannah to see how the potential tuskers were doing. It was an extraordinary trip as the animals gave me the brilliant answer themselves.

From the top of a hillock covered with spekboom, the miracle carbon-eating plant that grows prolifically on these lands, I watched the Tembe duo emerge from the dense Albany thicket. Their skins, glistening from frolicking in the Kowie River headwaters snaking lazily below, glowed with exuberant health. Dawn was glinting fractionally above the horizon and, as one of the askaris lifted his head, a burst of sunlight seemed to splinter off his elongated tusks like shards of gold.

It was how the planet should be.

Useful Organisations

Addo Elephant National Park – www.addo.org.za
African Conservation Trust (ACT) – www.projectafrica.com
African Parks – www.africanparks.org
African Rhino Conservation Collaboration (ARCC) –
www.arcc.org.za
Amakhala Game Reserve – www.amakhala.co.za
Aspinall Foundation – www.aspinallfoundation.org
Black Rhino Range Expansion Project (BRREP) –
http://www.wwf.org.za/our_work/initiatives/black_rhino_
expansion.cfm
Buffalo Kloof – www.buffalokloofsafaris.co.za
BuyNoRhino – www.buynorhino.co.za
Chipembere Rhino Foundation – www.chipembere.org
Communal Wild Conservancies Africa (CWC Africa) –
www.cwcafricaproperties.com
Compañia Humana – www.lafundacionhumana.org
The Conservation Imperative –
www.theconservationimperative.com
Conservation Initiative of Ven-Africa (CIVA) –
www.cova.org.za

Elephant Crisis fund – https://www.elephantcrisisfund.org
Elephants, Rhinos & People (ERP) – www.erp.ngo
Ezemvelo KZN Wildlife – www.kznwildlife.com
Freeland Foundation – www.freeland.org
Global Conservation Force – www.globalconservationforce.org
Gorongosa National Park – www.gorongosa.org
Hluhluwe-iMfolozi Park – www.hluhluwegamereserve.com
Hoedspruit Endangered Species Centre (HESC) –
    www.hesc.co.za
Human Elephant Foundation – www.humanelephant.org
iSimangaliso Wetland Park – www.iSimangaliso.com
Ithala Game Reserve – www.ithala.info
Jane Goodall Institute – www.janegoodall.org
JuMu Rhino Fund – www.jumurhinofund.com
Kageno – www.kageno.org
Kingsley Holgate Foundation and Rhino Art –
    www.kingsleyholgate.com
Loziba – www.loziba.com
Mount Camdeboo Private Game Reserve –
    www.mountcamdeboo.com
Mziki Game Reserve – www.mziki.co.za
National Geographic Exploration – www.nationalgeographic.
    co.uk/topic/subjects/exploration
Nkombe Rhino – https://www.nkomberhino.org
One More Generation – www.onemoregeneration.org
Operation Rhino – www.operation-rhino.com
Pilanesberg National Park – www.pilanesbergnationalpark.org
Pole Pole Foundation – www.polepolefoundation.org
Project Rhino – www.projectrhinokzn.org
Rhino 911 – www.rhino911.com
Royal Jozini Private Game Reserve – www.royaljozini.com

Saving the Survivors – www.savingthesurvivors.org

Space for Elephants Foundation (SEF) – https://spaceforelephantsfoundation.wordpress.com

Stop Poaching Now USA – https://www.stoppoaching-now.org

Tanglewood Foundation NZ – https://www.tanglewood.org.nz

Tembe Elephant Park – www.tembe.co.za

Transfrontier Conservation Areas (TFCA) – www.tfcaportal.org

Traffic – www.traffic.org

Tusk – www.tusk.org

12hours/Project Thorn – www.projectthorn.com

Vets Go Wild – www.worldwideexperience.com/vets-go-wild/

WildAct Vietnam – www.wildact-vn.org

Wildlands Conservation Trust – www.wildtrust.co.za/wildlands

Wildlife Conservation Society (WCS) – www.wcs.org

WildlifeDirect – www.wildlifedirect.org

Wildlife Justice Commission (WJC) – www.wildlifejustice.org

World Wildlife Fund (WWF) – www.worldwildlife.org

Index